The Remarried Family

CHALLENGE AND PROMISE

Esther Wald

FAMILY SERVICE ASSOCIATION OF AMERICA
NEW YORK

Library of Congress Cataloging in Publication Data

Wald, Esther.
  The remarried family.

  Bibliography: p. 2 3 3
  Includes index.
   1. Stepparents—United States. 2. Stepchildren—
Unites States. I. Title.
HQ759.92.W34   306.8'7   80-20598
ISBN 0-87304-184-4
ISBN 0-87304-183-6 (pbk.)

Printed in the United States of America

It is very unfair to judge of any-body's conduct, without an intimate knowledge of their situation. Nobody, who has not been in the interior of a family, can say what the difficulties of any individual of that family may be.

JANE AUSTEN
Emma

CONTENTS

FOREWORD

In this last half of the twentieth century there has been wide-spread concern and discussion about the current state and the future of the American family. The acceleration of the divorce rate, the development in the 1960s of alternative lifestyles of families, as well as the women's movement are cited as evidence of revolutionary change in attitudes toward the family as the basic unit of society, as well as changes in the structure, functions, and evolution of the family. Statistics are offered to support the underlying notion of the erosion of the family in our society and, therefore, of our society, with the result that there is more viewing with alarm than careful examination of the meaning, in human terms, of both the statistics and the apparent developments in family structure and family life. As might be expected, documentation for the alarm or for the contrary idea that all is well with the American family is still hard to come by because we are presently living with and through whatever real changes are taking place.

One of the changes that is visible and accessible to documentation is the increase in the incidence of remarried families, even though this increase is not fully or systematically counted. *The Remarried Family: Challenge and Promise* by Esther Wald is one kind of documentation of the significance, in human terms, of the acceleration of divorce rates and, subsequently, of remarriages. It also provides the basis for further examination, documentation, and knowledge development of this startling numerical change in family structure and relationships.

Based on Mrs. Wald's long experience in social work practice with nuclear and remarried families, her far-ranging study of developments in the family, and her orientation to research in this aspect of family structure and functioning, this book is both a milestone and a model of a social work approach to a basic societal issue. In addition to its felicitous readability, it combines compassion and clarifying and creative thinking about a tangled subject that is inherently complex but also carries considerable cultural and emotional baggage. The complexity is addressed, paradoxically, by specification of its details, and the cultural and emotional overtones are dealt with through identification of their origins and current manifestations. Compassion is evident throughout but specifically in the use of case material that is disciplined and systematic yet retains the poignancy of the human dilemma at the center of concern.

The contributions of *The Remarried Family: Challenge and Promise* are many. Important among them is the solid social work practice base from which Mrs. Wald's study and treatment of remarried families emanate. Her work is centered in the function of social work in relation to the dynamic interactions of person (family)-problem-situation. This is the enduring and nearly universally accepted view of the focus and locus of social work practice, no matter what the human problems being addressed. Mrs. Wald understands and clearly sets forth that this focus requires precise individualization of personal and familial psychodynamics, of the nature and significance of problem, and of the cultural, social, and economic context in which the specific people function and in which there is reciprocal impact. Her grasp of the various interrelationships of the many-faceted factors in the person-problem-situation configuration is so firm and so deep that she gives new meaning to the concept of "psychosocial" in and of itself and as it is unequivocally applied to understanding and treatment of the remarried family.

The author sets out to look at the remarried family as a "special case of family." This view arises from her conviction, derived from study and practice, that although there are, of course, basic similarities between nuclear and remarried families, there are profound differences in the structure, dynamics, and relationships in the remarried family. These profound differences are differences in kind that demand thorough understanding so that treatment may be affectively and substantively relevant to the concerns that these families bring to helping professionals. The author is passionate in her argument that understanding of the unique characteristics of the remarried family as a category, as well as individually, is absolutely necessary for any professional who takes a hand in the lives and life of people involved in this burgeoning class of family. Esther Wald does not "make a case" for her position in the forensic sense of the term. Rather, she documents the differences and complexities of this kind of family life from the research and theory from various disciplines, from clinical experience, and from hypotheses that have been developed from her study and practice. The "special case of family" emerges concretely from these sources so that one not only understands the complexities and differences of the remarried family as general propositions but can also identify the unique ways in which these propositions are manifested in individual family situations.

In addition to the explication of individual and family dynamics and transactions in the remarried family, The Remarried Family: Challenge and Promise provides a framework derived from theories about family structure and functioning that serves as guide for understanding specific families, their problems, and contexts so that precise assessments may evolve to direct individualized treatment that has the real possibility of being truly differential. The practice utility of the structure for assessment and treatment is clearly demonstrated in the judicious and generous use of case examples. The important learning usefulness of the case examples is found in the close analysis that is made not only of the specific case material but also of the actual application of theories about individuals, families, and interactional and ecological processes to assessment and treatment. The structure for studying remarried families has the added advantage of offering a potential point from which various forays into research of this family might be undertaken.

The specific examination of individual and family internal processes and of interpersonal and societal transactions is deepened and broadened by the careful setting forth of the origins and condition of the knowledge that informs the identification of the meaning of the human scene that confronts the practitioner. This substantive richness covers the historical, societal, cultural, and legal factors that contribute to the complexity and uniqueness of the remarried family. Thus, this family is squarely placed in its ecological context. As squarely placed is the demand for the practitioner to look microscopically at the remarried family and to raise eyes to the broader spectrum of the family's situation and life in order to understand them as equal forces in the coping and adaptation that is required. The sources for understanding and treating this special case of family are truly interdisciplinary. Mrs. Wald's "tour de force" is not only the identification of these sources, but also the integration of them always for social work utility and the demonstration of their applicability to real social work practice. She moves from clinical to theoretical considerations and back to clinical with such ease that one is carried along on a learning adventure of considerable excitement. The application and integration of scientific data to clinical practice is no small part of the excitement. Parenthetically, one can discern in this the author's development as practitioner-scholar-practitioner in the study and treatment of this category of family living.

Mrs. Wald recognizes that what she has to say in *The Remarried Family: Challenge and Promise* is derived from study and treatment of families who believe that they are in need of help and who have had that belief corroborated by the agency that accepts them for service. And, the purpose of this book is to offer systematic knowledge, theoretical and practical, to professionals who work with the remarried family in trouble. Nevertheless, there is much here that can contribute to general knowledge of this social phenomenon. This is underscored in the final chapter, which emphasizes broad societal considerations and offers recommendations for support of untroubled families, for community education, for prevention of troubles, and for addition to and refinement of knowledge about and treatment of the troubled remarried family. Finally, this book contributes new learning and new ways of work. There is also embedded in it a model for social work knowledge-building that originates in careful examination and conceptualization of clinical practice, that integrates interdisciplinary theory and research to enhance and support the conceptualization from which new theory for practice then evolves. Centrally this is a book for social workers, practitioners, and students, but any professional interested in families and this special case of family has much to gain from it to enrich practice and to emulate in ways of thinking about clinical work.

BERNECE K. SIMON
School of Social Service Administration
University of Chicago
Chicago, Illinois

ACKNOWLEDGMENTS

The dream for this book began ten years ago in a family service agency in response to the anguished plea of a stepmother for a more accurate perception and a deeper understanding of the remarried family situation by the therapeutic community. It has been written with the hope of contributing knowledge about this family situation that is both objective and sensitive to its dilemmas and struggles. It is indebted to and builds on an interdisciplinary body of theory about the family that has evolved over many decades. It builds, also, on ongoing dialogue with colleagues, friends, and relatives about the remarried family as a special case of family. The book, therefore, represents a synthesis of many of the ideas and concepts of existing family theory and fresh insights derived from continuing search and discussion. It is based on the humanistic value tradition that people can grow and change and that triumph can follow trauma.

I am especially grateful to Mrs. Martha Winch, executive director of the family service agency in which this study was launched, for teaching me the excitement of identifying a vulnerable population in clinical practice and using the social agency as the laboratory for a dual research-clinical model. Her encouragement and support was the beginning of the search for answers to the recurrent question remarried family members ask: Why is this such a difficult situation? Above all, I am grateful to the many remarried families who willingly and, indeed, eagerly participated in this research so that others in similar situations could be helped. Through the stories they told of their life experiences, I gained an understanding of the complexities, pain, and joy of the remarried family situation. The motivation and the hope of these families for a better life was the consistent inspiration for this book.

I would like also to thank the faculty members at the University of Chicago, School of Social Service Administration, and my doctoral committee, in particular, Bernece Simon, David Schneider, Eleanor Tolson, and Judith Nelsen for the intellectual stimulation they offered, the demand for disciplined analysis, and the requirement for clarity in conceptualizing and ordering the vast array of information gleaned from clinical interviews with remarried families. Their thoughtful criticism and suggestions helped me to formulate the schema for study of the remarried family that became the organizing structure of this book. I must also make special mention of the patient listening, valuable advice, and careful reading of this manuscript by my good friends Anne O. Freed, director of professional counseling of the Family Service Association of Greater Boston, and Pearl Slaton, teacher in special education of many children who live in remarried family situations. To all other faculty members, practitioner-colleagues, and members of related professions, too numerous to mention here, who gave generously of their time and thought about some of the issues, questions, and concerns in working with remarried families, a special word of thanks.

I owe a debt of gratitude to the many participants who came to the workshops I have led on theory and practice issues in work with remarried families. Their willingness to respond to surveys and polls of various issues relevant to the remarried family and their probing questions, challenges, and affirmations of the concepts and approaches presented constantly helped to test and refine the evolving body of knowledge about the remarried family. The generous sharing of their personal life experiences as members of remarried families or vignettes from their work with members of such families helped to identify and validate issues unique to the remarried family experience that transcended socioeconomic and ethnic differences.

There is no way I can properly thank Margaret Mangold, former director of publications of Family Service Association of America, who attended one of my workshops and encouraged me to write about the remarried family for the broader professional community. Her support and confidence in this effort, along with that of Jacqueline Marx Atkins, a subsequent director of publications, and Eileen Graham, assistant editor, have been invaluable during the writing and editing of this book.

Acknowledgments

Finally, I must thank my husband and my children for their patience, support, and love during the many months when this book was a dream and a work-in-process. To all others who helped to make this book a reality, a warm and heartfelt thank you.

1

A SPECIAL CASE
OF FAMILY

"How can I be a parent to a child I hardly know?"

"What do I call my father's new wife?"

"No matter how hard I try, I will never make it with my husband's daughter."

"My mom is so busy with the new kids, she never has time for me anymore."

"How can you love two fathers at the same time?"

"I always end up feeling like the 'wicked stepmother'."

"Why can't you be like my 'real' mother?"

"How do we blend our different lifestyles?"

Vignettes like these, drawn from conversations and interviews with persons who live in remarried families, testify to only a few of the unique concerns and critical issues such family members experience. They dramatize some of the universal dilemmas these families face that are both *different from* and *in addition to* those of other kinds of family units. Such unique concerns and issues occur only in the remarried family and, thus, have put it in the position of being "a special case of family."

Specifically, the term *remarried family* refers to a two-parent, two-generation unit that comes into being on the legal remarriage of a widowed or divorced person who has biological or adopted children from a prior union with whom he or she is regularly involved. Or, either husband or wife or both may have children who live elsewhere but interact with the remarried couple on a regular and sustained basis. Thus, the children may or may not live with the remarried couple, but, in either case, they have on-going and significant psychological, social, and legal ties with them. Sometimes the couple are not legally married but live together with his or her children of a prior union "as if" they were. These families are often referred to as *live-in* arrangements or *socially remarried families*. Because many of the issues and problems of the socially remarried family are similar to those of the legally remarried family they are included in this definition.

To the casual observer, the remarried family, whether legal or social, looks no different from the predominant nuclear or conjugal family considered to be the norm and the ideal in the United States; that is, a two-parent, two-generation family unit consisting of a man and a woman who live as husband and wife with biological or adopted children. Although it is possible that husband or wife or both may have been married before, the children with whom they are living belong to both and are children of the current union only. In contrast, one of the conditions of the remarried family is that at least some of the children in the family belong to one spouse and not to the other.

These definitions highlight that the major differences between the remarried and nuclear families are in the parent-child unit and in the sibling relationships that follow. These key differences are known as the *step situation* and have significance for many of the special problems that remarried families encounter. The remarried family has, in fact, been a part of our culture for thousands of years. It is identified by the presence of stepparents and stepchildren. Many people know such families among friends and relatives, or perhaps may even be members of remarried families. However, the increased numbers and visibility of this family during the past few decades makes the remarried family a phenomenon of our times.

THE INFORMATION GAP

The lack of pertinent literature about the remarried family population has been noted by both remarried family members and the professionals with whom they work. People in remarried families have commented that, except for personal and anecdotal accounts written by stepparents, there is little to guide them in their search for answers to some of the special problems they encounter. Professionals working with such families have also searched for literature to guide them in understanding the remarried family. They have found that although the family as a significant, evolving, and complex institutional structure has been studied extensively by many in a wide range of disciplines, the remarried family as a specific variant of the nuclear family has only occasional and limited mention. Moreover, what does exist is fragmentary and often contradictory. What is needed is documented and sound information that is sensitive and empathic to the remarried family situation without being sentimental; objective and factual without being oversimplified. Professionals, as well as the families themselves, need a body of basic information that explains the remarried family situation. This would address the critical information gap identified by both groups. It would provide a readily accessible systematic presentation of the facts and meanings of life in this family situation.

Recognition of the need for such a presentation emerged first from the combined frustration of professionals and their remarried family clients, and was compounded by the large numbers of remarried families who applied to social agencies for help. For many of these husbands and wives, the decision to reestablish intimate relationships in a remarried family structure reflected their hope and their need to satisfy enduring drives for meaningful social, psychological, and sexual relatedness. Therapists* commented on the poignancy of clients' feelings of bewilderment and disappointment that the "hope and the promise" of a better life in remarriage had eluded them.

Many remarried persons spoke of their lack of preparation for living in this kind of a family unit. Husbands and wives discussed the surprise and the frustration they experienced when the new life had a set of problems and pressures they had not anticipated. Two recurrent questions they asked were: "Why is a remarriage where there are children of a prior marriage so difficult?" and "What can we do to make this family a 'real' family?" Frequently, these families were characterized by a high degree of social dis-

---

*The terms therapist, practitioner and clinician are used interchangeably in this book.

organization. Often the threat of another divorce was imminent.

In interviews with practitioners, clients often despaired when the complexity and the uniqueness of their life situation was not grasped by those to whom they turned for help. It was not uncommon for a client to say to a therapist, "I don't think you really understand how complicated and difficult life in our kind of family is" or "I feel that no one in the whole world knows what I am going through." On the other hand, practitioners were concerned with their lack of success in working with this particular family unit. Thus, both therapist and client were acutely aware that the existing repertoire of skills and interventions for work with remarried families was inadequate for the needs of the situation.

EMERGENCE OF SELF-HELP GROUPS

In light of these frustrations and needs, it is not surprising that spontaneous grass-roots efforts for self-help emerged in both the remarried family population and in the professional community. Traditionally, self-help groups are established either when there is a lack of professional services or when available professional services are ineffective or inadequate. Remarried Parents, Inc., and Stepfamily Foundation are examples of self-help groups that have organized among the remarried family population. These self-help groups believe that the professional is not sufficiently acquainted with the background or particular circumstances of their situation and, therefore, members join together to reduce their sense of loneliness and alienation from the mainstream of society. A demonstration of these views is expressed in quotations from a brochure of the Stepfamily Foundation of California, Inc.: "Stepfamilies tend to feel isolated and alone" and "Through this organization, stepfamilies can meet with other stepfamilies." The Stepfamily Foundation sees itself as providing a forum for families of similar life experiences to develop a sense of community and affiliation to share their common concerns.

Self-help groups for professionals have taken the form of seminars, workshops, and staff development programs in social agencies. In these groups, differences between various family structures have been analyzed with specific attention to the remarried family. Participants have begun to identify some of the essential aspects of life in the remarried family. They have shared with each other their need for more knowledge about stepparenting, blending different lifestyles, affiliating, and bonding. Such groups reflect the professional search for a theoretical, explanatory framework, dif-

4

ferent from that designed for other families, to guide practice interventions with the remarried family. They have identified that the principle of differential diagnosis in work with families is essential, just as it is in work with individuals.

REFLECTIONS OF THE POPULAR INTEREST

Although the shared frustration of therapist and client unfolded in the privacy of the social agency interview, and spontaneous self-help groups arose to cope with the unmet needs of this specific family unit, the general population outside of the social agency has also shown significant interest in the remarried family population.

Communications media, particularly television and popular magazines, have recognized the widespread interest in the remarried family and that it comprises a substantial constituency. Thus, increased time and space have been devoted to the remarried family. At one extreme, the ever-popular soap operas of daytime television spin complex tales of custody battles, divided loyalties of children, and other kinds of remarried family problems; at the other, the blithe, fun-loving families of situation comedies spin myths of easy and happy family adjustments for all.

Popular magazines have featured articles that dispel the myth of the "wicked stepmother" and have offered suggestions for successful living in the step situation. Newspapers, always responsive to human interest topics, changing lifestyles, and family problems, have reported on the phenomenon of remarriage; its trials and its rewards. Newspaper-syndicated columns like "Ask Ann Landers" or "Dear Abby" feature letters and answers to those seeking advice in adjusting to the strains of living, often in remarried families. Approximately 20 percent of this mail is estimated by these columnists to be from persons seeking direct answers to questions about life in the remarried family situation.

A POPULATION AT RISK

Remarried families are drawn from the pool of single-parent families that comprise 19 percent of all families with children under eighteen in the United States.[1] Because 75 to 80 percent of those who are divorced or widowed single parents remarry legally within three to five years and many others establish social remarriages, most single-parent families become legal or social remarried families. In addition, there is a growing population of unmarried single parents who later marry and, thus, introduce the step situation into their family.[2] Increasing numbers of families involved in the step situation are found in social agency caseloads.

Family service agencies report that "the reconstituted or remarried family comprises a significant client population."[3] Practitioners from a wide range of social agencies report that most agencies do not differentiate between nuclear and remarried families. Figures on the proportion of remarried families in their caseloads are, therefore, estimates that range from 5 to 60 percent, depending on the function of the agency and socioeconomic populations served.

Probation officers, juvenile court workers, and youth service agencies report concern that many of the children with whom they work are runaway stepchildren; workers in child abuse programs estimate disproportionate numbers of stepchildren are abused.[4] Child welfare agencies report that a high proportion of children in foster homes are stepchildren who have not been able to adjust in the remarried family situation.[5] A recent study commissioned by the United States Children's Bureau has identified the need for special attention to children who live in step situations.[6]

In addition, many school social workers, counselors, and teachers have expressed concern about academic and familial problems that children in remarried families present. Although few schools have reliable statistics about the number of stepchildren they educate, some limited estimates are drawn from counts of children who have different surnames from the parents with whom they live. There is general agreement that these and many more children are members of remarried families that are not adequately identified or verified.[7]

Failure to establish categories to differentiate the remarried from the nuclear family is not limited to social agencies and schools. The United States Census Bureau makes no definitive distinctions either. Paul C. Glick, senior demographer for the United States Census Bureau, has said that at present there is no specific category for remarried families or stepchildren. Figures on the incidence of remarried families and numbers of stepchildren in the general population are, thus, inferred from related questions and government documents. They are, therefore, estimates and do not reflect a direct census count.[8]

According to recent census figures, 42 percent of the almost 58 million families in the United States are comprised of a husband and wife and one or more children, a two-parent, two-generation family.[9] Not indicated, however, are the number of remarried families that are a part of this population. In an earlier study, Marvin B. Sussman did differentiate two-parent, two-generation families into nuclear and remarried, and found that 22 percent or approximately one out of five of the two-parent, two-generation families in this country were remarried families.[10]

Not included in these data are the live-in or socially remarried families defined earlier. Although no hard data are available on the number of these families, census figures indicate that during the past decade the number of unmarried couples who live together and have children of a prior marriage has increased.[11] A more comprehensive view of the remarried population that includes the socially remarried families along with those who are legally remarried would result in estimates that exceed those mentioned above.

The number of stepchildren who live with a natural parent and a stepparent has also grown. (For purposes of simplification, the text does not always indicate that natural parent also includes an adopted parent. This follows the convention of the United States Census Bureau.) In 1960, it was estimated that one out of ten minor children was a stepchild residing with a natural parent and a stepparent.[12] By 1978, estimates reflected that one out of eight children under eighteen was a stepchild living with a natural and a stepparent.[13] Most stepchildren are children of divorce.[14] Not reflected in estimates of stepchildren residing with stepparents are the many children who live with a single parent whose absent parent has remarried, thus establishing a category of nonresidential stepchild.

Projections are that if no interventions occur to modify existing and identified trends, 45 percent of children born in 1977 will live for some period of time during their first eighteen years (to 1995) as a child in a single-parent family. Children in this pool, whose parents were divorced, widowed, or unmarried have the potential to become stepchildren. Glick estimates that 32 percent of these children will be children of divorce.[15] Assuming that current trends remain essentially the same, and that 75 to 80 percent of divorced parents continue to remarry, one out of four children, or 25 percent of these children, will have experienced the stepchild role for some period of time during their childhood.[16] This number would be somewhat larger if children who have become stepchildren when an unmarried parent marries or a widowed parent remarries were included. Nonetheless, based on available statistics, the magnitude of the step experience for so many children for some period of their childhood is dramatic.

At the present time, information on those who divorce a second time is sparse and tentative. However, what evidence is available indicates that there is a higher divorce rate among the remarried than among those married for the first time. Recent figures show that the rate of those who divorce after remarriage is 44 percent compared with 40 percent for first marriages.[17] Moreover, 60 percent of these first marriages have children of a prior marriage.[18] Unfortunately, there are no figures of the numbers of children involved in situations of those who divorce again. However, analysis of divorces after remarriage indicates that the presence of at least one child at entry into a second marriage increases the probability of marital dissolution.[19] Given that many remarriages involve children of prior unions and those who remarry without children may have children in their remarriage, it seems safe to assume that substantial numbers of children are involved in divorce after parental remarriage.

More definitive research is needed to establish the factors that contribute to higher divorce rates after remarriage than after first marriage, and learn whether stepchildren are more vulnerable to social and emotional problems than their nonstep peers. However, the cumulative concerns of large numbers of professionals from a wide range of agencies and disciplines about the step situation and remarried family stress cannot be ignored or minimized. It would appear that a high-risk population with the potential for many social problems has been identified.

MOTIVATION AMONG REMARRIED FAMILIES

But this account of the current remarried family scene, although sobering, is incomplete. It does not properly emphasize the many strengths that remarried family members often bring to their family situation and to the treatment process. Therapists who have worked with these clients have reported that typically such persons come with a high level of motivation, readiness, and capacity to confront and work through the unique challenges of their situation. They are eager to examine the problems and interactions within the family unit, as well as unresolved issues within themselves as individuals. Many have made a stronger commitment to seeing their family survive and be successful than was true of their

8

earlier nuclear family situation.

Some remarried family members have already confronted fantasies and faulty expectations that were barriers to the survival of their earlier family unit. They are eager and ready to explore the myths and unrealistic hopes they may have in their remarried family situation. Thus, they come for help in mastering the difficulties involved in the remarried situation with considerable capacity for self-observation and change.

The high level of motivation and capacity to consider and examine the interactions and dynamics of the new family unit are resources the therapist can and must tap in work with this family. However, the therapist must bring to the exchange a firm theoretical and differential knowledge base about the remarried family as a variant of other family forms. When this understanding is conveyed to the client, he or she no longer need feel that "No one understands how complicated and different our kind of family is." Practitioners can then provide services that are sensitive to the universal realities of the remarried situation. In this way, empathic bridges between therapist and client, so essential to successful outcomes, can be built.

PLAN OF THE BOOK

The intent in this book is to articulate a body of substantive knowledge about the remarried family system that narrows the existing information gap and provides the therapist with an objective understanding of the factors that make it a special case of family. This knowledge base is grounded in the author's research and clinical experience with this family and, in addition, derives from information gathered from participants in professional workshops and family life education courses on the remarried family. Although the focus is on remarried families who sought professional help, it is possible, and in fact very likely, that many of the issues and problems these families report exist in remarried families who have never sought such help.

The first three chapters of this book identify the remarried family as a population at risk, discuss some of the recurrent problems and dilemmas for which these families seek professional help, and present a five-part dimensional schema for study of the remarried family situation. Chapters four through eight develop the substantive knowledge base of the remarried family and identify some of its unique and inherent realities through elaboration of each dimension of the schema. Case materials illustrate issues such as blending different lifestyles, defining the step role, forming new attachments while maintaining ties with the old, and achieving a new remarried family identity. The remainder of the book focuses on clinical intervention. It presents a problem-process profile for diagnostic assessment, and demonstrates the application of selected aspects of the knowledge gained in the therapeutic process. Finally, new directions in programs, research, and policy are suggested.

Overall, the goal of this book is to provide some reasonable answers for therapists to use in their work with families who ask the recurrent questions:

"Why is remarriage where there are children from a prior marriage so difficult?"

"What can we do to make this a 'real' family?"

NOTES

1. United States Bureau of the Census, "Divorce, Child Custody and Child Support," *Current Population Reports: Special Studies,* Series P-23, no. 84 (Washington, D.C.: U.S. Government Printing Office, 1979), p. 1.
2. Paul C. Glick and Arthur J. Norton, "Marrying, Divorcing and Living Together in the United States Today," *Population Bulletin* 32, no. 5 (October 1977): 4–8.
3. Robert M. Rice, ed., *Family Listening Post* (New York: Family Service Association of America, 1977), p. 15.
4. Esther Wald, "Remarried Families in Practitioner Caseloads," unpublished study, 1975–1978.
5. Helen R. Jeter, "Child Problems and Services in Child Welfare Programs," *U.S. Children's Bureau Publication,* no. 403 (Washington, D.C.: U.S. Government Printing Office, 1963), p. 107.
6. Shirley Jenkins, *Planning for Children of Divorce* (New York: Child Welfare League of America, 1976).
7. Wald, "Remarried Families in Caseloads."
8. Personal communication with Paul C. Glick, Senior Demographer for the United States Bureau of the Census, August 1980.
9. United States Bureau of the Census, "Population Profile of the United States: 1979," *Current Population Reports,* Series P-20, no. 350 (Washington, D.C.: U.S. Government Printing Office, 1980), p. 9.
10. Marvin B. Sussman, "Family," *Encyclopedia of Social Work* (Washington D.C.: National Association of Social Workers, 1977), p. 359.
11. United States Bureau of the Census, "Marital Status and Living Arrangements: March 1979," *Current Population Reports,* Series P-20, no. 349 (Washington, D.C.: U.S. Government Printing Office, 1980), p. 3.
12. Paul C. Glick, "Children of Divorced Parents in Demographic Perspective," *Journal of Social Issues* 35, no. 4 (1979): 170–75.

13. United States Bureau of the Census, "Population Division: American Families and Living Arrangements," prepared for the White House Conference on Families (Washington D.C.: U.S. Government Printing Office, 1980), p. 11.

14. United States Bureau of the Census, "Population Profile of the United States," p. 9.

15. Glick, "Children of Divorced Parents," p. 176.

16. Personal communication with Glick about verification of estimate of figures cited, August 1980.

17. Glick and Norton, "Marrying and Divorcing," p. 37.

18. Glick, "Children of Divorced Parents," p. 174.

19. James McCarthy, "A Comparison of the Probability of Dissolution of First and Second Marriages," *Demography* 5, no. 3 (August 1978): 354.

2

~~~~~~~~~

THE CLIENT'S STORY

L ike any other client who first seeks professional help, a member of a remarried family does so when the "felt" problem or stress of the situation exceeds his or her coping and problem-solving capabilities. As therapists have listened to the stories remarried family clients tell when they come for help, they have been impressed with the wide range and complexity of their problems. The heavy demand these problems make on individual and family coping and problem-solving capacities is, of course, the heart of the challenge to these families. For the therapist, the challenge is one of providing a relevant and informed knowledge base so that the mutual work between the client and therapist can be facilitated.

PROBLEM AS THE POINT OF ENTRY

The problem for which the client seeks help is the point of entry into work with the therapist. *Problem* is defined here as some difficulty or obstacle the client perceives as interfering with the social and psychological functioning of one or more members in the remarried family unit. Problems are outcomes of tension within the individual, within his or her situation or between the individual and the situation. Thus, the social work framework of person-problem-situation is accepted as relevant for study of the remarried family. Frequently, one problem gives rise to others, so that they create a multidimensional and interrelated network. At times, this results in problems that are so enmeshed that their boundaries are indistinct.

Professionals in both clinical and research environments have worked with families of all socioeconomic classes, in rural and urban environments, and among black and white populations. Out of this cumulative experience, two potential areas of stress and problems for the remarried family have been identified. First, this family has all of the same growth and developmental problems that any other family has; second, it has additional problems that are rooted in the remarried family situation itself. These two major potential sources of problems combine to produce a lattice of interwoven pressures and dilemmas. They can be observed in individual, social, and psychological functioning; interpersonal relationships within the remarried family; and between the re-married family, absent parent, and extended family.

Although these problems are highly particularized within each family in terms of content, persons involved, onset, duration, and intensity, some recurrent issues and concerns have been identified that are unique to the remarried family. They often involve the reorganization and "blending" of lifestyles of two prior family units, overcoming the "stranger" phenomenon, and achieving consensus on family rules and child-rearing practices. Other is-sues are focused on the step relationship. These issues involve learning new roles and affiliation with and inclusion of the new remarried family members. Still others revolve around issues of individual and family identity and the process of becoming a remarried family. The impact and intensity of these problems are often heightened by lack of knowledge of or preparation for the dilemmas that are inherent in any remarried family adjustment. Consequently, many who enter into remarriage where there are children from prior relationships bring with them myths and fan-tasies that are not consistent with the realities that are part of the remarried family situation.

INITIAL INTERVIEWS

The initial interviews with remarried family members that fol-low, drawn from clinical practice and family life education groups, illustrate some of the problems these families experience in their day-to-day lives. The names of all persons used in case examples throughout this book are, of course, invented.*

THE BRENT FAMILY

Mrs. Brent initiated application for service at her local family service agency. She had been referred by the minister of her church. At the time of her request, she said that hers was a "new" family and that things were "not going well." She asked that the entire family be seen by a counselor.

The Brent family consisted of Mr. Brent, thirty-nine, Mrs. Brent, thirty-five, and four sons, Bob, sixteen, and Tom, fourteen, from Mr. Brent's first marriage, and Rick, fourteen, and Fred, thirteen, from Mrs. Brent's former marriage. Mr. and Mrs. Brent had met each other at a church social for single parents and had been married four months earlier. Mrs. Brent had been divorced for three years after thirteen years of marriage, and Mr. Brent had been divorced for one year after seventeen years of marriage. Each retained custody of his or her children. In both cases, the absent parent had no contact with the children. Mr. and Mrs. Brent had each grown up in intact nuclear family households.

The problem as Mr. and Mrs. Brent saw it was that they lived in a "house of strangers," and that the boys did not seem to have any desire to become a part of a "whole" family. The parents had expected the children to share their joy at being once again a "real" family. The behaviors of the children resulted in parental anger and frustration because they saw the children as jeopardizing the new family. The boys listened, but were sullen and morose. They resisted the therapist's and parents' efforts to involve them in the discussion until very much later in the interview.

Single parenting had been difficult for both Mr. and Mrs. Brent, as each had attempted to fulfill the dual roles of mother and father. Mrs. Brent talked of the difficult time she had in adjusting to the role of being the breadwinner. She had married soon after graduation from high school, and had only very limited prior work experience. Irregular and insufficient support payments from her ex-husband left her no choice but to go outside the home to work. Even more difficult for her was giving up many of the homemaking and child-rearing practices to which she was firmly committed, such as "being home when the boys came home from school, attending all school functions, and maintaining a smooth and efficient household." Fortunately, a spirit of cooperation prevailed, and a teamwork approach to cooking and cleaning was worked out that spoke well

---

*For purposes of convenience, the remarried couple's surname will be used in labeling case example material throughout, although children of a prior marriage may retain the legal name of their prior nuclear family unit.

of the children's adaptability to the change in their lifestyle. Although her sons did not complain, Mrs. Brent was certain that they were unhappy and lonely for a father who could become involved in male activities with them. Mrs. Brent also longed for a "man at home," someone who could provide adult companionship and help her feel like a "woman" once again, not "just a mother." She was certain that her sons would welcome her remarriage.

Mr. Brent also found single-parent family life difficult to manage. For him, the assumption of the dual-parent role meant running the household in addition to a full-time job. He, too, valued a smoothly run household, but this was not achieved. Instead, "meals were on the run, laundry was never done, and the house was not to be believed." Although he described a chaotic household, he was proud that he and his sons had achieved an easygoing communication pattern and lifestyle of good humor and fun. Like Mrs. Brent, Mr. Brent was pleased at the adaptation his sons had made to the changes in their life precipitated by their mother's departure. He, too, assumed that his children would welcome his remarriage. "Isn't it better," he argued, "to sit down to a hot meal, find a clean shirt when it is needed, and live in a house that does not look as if it has been hit by a tornado?" Mr. Brent also said he longed for an ongoing stable relationship with a woman, which would repair the damaged self-concept he suffered when his first wife abandoned the family.

Later in the interview, Bob spoke up and said that from his point of view things had been going well before the remarriage. He talked of the fun they had had "batching" it, and resented the new rules and regulations of "order and routine." In addition, he felt angry at having to share his house with "strangers," and resented his father's time and effort in "winning over the new kids." He was supported by his brother Tom, who, in addition, did not like his stepmother's cooking and insistence that everyone sit down at the dinner table at the same time. He didn't see what was so great about being a "whole" family anyway. Neither Bob nor Tom liked being "one of those stepfamilies."

Rick and Fred were not as vocal as their stepbrothers, but talked of how hard it had been for them to move out of their old neighborhood and go to a new school. Also, they resented Bob and Tom's lack of appreciation of their mother. From their point of view, things had been a lot better for them before, too. But they were glad that their mother was happier.

Mr. and Mrs. Brent were shocked at the intensity of feeling that was expressed by the children. They simply could not understand or accept that what seemed so right for them did not seem right for their children. To Mr. and Mrs. Brent, having a two-parent household again had seemed the "perfect" answer for all of them.

At first glance it is indeed hard to understand why everyone in the Brent household did not embrace the parental goal of a "whole" family as an opportunity for an improved quality of life. On examination of the Brent story in greater depth, however, the "fairy tale" hopes and lack of preparation to face important issues and dilemmas begin to come to the surface. Neither Mr. nor Mrs. Brent was prepared for some of the adjustments entailed in the reorganization of their separate families into a "new" family. Each held to a myth that they need only to reconstitute themselves as a two-parent, two-generation family, similar to the "ideal" nuclear family, and "all would live together as a 'new' family happily ever after." The issue for therapeutic consideration was the fact that what is right for parents seeking to grow beyond their earlier loss may not always be accepted as right by their children (see chapter ten). The critical question then becomes, "How can these tensions be reconciled?" The situation in the Gray family illustrates another aspect of this same problem.

THE GRAY FAMILY

When a complete, hospital-based examination for chronic backache revealed no organic basis for her pain, Ellen Gray was referred to the psychiatric department of the hospital.

Ellen's first husband had been killed in an automobile accident when her only daughter, Nancy, was four years old. Prior to the accident, the three of them had been a close-knit family. After her husband's death, Ellen, then twenty-six, was sure she would never be happy again, and she devoted herself to Nancy in an effort to rebuild her life.

Six years later, Ellen met Jim Gray, an attractive bachelor in his mid-forties. Ellen described feelings of incredible excitement that she could once again experience deep love for a man. She and Jim were married after seven months of whirlwind courtship. She fully expected that she, her new husband, and her daughter would "all love each other and live together as a united and happy family."

However, after more than a year of marriage and life together as a remarried family, Nancy and Jim did not love each other, and the family was not the united and happy one Ellen had fantasied it would be. Instead, there was a pattern of mutual reserve and distance between Nancy and Jim, with each complaining about the other, and each resentful of the time Ellen spent with the other. The matter became further complicated because Ellen resented Jim for his difficulties in accepting Nancy as "his own child," and was angry at Nancy when she did not respond enthusiastically to whatever efforts Jim did make to include her in his life. In her efforts to bring about a better understanding between her husband and daughter, Ellen found that she was alternately an advocate for one or the other or frustrated and immobilized because she understood the complaints that each had of the other. She found that she was "torn between her old love for her daughter and her new love for her husband." She asked, "How can it be that the two people I love more than anything ele in the world seem unable to love each other?" She wondered if the tension she experienced because of this could be related to her backaches?

As in the situation with the Brents, the dream of a whole and united family was not realized for Ellen. She, too, had had no preparation for the issues involved in the step situation and had built a fantasy of mutual love in a tightly knit family. She made the faulty assumption that adjustments would be easy and all would love each other, as had been true in her first marriage.

Children as well as adults who are seen in professional counseling come with faulty assumptions and myths. It is not uncommon for them, in the case of divorce, to cling to hopes that because both parents love them and this love is returned by them to each parent, that their parents must, in fact, still love each other. Some children assume that this hope can be a reality and dream about expulsion of the stepparent and reunion of their parents.

Billie, age seven, was referred to a child guidance clinic for daydreaming and inattention in the classroom. In play therapy, he expressed confusion because his parents no longer lived under one roof. He had assumed from the time his parents were divorced that they would, undoubtedly, be reunited. However, when his mother remarried, this hope of certain reunion was shattered. His daydreams were concerned with how he could get his stepfather to leave. Billie was sure that if he did, his mother and father would once again live together.

Another child, whose mother had remarried a man with two children, solved the problem of parental reunion in a fantasy she reported that her absent father and the absent mother of her step-siblings would marry each other. In this way, all of the parents would be in the same family. Still another poignant story was told by a forty-two-year-old woman whose parents had divorced when she was seven years old. Although each had remarried and she had enjoyed a good relationship with each stepparent, recently her stepfather had died, and not long after, her father's wife, her stepmother, had also died. Although both of her parents were now almost seventy, she recounted that one of her first hopes on learning that her stepmother had died was that now her parents would remarry each other. It is apparent that the myth of parental reunion is not limited to the young child or easily overcome. It surfaces in many different ways and is often a threat to a remarriage. Such a situation existed for the Maynors, when adolescent children could not give up the hope of parental reunion many years after their parent had remarried.

THE MAYNOR FAMILY

The Maynors, a couple in their mid-forties, came to the agency for their appointment a day after Mr. Maynor had called a crisis center for emergency help. Mrs. Maynor clarified immediately that she was an unwilling participant. She had made up her mind that there was no place for her in this family, and she planned to file for divorce. The current crisis was precipitated by the seating arrangement at her stepson's wedding a few days earlier. The wedding had taken place in another state, and the Maynors had not been involved in the planning in any way. The details of the seating plan had been completed by Mr. Maynor's two sons, Bert, twenty-one, the bridegroom, and his brother, Howard, eighteen. When Mr. and Mrs. Maynor arrived at the wedding they found that Mr. Maynor, his former wife, and his children were seated together, while Mrs. Maynor and her two children were seated with other guests. Mr. Maynor's acceptance of the seating arrangement was perceived by Mrs. Maynor to be a public statement that she did not belong in this family.

At the time of the interview, the Maynors had been married for seven years. For five years prior to the remarriage, Mrs. Maynor and her two children, Mike and Beth, had lived together as a single-parent family unit. During this period, the children had only sporadic contact with their absent father, and child support payments by him were most irregular. Mrs. Maynor was divorced from her first husband after six years. At that time, Mike was five and Beth was two.

Mr. Maynor reported that his first marriage had been a happy one until all of the children were in school. At that time, his wife became restless and began to work outside of the home. She was unable to balance her family and work responsibilities, and Mr. Maynor said that he became both father and mother to his children. Although he enjoyed the opportunity to function as a "nurturing parent," he resented his wife's separate interests and relationships. Ultimately, the marital conflict escalated and a divorce was obtained. Mr. Maynor had been married thirteen years at the time of his divorce. All of his children, Bert twelve, Howard nine, and Jane eight, continued to live with their mother, who remarried within a few months. Mr. Maynor lived alone, but maintained consistent contact with his three children through twice-weekly visits; he made regular support payments. He remarried two years after his divorce.

Mr. and Mrs. Maynor had known each other for about a year prior to their remarriage. During this period, there were frequent shared afternoons with both sets of children. Mrs. Maynor was impressed with the warmth and sensitivity of Mr. Maynor's relationship with his children.

19

She assumed that this quality would also be true of his relationship with her children.

At the time of the remarriage, Mrs. Maynor's children, Mike, ten, and Beth, seven, lived with them, while Mr. Maynor's three children continued to live with their mother and stepfather. Both Mr. and Mrs. Maynor reflected that things seemed to go well early in the remarriage. Her children seemed happy and related well to Mr. Maynor. They spontaneously called him "Dad" and chose to use Maynor as their surname in school. Mr. Maynor willingly assumed total responsibility for their financial support, and beginning discussions of his legal adoption of them were underway. Mr. Maynor's children visited on weekends and seemed to be enjoying the new family situation. Mrs. Maynor felt that Bert and Howard accepted her as a "good friend", and did not demonstrate any evidence of resentment about the new marriage or the growing attachments between their father and Mike and Beth.

Mrs. Maynor said that she was especially grateful for the improved quality of life in the new family situation. Her first husband had been an alcoholic, had not supported the family, and was emotionally unavailable to her and the children most of the time. She could finally relax and felt that her children had a "good father" and that she had a "good life."

Two years later, when Bert and Howard, then sixteen, and fourteen, asked to come to live with them because they did not get along with their stepfather, Mrs. Maynor felt no threat and looked forward to a continuation of the same good relationships the "weekend" family had. Mr. Maynor had been elated about the "parent-switch," because the one thing that had been missing in his life was the day-to-day contact with his children; now, this would be possible. Mrs. Maynor's children also looked forward to Bert and Howard's coming to live with them.

Mrs. Maynor was, therefore, totally unprepared for the change in the quality of their family life after Bert and Howard moved into their home on a permanent basis. Bert and Howard seemed intent on proving that they were more important to Mr. Maynor than either she or her children were to him. She had expected her husband to convey to his children that she was the parent in charge of the home, and that he would continue the warm and giving relationship he had toward her own children. However, neither of these expectations was realized. Instead, Mr. Maynor seemed to have time only for Bert and Howard. When conflicts arose between Mike and Howard, as they often did, Mr. Maynor invariably assumed that Howard was right. Moreover, Mr. Maynor had become much more harsh and demanding of Mike, in contrast to his easygoing disciplinary attitude toward Howard. Mrs. Maynor found herself an advocate for Mike, while Mr. Maynor took this role for Howard.

This stressful family situation was compounded further a few years later, when Bert and Howard's mother divorced her second husband. It seemed to Mrs. Maynor that Howard undertook an unrelenting campaign at the time to reunite his mother and father. Mrs. Maynor said that although she called this to her husband's attention and suggested that they seek professional help, he discounted her observations. Moreover, he did nothing to clarify for his children that his reunion with their mother was not a possibility. This situation created feelings in Mrs. Maynor of being depreciated by her husband and of being "second best" to her stepchildren. She saw herself as nothing more than a "housekeeper" in her own home. The seating arrangement that Bert and Howard had evolved at the wedding was the last straw and convinced her that she had been right all along in her perception of what Bert and Howard felt toward her. She described the intensive welcoming efforts she had made when they first came to live with them, and said she felt betrayed by her husband and his sons.

When Mr. Maynor responded to his wife's story, he affirmed that his wife had indeed made intensive efforts to make his children feel a part of the home. He talked of how much he loved his children and how hard it had been for him to be without them during the years they lived with their mother. He felt that he had to "make it up to them" because their family had been broken. No one else in his family had ever been divorced and this was a hard situation for him to accept. He admitted "hearing for the first time" the extent of his wife's despair. The planned seating arrangements by his sons had jolted him so that he felt he could no longer close his eyes to the need for professional help.

The issues presented by the Maynor family pinpoint the complex, multidimensional, and causal chain network of problems so often true of remarried families. Of primary importance for Bert and Howard were issues of grief and unresolved mourning for their prior family structure. That this issue had never been addressed with them contributed to behavior that sought to reunite their parents. This, in turn, set up barriers in the step relationships and infiltrated into the marital relationship.

Feelings of being "second best to one's stepchildren" can also occur between couples where one partner has children of a former marriage, even if the children live elsewhere and there are no other children in the home. Moreover, when the newly remarried couple disagree about the extent of responsibility toward children of a prior marriage, as it pertains to a wish to start a new family, other strains are added. In the following case example, Greg and Janet Ronson discussed this problem with a group of remarried parents in a family life education course sponsored by their local mental health association.

THE RONSON FAMILY

Greg placed the problem before the group the first day it met. He felt that Janet was trying to force him to make a choice between her and his children, who lived with his ex-wife. Both Janet and Greg agreed that most of their arguments were about "who came first," and about starting another family. Both agreed that the marriage was deteriorating, and that unless these issues could be resolved they were headed for divorce.

Greg told the group that Janet and he had been married for three years. She knew before the marriage that he had two children to whom he was deeply attached. He saw his children twice a week, and said that the visits were the high point of his week. Janet interrupted to say that when the children, nine and seven, came she felt that she "did not exist for Greg." He was so involved with them at those times that there was no room for her; she was "second best." She felt that in any marriage, "the wife should come first."

Not only did Janet feel excluded and second best at these times, she also felt that she had failed to meet Greg's expectations. He assumed that she would accept and love his children as her own and, thus, they would have no need to begin a second family. Janet said that she had tried to love Greg's children as her own, but just did not seem able to do so. Although she liked them, she was unwilling to give up the hope of a family of her own. Janet said that she felt she had been understanding of Greg's prior family commitment. She had worked long hours as a hairdresser to help him meet his financial obligations for child support and alimony. She could accept these responsibilities, but she was resentful of Greg's ex-wife's frequent requests for "extras." His quick compliance furthered her feelings of being second best. She wondered what Greg's responsibilities were toward her.

Working out a balance between "old" and "new" ties is vital to the remarried family situation. It is not only a problem for husband and wife but also for children, who are trying to define a place for themselves in the new family. For instance, an alert and sensitive teacher noticed that six-year-old Nellie was not herself and referred her to the school counselor.

Nellie was easily distracted and unable to concentrate. This was in sharp contrast to her usual eager participation and involvement in studies and with her classmates. It did not take the school social worker long to learn that Nellie was confused because she now had two fathers, an "old" one and a "new" one. She loved them both, and thought that she had to make a choice.

The issue of multiple parents is a complex one for many children. They wonder how one can love two parents of the same sex and, if so, what are the risks of losing one or the other. In Nellie's situation, a cooperative and child-centered focus on the part of all of the parents gave her permission to love two fathers, so that she did not have to make a choice. However, this kind of support for a child is not always available.

The problem of dealing with feelings about having multiple parents had different manifestations for nine-year-old Kim, described below, who was also referred to the school counselor by her teacher. Her problem was manifested by defiance of authority and poor school performance. However, when she was seen by the counselor, it became clear that these behavior difficulties were only outward signals of Kim's confusion about parental authority. She was referred to a family service center.

THE DEAN FAMILY

When the therapist at the center explored this family situation, she learned that Kim had recently been enrolled in the local elementary school. Prior to this, Kim, her two older brothers, Frank, thirteen, and Dennis, eleven, and her mother lived in another part of the city. However, her mother had recently remarried, and the family had moved, in order to discourage frequent visitation with Kim's noncustodial father, Mr. Wilkins. Mr. Dean, Kim's stepfather, had two children, seven and four, who lived with his ex-wife and visited regularly into the remarried household.

Mr. Dean talked of his efforts to win Kim over, but said she insisted that she had no need to obey him because he was not her "real" father. Except for Kim's defiance and rebellion, the parents and boys saw the new family situation as a good one for all. Frank and Dennis had accepted their stepfather, and even used his surname in school. Kim, however, adamantly called herself Kim Wilkins. Her attitudes and behaviors were in such sharp contrast to that of her brothers that her mother, Frank, and Dennis were fearful that Mr. Dean would give up on all of them if Kim's negative behavior continued. Mrs. Dean described a stormy first marriage; one in which she and her children were abused. Only Kim, the youngest and the favorite of her father had escaped. The older boys had refused to have anything to do with their father because of his mistreatment of them and their mother. They perceived Kim as disloyal because she did not join with them in rejecting their father and allying with the new family unit. But, although Kim remembered her father's rages and uncontrollable anger toward the others, she enjoyed her visits and wanted to continue to see him.

She did confide, however, that there were some very difficult aspects to these visits. She said her father asked her many questions about the activities of the new family and instructed her not to obey her stepfather because he was not her "real" father. On the other hand, her brothers *and mother instructed her not to discuss the activities in the new home with her father and expected her to obey her stepfather. Kim was indeed confused about whose instructions she had to obey.*

The Dean situation poses some very difficult questions. How can problems related to multiple parenting be effectively handled in the service of the child's growth and family cohesion? The issue of maintaining prior ties had become a point of dissension between Kim and her mother and her brothers because they felt that the security of their new family unit was jeopardized by Kim's relationship with her father. Questions that were raised for therapeutic consideration were: How could Kim be helped to deal with the contradictory instructions from her resident and absent parent families? How could her stepfather be helped to parent a child who resisted his positive efforts? How could the new family unit be stabilized and strengthened, yet permit Kim the freedom to maintain a relationship with her father? The Dean family problems highlight only a few of the issues of relating to multiple parents.

At times, some of the problems and stresses that stimulate a member of a remarried family to seek professional help are more focused on distress within the person. In such cases, the stress may derive from the incongruity between self-expectations and actual performance. The case of Ginny Blake illustrates this kind of situation.

THE BLAKE FAMILY

Ginny, twenty-five, had been referred to a local mental healt clinic by her physician because of deep feelings of depression, for which no organic basis could be found. Ginny lived with her thirty-one-year-old husband, George, stepdaughter, Amy, eight, and son, Jeff, nine months old. She insisted that her husband not be contacted, that her problems related only to her own individual adjustment.

In her first interview with a therapist, Ginny related that she had been a stepchild. Her natural mother had been killed in an automobile accident when she was nine years old. Two years later, her father remarried a woman who had been divorced but had no children. Ginny described that she felt isolated and excluded in the remarried family unit in which she grew up. This was especially true after her father and stepmother had a baby, one year later. Because of these feelings, Ginny vowed that if she were ever a stepparent she would never treat a stepchild as she had been treated.

When Ginny was twenty-two, she married George, who had been divorced for four years, and had a five-year-old daughter, Amy, who lived with his former wife and stepfather. Before the marriage, Ginny spent many hours with Amy in an effort to establish a relationship with her. After the marriage, a pattern of regular visitation was established when Amy visited their home. Three years later, George and Ginny had a son. They anticipated that they would include Amy in the family activities whenever she came to visit, and that she would not be made to feel excluded because of the birth of their baby.

Two months after the new baby was born, Amy's mother suddenly died. Although her stepfather asked if Amy could continue to live with him because she had two half-siblings to whom she was very attached, George brought Amy home to live with him. He felt that Amy was "his" daughter, and now that her mother was no longer alive she belonged with him.

Ginny described the difficulties of helping Amy adjust to her mother's death. She felt growing irritation because Amy's needs intruded on her privacy with George and with the baby. George left all of the caretaking to Ginny. Increasingly, Ginny thought of Amy as an intruder; she wished that Amy had stayed with her stepfather and had never come to live with her and George. She expressed guilt about her resentment toward George for burdening her with the total caretaking of Amy; she did not feel she had a right to such feelings.

Ginny described a deep pervasive sense of guilt and shame that her performance in the role of stepmother did not match the expectations she had of herself. In addition, she found herself reviewing her earlier feelings of anger toward her family and castigating herself for not having understood the needs and feelings of her father and stepmother. She wondered if the estrangement that existed between her parents and herself could ever be erased.

The kinds of life experiences one has had in childhood are universally accepted as a significant determinant of one's self-expectations in adulthood. In Ginny's case, because of her experience of feeling excluded and deprived as a child with a step-parent, she had then developed an idealized version of how she, as an adult, would behave toward a stepchild. When the dual roles of natural parent and stepparent created tensions within Ginny, she had to cope with the disparity of thoughts, feelings, and behaviors between her idealized self and her actual self. The threat to her self-esteem that this disparity posed was the therapeutic issue. (For a fuller discussion, see chapter ten.)

Still another aspect of remarried family adjustment involves the complex tasks of redefining old roles, learning new roles, and breaking down barriers to positive ties. Struggle with environmental stresses of insufficient money, space, and time in day-today life often delays the formation of new attachments and bonds. The struggle with insufficient resources is a problem for many families who come to social agencies, but it can take on additional proportions in the remarried family. Marcia and Jack Carr told a group of remarried couples their story of repeated crisis, disorganization, and chaos, as they struggled to provide for their remarried family.

THE CARR FAMILY

When Marcia and Jack came to a family life education course at their local community center, they spoke of how overwhelmed they felt in their new family situation. They said that they were so busy "mending fences," they rarely had time to themselves to build their own relationship.

Marcia and her four children had lived in a crowded city apartment after her divorce. When she and Jack were married it seemed logical to move into the home where Jack and his four children lived because it was a better neighborhood. Jack's wife had died three years earlier, and he had worked very hard to keep things going so the children would not be "uprooted."

Despite extensive repainting, Marcia never felt that this was "her home." The furniture was not the kind she would have selected, the curtains were wrong, and the rugs were not the right color. But the cost of supporting eight children made the hope of replacing these things or of moving into another house unrealistic. Even if she had been able to erase the reminders of living in "another woman's house," as she put it, there were still the pictures that Jack's children prominently displayed of their mother. Added to this, his children frequently made negative comparisons of Marcia's cooking, looks, and general skills with those of their deceased mother. Marcia felt constantly undercut, but could understand it because, as she said, "after all, I am living in their home."

Jack's oldest daughter, Lynn, age sixteen, felt especially angry and displaced. She was bitter about the changes Marcia made in "her home." During the three years since her mother's death and for two years prior to it, when her mother was dying of cancer, Lynn had taken charge of the household and run things with skill and responsibility. She felt that she was the "mistress" of the house. She bitterly resented giving up the companionable conferences with her father about the "younger children" and their joint planning of family activities. The younger children resented changes in sleeping arrangements to include the new family members. Only Lynn Carr kept her bedroom.

Marcia's oldest daughter, also called Lynn and also sixteen, was angry at what she perceived as special treatment of her stepsister. She was also angry about leaving the old neighborhood and being "bossed" by Lynn. She was uncomfortable with the middle-class lifestyle of the kids she *was meeting in school, and was sure they were trying to "put her down." Most of all, she resented having to use her middle name of Jean or be addressed as Lynn Hudson, in order not to be confused with the "other Lynn."*

The cost of supporting a household with eight children who ranged in age from four to sixteen was staggering. Marcia kept her old job as a waitress; Jack did extra work as a carpenter for friends and neighbors at night. The older children were expected to take turns babysitting for the younger children. When Jack and Marcia returned home from work, tired and eager for some time together, they were instead greeted with horror stories of how "his" children mistreated "hers" or how "her" children mistreated "his." His children said her children "took over" and things that they had prized as their own were appropriated without their permission. Her children felt that anything they wanted suddenly became someone else's "prized possession."

The time that Marcia and Jack had looked forward to spending with each other suddenly melted away. The question they posed to the group was, "Where do you start?"

The story the Carrs told reflects problems that can be generalized to many remarried families who combine children of prior family units and live together under one roof. It often happens that when one family moves into the same quarters that previously housed the other family, issues of not enough space and whose space are crucial and recurring ones. Decisions such as which family moves, who changes schools, and who stays in the same neighborhood often stimulate much conflict and dissension. At a deeper level, the issue is often one of territoriality; whose turf is invaded, who are the invaders, and who are the defenders. Often a child's space in the family hierarchy is preempted when both spouses bring children of former relationships into the new, remarried family. Sometimes it happens that a child who has been the oldest or the youngest in the former family situation had to yield that position to another and become a middle child in the new family situation. This kind of change in ordinal position has ramifications for the nature and quality of individual identity and family interaction.

The stresses are further amplified when children are the same age and sex and have the same name, as in the case of the two sixteen-year-old Lynns. Given that names have popularity cycles, it does often happen that remarrying families have children of approximately the same age who bear the same first names. Issues of individual identity, who keeps his or her name and who changes it, must be included among the problems that need to be addressed in working out the conflicts, pressures, and dilemmas in the re-married family.

For parents, the task of maintaining the expanded family may mean that additional sources of income must be generated. Some-times support from an absent parent can be counted on, but fre-quently this is not the case. Also, it is often necessary for a husband to send money out of the home to support one or more children who live with an ex-spouse. Whatever the variations in income and outgo of money, the concern of parents about having enough money to support the remarried family is a real and recurrent one. It is not uncommon to hear of husbands who take extra jobs to maintain the household, as in the Carr situation. Sometimes when support payments are sent to a former wife and children there is tension because the new wife resents working "to support the husband's former family." As with any family, financial pressures cause stress and radiate out to create interpersonal and familial problems. The necessity of earning extra money initiates another problem, because it means more time away from home.

In remarried families, when there are new relationships to be fostered and old relationships to be maintained, the issue of too little time for too many people is a frequent and repeated one. Time, thus, becomes the scarce commodity. It must somehow be distributed so that each member of the family can have what he or she needs in learning to know the other. But the reality is that there is a poverty of time. As one father in a family life education course said, "The marriage is the last item to have time devoted to it to work out the concerns that confront any newly married couple." One mother added, "When we finally do manage to get some private time, we find ourselves worrying about the children and talking about their problems instead of building on our own relationship."

In the Carr family, the adjustment problems were an inter-weaving of issues related to inadequate time, space, and money. In an effort to save money, children were pressed into service as babysitters for stepsiblings they wished lived elsewhere. Sibling interactions of "you don't belong" complicated the normal sibling rivalries common to any family. Lynn Carr had to adjust to the change in her role from spouse and parent surrogate to that of one of eight children. For all members of the remarried family there were new roles, bonds, and affiliations to be established and in-tegrated with prior ones, so that a new family identity could be achieved.

And so the stories go. Each has its own particular pain yet is sufficiently universal to encompass the stress felt by many remarried families. These experiences from the client's perspective are only a few of the many that might have been selected to make visible the recurrent strains. However, these examples begin to illuminate some of the repeated themes and patterns of feelings and behaviors that professionals hear as they listen to clients in remarried families.

RECURRENT ISSUES AND DILEMMAS

Overall, these nine remarried family situations came to professional attention through many different channels and were seen in many different settings. Behavior difficulties, poor peer relationships, and deteriorating academic performance at school were signals to teachers that Billie, Nellie, and Kim were in trouble. Other clients, like Ellen Gray and Ginny Blake, were referred by physicians because no organic basis for their physical or emotional difficulties could be found. Still other families came to therapy because the stress was immediately identifiable in family relationships. Thus, the Maynors and the Ronsons came because their marriages were in jeopardy. On the other hand, the Brents and the Carrs sought help for difficulties clearly rooted in the strains of combining two prior single-parent family units into one remarried family.*

Broadly speaking, the problems and the issues that challenged these families fall within three major classifications familiar to professionals in a social work context, namely; insufficient environmental resources, intrapersonal difficulties, and interpersonal adjustment areas. A more detailed categorization of problems and processes with these families is shown in chapter nine, while chapter ten will expound on the process of intervention with the Brents, Maynors, and Blakes.

Beyond identification of the issues and dilemmas that challenge remarried families, it is important to understand the forces that consistently generate problems unique to this family situation. Myths and fantasies that lead to misguided hopes and, ultimately, disappointments, must be recognized for what they are. Furthermore, clients can be helped to recognize some of the normal and expected kinds of adjustments to be made that are specific to the remarried family. When these are seen in the context of normal,

*These cases are referred to throughout the book.

individual, and family stages of growth and development, a more realistic view of the family situation is obtained. This knowledge can free both client and therapist from assuming labels of pathology and failure. Remarried family members can, thus, anticipate problems and develop strategies to facilitate adjustments within their new families.

3

MISSION AND TASK

From its early beginnings in the nineteenth century the mission of social work has been to help man in distress. Implicit in this aim is the professional responsibility to identify populations at risk. During the twentieth century, the mission of social work has been joined to an increasing commitment to scientific inquiry into the factors which generate, maintain, or change vulnerable states into high-risk populations.[1] Through the development of specific knowledge grounded in clinical and research experience, professionals continue to seek ways to alleviate client distress.

In the context of this mission and task, the remarried family, a highly stressed population in need of systematic study, has been identified in clinical practice. The urgent clinical need is for a substantive knowledge base that expands understanding of the nature of the remarried family. The expectation is that if practitioners have access to such a knowledge base they can more fully and accurately comprehend the factors related to recurrent remarried family problems and dilemmas. Goals can then be more realistically determined, and therapeutic interventions can be more responsive to client distress.

As in all endeavors which seek to develop knowledge, study of the remarried family first clarifies what is already known, identifies gaps in existent information and theory, and specifies what more needs to be known. If this proves insufficient to provide useful directions, the task can be expanded to include exploration and study of analogous populations and of related information. Finally, it is necessary to synthesize and reformulate what has been learned into a usable framework so that the significant details about the remarried family population can be specified.

This chapter reports on the three-stage process involved in the search for knowledge. It comments on existing research and the lack of current and relevant theory to explain recurrent problems and strains in the remarried family, highlights some key reference points in the study of the nuclear family that are appropriate to study of the remarried family, and suggests a schema for that study. In describing this process, Robert Merton's suggestion of including tangential inquiries is followed. He has observed that reports of studies could be enriched by inclusion of many of the source materials which are often omitted. He urges that "intuitive leaps, false starts, mistakes, loose ends, and happy accidents that actually cluttered up the inquiry" be integrated in the final report.[2] Thus, some of the author's "loose ends" in the form of early, unpublished surveys, polls, and pilot study have been interwoven in the discussion as they have relevance to the remarried family.

THE THEORETICAL LAG

The theoretical lag in knowledge development on the remarried family is demonstrated by the paucity of research about this family in contrast to extensive empirical study and theory development about the nuclear family. The need for more extensive documentation of the remarried family experience has, except for personal accounts and books of instruction by stepparent authors, remained largely unattended.

One possible explanation for this is that the external similarity of the remarried family to other two-parent, two-generation families obscures significant differences so that nuclear and remarried families are considered to be the same. Another explanation is that many remarried family members and professionals need to perceive the remarried family as no different from the nuclear. Because of the lack of recognition or the denial of significant differences between remarried and nuclear families, the remarried family has not yet assumed an identity of its own in the constellation of families.[3] The multiplicity of names by which this family is known underscores this point and emphasizes its uncertain status. Indeed, a survey of the literature uncovered seventeen names to describe this family as follows: aggregate, amalgamated, blended, combined, compound, composite, consolidated, joint, merged, mixed, multimarriage, multiparent, reconstituted, reconstructed, recoupled, split, and step.

Clinical studies adopted the traditional stereotyped term *step-family*, while most sociological studies chose technical, value-free terms like *reconstituted* and *reconstructed* to neutralize the negative images stimulated by *step*. Currently, there is a growing body of literature, largely in use by practitioners, that refers to remarried families with such value-laden terms as *blended* and *merged*, thus implying the achievement of the goal of family cohesion.[4]

The choice of the term *remarried family* for this book is the result of polls taken of professionals who attended seminars and institutes given by the author on theory and practice issues in working with this family constellation. Students were asked to rank the list of designations given above according to greater or lesser preference, or to suggest a term that they believed was more suitable. Participants found limitations to all of the existing names, and no new ones that seemed any better. A significant finding of these polls was that there was no uniform favorite name, and that what one group selected as a first choice could be and sometimes was a last choice for another group of participants. *Remarried family*, was, however, never a last choice, sometimes a first choice, and often a middle-ranking choice. Despite its limitations, it is accurately descriptive, nontechnical, and value-free, and does not imply goals achieved. Moreover, it does not carry old negative stereotyped associations and is easily understood by professionals and lay persons alike.[5]

An overview of studies on the remarried family indicates two major methods of study—clinical and sociological surveys. Clinical studies have obtained their data from social agencies and therapists' files, and have, therefore, focused on remarried family members who sought professional help. In contrast, sociological studies drew data from remarried families in the general population. Both clinical and sociological studies were identified as early as 1930, but interesting differences in findings appear within these two major methods of study.

Clinical studies reveal consistent findings that the step situation was a high-stress experience for both stepmothers and stepchildren.[6] In contrast, sociological studies do not provide such consistent conclusions. Some found that stepchildren experienced the step situation as stressful and were not as well-adjusted as their nonstep peers.[7] Others, on the contrary, found that stepchildren were as well-adjusted as their nonstep peers.[8] Another interesting finding related to studies on stepchildren adjustment was the difference between children and parents in their perceptions of stepchild adjustment in the remarried family. Thus, when children were queried about their feelings of adjustment in the step situation they reported less satisfaction than they had felt in earlier family situations.[9] However, when mothers were questioned about their children's adjustment in the remarried family situation they reported the reverse.[10] After World War II, research interest shifted from studies focused on stepchildren and parent-child relationships to studies of marital satisfaction in the remarriage. Many of these studies found that remarried men and women were as happy or happier than men and women in first marriages.[11] However, other studies did not confirm these findings.[12]

A RESEARCH PILOT STUDY

Practitioners' discomfort with this state of contradictory knowledge caused them to press further explorations. They questioned why so many remarried families were seeking professional help, why so many stepparents sought to share their experiences with other stepparents through autobiographical accounts in books and newspaper columns, and why the remarried families who came for help were so highly distressed. In 1970, one family agency undertook a clinical-research pilot study to explore marital couples' perception of the "most burdensome" problem for them in their family situation and to inquire into what they hoped professional help would accomplish. *Burdensome* problem was defined as the client's perception of the problem seen to be interfering most greatly with his or her satisfaction within the remarried family situation.

This study found that stress between stepparent and stepchild and between stepsiblings was the "most burdensome" problem in the remarried family situation. In those situations where marital difficulties were identified as a problem, they were perceived by the marital partners to result from tension between step-related persons that infiltrated the marital situation.[13] These findings, therefore, confirmed earlier clinical studies that found the step situation to be a high-stress event for children and parents and, at times, a threat to marital happiness. Research since 1970 also found the step situation to be highly stressed, and reports of marital happiness were more mixed than earlier studies had indicated.[14] The proliferation of recent books on this subject by stepparents is further confirmation of the difficulties remarried families encounter.[15]

A limitation of existing research on the remarried family is that dynamics of the total family as a unit have not been considered because observations have been focused on only one part of the family system: stepchild, stepparent, or marital couple. In addition, these studies have failed to provide a theoretical basis for understanding the factors that contribute to remarried couple happiness and stepchild adjustment. Future studies should include an examination of the dynamic problems and processes within the remarried family that reflect perceptions of both parents and children. It is also necessary to identify an approach to the study of the remarried family that begins to contribute to substantive knowledge about this family and to explain their unique problems and processes at a theoretical level.

APPROACHES AND KEY REFERENCE POINTS

From a review of existing literature, the search for knowledge about the remarried family included an exploration of approaches to the study of the nuclear family. The underlying assumption was that significant concepts in the study of the nuclear family would be applicable to study of the remarried family, and the selection of appropriate concepts would permit comparative analysis of the similarities and differences between nuclear and remarried families. In addition, variations among remarried families could be specified. The approaches noted below have been identified as key reference points for inclusion in the development of a schema for study of the remarried family.

Throughout the twentieth century, scholars in the social and psychological sciences have developed various approaches to the study of the family. These approaches have been broadly classified into macro- and microanalytic perspectives. The macro perspective looks outward to global linkages between the family and society. The micro perspective looks inward to face-to-face encounters and relationships between family members and examines the family as a system in its own right. Ultimately, a perspective that combines both macro- and microanalytic perspectives is useful for comprehensive analysis of the family. This derives from the reality that families function in ways that contribute to the larger external goals of society, as well as to the needs and goals of its internal membership. At the present time, the social systems approach, widely used by practitioners, encompasses macro- and microanalytic perspectives. Because there is a broad body of literature in each of these approaches, only the most salient aspects will be presented.

The Institutional Approach: An early and foremost approach to study of the family, the institutional approach is macroanalytic in perspective and is widely used by historians and social scientists. It examines the family as one of society's major adaptive and evolving institutions. Social change and family change are interrelated. Cultural values and norms, as the cumulative expression of views over many centuries, are transmitted from one generation to the next. These values and norms eventually become incorporated into the legal codes that regulate the family.[16] This approach has utility for practitioners working with families because it identifies the broad social forces and cultural orientations of society that have shaped the current American family.

The Structure-Functional Approach: Rooted in sociology and anthropology, this approach has been applied to family analysis at both macro and micro levels of analysis, and can focus on one or both. At the macro level, this approach studies generalized family structures as they contribute to societal goals. Family structures are analyzed in terms of kinship roles, lineage, authority, and inheritance. Rules of residence, marriage, divorce, remarriage, and incest taboos are also important aspects of family analysis. All family theorists are in agreement that family functions have changed over time and that the universal function of the family today is the socialization and physical and emotional care of children so that they may eventually take their place as adults in society. Other family theorists include an affectional function and provision of a stable milieu for emotional and sexual gratification of adult members. The companionate aspect of marital relationships is emphasized. Still other theorists include the status-conferring aspect of the family as a major function.[17]

At a micro level of analysis this approach starts with the nuclear family as a stable referent and recognizes the universal influence of the family on individual personality and development. It examines the patterned relationships and processes within and between family subsystems, role behavior, bonding patterns, and ways in which families function to maintain their social system.

Values, norms, and priorities absorbed from the larger society are an important aspect of analysis of family interaction, identity, and status.[18] The structure-functional approach has value for practitioners because it provides a holistic view of the family at the interface between the individual and larger society. It combines analysis of social as well as psychological factors that affect individual behavior and family functions.

The Interactional Approach: This approach, microanalytic in perspective, draws from a large body of cumulative theory developed since the early twentieth century by sociologists and social psychologists. The family is perceived as a small primary group of interdependent persons in a field of interaction. This approach moves away from the focus on the relationship of the family to society and studies internal dynamic processes within the family. A cornerstone concept of this theory, first articulated by Ernest Burgess in 1926, is that the family is a "unity of interacting personalities."[19] Behavior is jointly determined and a function of the interactions of persons and the situation in which it occurs. Major contributions of this approach are its emphasis on role behavior and analysis of repetitive and reciprocal processes of interpersonal and collective behavior within the family.[20] Practitioners have found this approach productive because it encompasses family and small group therapy. It focuses on relationships between and among family members in such interactions as communication, role performance, decision making, conflict resolution, socialization, and bonding. Its attention to the situational constraints that influence behavior is congruent with the person-problem-situation focus of clinical practice.

The Developmental Approach: Also microanalytic in perspective, and conceptualized by developmental psychologists and sociologists, this approach builds on the structure-functional and interactional approaches. Its salient contribution to family analysis is its delineation of normal developmental family life cycle stages and the developmental tasks for mastery that accompany each stage. This makes possible the study of the impact of universal significant life events on family interaction and adaptation and prepares the way for analysis of the effects of life stress events on family development.[21] Practitioners have found this an enriching approach in examining the interrelationship of individual developmental dynamics and family processes.

The Situational Approach: Used predominantly by sociologists and psychologists, this approach is still another reference point. Although it has its roots in interactional theory, it has been developed as an approach to the study of the family in its own right. A situation can be identified at either micro or macro levels of analysis. The situational approach assumes that situations exist as objective and separate realities. The family is perceived as a social situation affected by external forces. Behavior is said to be purposive and interaction is responsive to specific aspects of the situation. The goal of the situational approach is to provide objective data on uniformities, recurrent problems and processes, cultural norms, sequences, trends, and other issues specific to the situation under study. Situations are studied inductively in order to identify the components that have relevance for behavior of individuals, problems, and processes within the family.[22] Practitioners working with families in multiple kinds of situations find this a useful approach in particularizing different types of conditions that affect the family.

The Social Systems Approach: This is the final key reference point from which the schema for study of the remarried family was developed. Introduced by social scientists in the 1950s, it integrates concepts from all of the approaches discussed, and expands the focus of analysis by the inclusion of such concepts as open and closed systems, boundaries, and family balance. This approach integrates both macro and micro levels of analysis because it examines the family as it relates to other social systems in society and, in addition, focuses on the internal structure and processes within the family. Although other approaches have implicitly recognized the family as a system, this approach makes the specific components of the family explicit.

The social systems approach is characterized by two major tenets. The first is a philosophy about the value of an interdisciplinary approach to the study and development of knowledge. The second is that a social systems approach is a tool for thinking about and organizing knowledge regarding social systems through the use of universal constructs, structure, function, and interaction.[23] When these constructs are elaborated on in connection with the key reference points discussed, an holistic view of the family is obtained. Practitioners have found this approach particularly useful because it is compatible with the historic social work tradition of interdisciplinary use of knowledge and, in addition, provides a systematic, coherent, and integrative framework for analysis of the family.

A SCHEMA EMERGES

The third stage in the process of expanding clinical understanding of the nature of the remarried family focused on the development of a schema through which this particular family unit could be studied. The process evolved to this stage because of the dearth, inconsistencies, and gaps in extant research and theory about this special case of family. Although each of the reference points discussed was a landmark contribution to the study of the nuclear family, a comprehensive theoretical orientation to the study of the remarried family required a selection and synthesis of the various approaches. The goal was to provide therapists and researchers with a basic organizing tool for acquiring facts about the nature of the remarried family.

The broad theoretical orientation that guided the selection and synthesis of concepts was that the remarried family was a significant aspect of the larger constellation of families and needed to be understood as a family in its own right. Within this perspective, the remarried family is defined as a primary, small-group social system. Drawing from the institutional and structure-functional perspectives, the expectation is that the remarried family contributes to larger society and, in addition, performs functions that meet the needs of its internal membership. It is assumed that both nuclear and remarried families share the same universal family functions of conferring status, socializing children, and providing a stable milieu in which adults can achieve emotional and sexual gratification. It is further assumed that a breakdown or conflict in these functions is often the basis of dissolution of the nuclear family and of recurring problems for which remarried family members seek professional help.

Overall, it appears that many of the problems and processes of the remarried family interaction are related to specific aspects of its situation. It was hypothesized that if the elements of the remarried family situation could be specified and examined in depth, some plausible explanations of the unique problems and processes of remarried family interaction could be made. Thus, problem and situation became the two major variables and the interactional and situational approaches were the two reference points. Some of the problems that are unique and recurrent to this family situation have already been delineated in chapter two. A problem-process profile based on content analysis of remarried families seen in family therapy by the author is shown in chapter nine. The rationale for this focus was based on the need to acquire knowledge from the perspectives of all family members.

A RESEARCH-CLINICAL FOCUS

The selection of the dimensions to explicate the remarried family situation was guided by two primary questions: (1) Does the elaboration of each dimension contribute to a beginning body of substantive knowledge that expands understanding of the unique and recurrent problems and processes in the remarried family? (2) Is this knowledge helpful to practitioners in their work with remarried families? Each of the five dimensions selected is an aspect of the family as a social system. However, each of the key reference points provides a broad literature, specific to each dimension, to which researchers and practitioners can refer. Thus, the schema that was developed was perceived to have a dual research-clinical focus. It is important to note that each of the dimensions selected as a discrete aspect of the schema is, in fact, intermeshed and closely interwoven with the others. However, for the sake of explication, it is necessary to consider each separately.

The first dimension, the social, cultural, and historical orientations of society toward the remarried family, draws from the institutional frame of reference. It examines specific literature that reflects cultural orientations that have contributed to the present negative images and stereotypes of the remarried family, and notes that the remarried family can and should be understood as part of a continuous process of social change.

The second dimension, the cultural orientations of remarried family members toward their own family situation and status, draws from the structure-functional and interactional perspectives. Its major focus is on the permeation of larger societal cultural attitudes into the interactions and identity of the remarried family.

The third dimension, the structural aspects of the remarried family, draws from the structure-functional perspective. It includes focus on family subsystems and boundaries, roles, and kinship complexities. Structural aspects of nuclear and remarried families as well as structural variations among remarried families are compared.

The fourth dimension, the developmental aspect of the remarried family, draws from the developmental approach. A comparative analysis of nuclear and remarried family developmental life cycle stages is demonstrated and essential tasks for mastery are discussed.

The fifth dimension, the legal aspects of the remarried family, draws from the institutional approach and examines legal doctrines over time that have relevance for remarried families. This examination is interrelated with the social historical context and cultural orientations of larger society toward the remarried family. In addition, the interactional approach is applied to analysis of these legal doctrines as related to problems and processes in family interaction. Structural and developmental aspects as well as cultural orientations of the family toward its identity and status are interwoven with the discussion of the legal doctrines. The legal dimension, thus, integrates all of the dimensions of the remarried family situation.

In summary, the remarried family has been identified in clinical practice as a vulnerable and distressed population. In the chapters that follow, the elaboration of each dimension in the schema provides information that contributes to the development of a substantive knowledge base about this family, and identifies some of its inherent realities. Ultimately, the usefulness of this body of knowledge in fulfilling the social work mission of "helping man in distress" will be tested in actual clinical practice with remarried families.

NOTES

1. Carel B. Germain, "Social Casework: An Historical Encounter," in *Theories of Social Casework*, ed. Robert Roberts and Robert Nee (Chicago: University of Chicago Press, 1972), pp. 14–15.
2. Robert Merton, *Social Theory and Social Structure* (New York: Free Press, 1957), p. 4.
3. Esther Wald, "Family: Multi-Parent," in *Encyclopedia of Social Work* (Washington, D.C.: National Association of Social Workers, 1977), pp. 390–96.
4. Ibid., p. 391.
5. Esther Wald, "Choose a Name," unpublished study, 1978.
6. See Louise Despert, *Children of Divorce* (Garden City, N.Y.: Doubleday, 1962); Irene Fast and Albert C. Cain, "The Step-Parent Role: Potential for Disturbance in Family Functioning," *American Journal of Orthopsychiatry* 36 (April 1966): 485–92; Clairette Armstrong, "Runaway Boys," in *The Stepchild*, ed. William Smith (Chicago: University of Chicago Press, 1953); Else Heilpern, "Psychological Problems of Step Children," *The Psychoanalytic Review* 30 (April 1943): 163–75; Nazre Kahlique, "A Study of Insecurity Feeling and Anxiety in Step Children and Non-Step Children," *Journal of Psychological Research*

The Remarried Family

5 (1961): 114–15; Janet Pflegler, "The Wicked Stepmother in the Child Guidance Clinic," Smith College Studies in Social Work 17 (March 1947): 125–26; Edward Podolsky, "The Emotional Problems of the Stepchild," Mental Hygiene 39 (1955): 49–53; and Annie M. White, "Factors Making for Difficulty in the Stepparent Relationship with Children," Smith College Studies in Social Work 14 (1943): 242.

7. See Charles E. Bowerman and Donald P. Irish, "Some Relationships of Stepchildren to their Parents," Marriage and Family Living 24 (May 1962): 113–21; and Meyer Fortes, "Step-Parenthood and Juvenile Delinquency," Sociological Review 25 (1933): 348–67.

8. See Lee G. Burchinall, "Characteristics of Adolescents from Unbroken, Broken and Reconstituted Families," Journal of Marriage and Family Living 26 (February 1964): 44–51; and Ivan F. Nye, "Child Adjustment in Broken and in Unhappy Unbroken Families," Journal of Marriage and Family Living 19 (November 1957): 356–61.

9. Judson T. Landis, "The Trauma of Children when Parents Divorce," Marriage and Family Living 22 (February 1960): 7–13; and Bernice Milburn Moore and Wayne H. Holtzman, Tomorrow's Parents: A Study of Youth and Their Families (Austin, Texas: University of Texas, 1968).

10. William J. Goode, After Divorce (New York: Free Press, 1956), pp. 307–29.

11. See Jessie Bernard, Remarriage: A Study of Marriage (New York: Dryden Press, 1956); and Harvey J. Locke and William Klausner, "Marital Adjustment of Divorced Persons in Subsequent Marriages," Sociology and Social Research 33 (November 1948): 97–101.

12. See Judson T. Landis, "Sequential Marriage," Journal of Home Economics 42 (October 1950): 625–28; Thomas P. Monahan, "How Stable are Remarriages," American Journal of Sociology 58 (November 1952) 280–88; Thomas P. Monahan, "The Changing Nature and Instability of Remarriages," Eugenics Quarterly 5 (June 1950): 73–85; and United States Bureau of the Census, "Marital Status, Number of Times Married and Duration of Present Marital Status: April 1948," Series P-20, no. 23 (Washington, D.C.: U.S. Government Printing Office, 1949).

13. Esther Wald, "The Multi-Marriage Exploratory Study," (Highland Park, Ill.: Family Service of South Lake County, 1970).

14. See Spencer J. Condie and Hans T. Doan, "Marriage—Second Time Around," Woman's Day 31 May 1977, p. 20; Lucille Duberman, "Step-Kin Relationships," Journal of Marriage and the Family 35 (May 1973): 283–92; Benjamin Schlesinger, "Husband-Wife Relationships in Reconstituted Families," Social Science (Summer 1977): 152–57; and Norval D. Glenn and Charles N. Weaver, "The Marital Happiness of Remarried Divorced Persons," Journal of Marriage and the Family 39 (May 1977): 331–37.

15. See Brenda Maddox, The Half-Parent (New York: Evans, 1975); Davidyne Mayleas, Rewedded Bliss (New York: Basic Books, 1977); June and William Noble, How to Live with Other People's Children (New York: Hawthorne Books, 1977); Jean and Veryl Rosenbaum, Stepparenting (New York: Dutton, 1978); Ruth Roosevelt and Jeanette Lofas, Living in Step (New York: Stein and Day, 1976); Leslie Aldridge Westhoff, The Second Time Around: Remarriage in America (New York: Viking Press, 1977); Carmel Reingold, Remarriage (New York: Harper and Row, 1976); and Suzy Kalter, Instant Parent (New York: A. and W. Publishers, 1979).

16. See Richard R. Clayton, *The Family, Marriage and Social Change* (Lexington, Mass.: D.C. Heath and Co., 1975); Robert W. Habenstein and Stuart A. Queen, *The Family in Various Cultures*, 4th ed. (New York: J.B. Lippincott, 1977); John N. Edwards, ed., *The Family and Change* (New York: Alfred A. Knopf, 1969); and Betty Yorburg, *The Changing Family* (New York: Columbia University Press, 1973).

17. See Rose Laub Coser, ed., *The Family: Its Structure and Functions*, 2d ed. (New York: St. Martin's Press, 1974); Bert N. Adams, *The Family: A Sociological Interpretation* (Chicago: Rand McNally, 1980); Bernard Farber, *The Family and Kinship in Modern Society* (Glenview, Ill.: Scott, Foresman, 1972); Robin Fox, *Kinship and Marriage* (Middlesex, England: Penguin Books, 1967); Claude Levi-Strauss, *The Elementary Structures of Kinship* (Boston: Beacon Press, 1969); and Alfred R. Radcliffe-Brown, *Structure and Function in Primitive Society* (New York: Free Press, 1965).

18. Norman W. Bell and Ezra F. Vogel, eds., *The Family*, rev. ed. (New York: Free Press, 1968).

19. Ernest Burgess, "Unity of Interacting Personalities," *The Family* 7 (March 1926): 3–9.

20. See Charles H. Cooley, *Human Nature and the Social Order*, rev. ed. (New York: Scribner's, 1922); George C. Mead, *Mind, Self and Society* (Chicago: University of Chicago Press, 1966); Herbert Blumer, *Symbolic Interactionism: Perspective and Method* (Englewood Cliffs, N.J.: Prentice-Hall, 1969); Ralph H. Turner, *Family Interaction* (New York: John Wiley, 1970); George C. Homans, *Social Behavior: Its Elementary Forms* (New York: Harcourt Brace Jovanovich, 1961); Dorwin Cartwright and Alvin Zander, *Group Dynamics* (New York: Harper and Row, 1968); Edward E. Sampson, *Social Psychology and Contemporary Society*, rev. ed. (New York: John Wiley, 1976); Jay D. Schvaneveldt, "The Interactional Framework in the Study of the Family," in *Emerging Conceptual Frameworks in Family Analysis*, ed., Ivan F. Nye and Felix M. Berardo (New York: Macmillan, 1968); Mary Louise Somers, "Group Process Within the Family Unit," paper presented at the Fourth Pacific Northwest Regional Institute, May 1964; Grace Longwell Coyle, "Concepts Relevant to Helping the Family as a Group," *Social Casework* 53 (July 1962): 347–54; and William C. Schutz, *The Interpersonal Underworld*, reprint ed. of *Firo: A Three-Dimensional Theory of Interpersonal Behavior* (Palo Alto, Calif.: Science and Behavior Books, 1966).

21. Nathan Ackerman, *Psychodynamics of Family Life*, rev. ed. (New York: Basic Books, 1970); Evelyn Duvall, *Family Development*, 2d ed. (New York: J.B. Lippincott, 1962); Joan Aldous, *Family Careers: Developmental Change in Families* (New York: John Wiley, 1978); Erik H. Erikson, *Childhood and Society*, rev. ed. (New York: W.W. Norton, 1963); Erik H. Erikson, *Identity and the Life Cycle: Selected Papers, Psychological Issues* (New York: International Universities Press, 1959); Daniel J. Levinson, *The Seasons of a Man's Life* (New York: Alfred A. Knopf, 1978); Jerry M. Lewis et al., *No Single Thread: Psychological Health in Family Systems* (New York: Brunner/Mazel, 1976); Bernice L. Neugarten, ed., *Middle Age and Aging* (Chicago: University of Chicago Press, 1975); Theodore Lidz, *The Person: His Development Throughout the Life Cycle* (New York: Basic Books, 1968); Harry Stack Sullivan, *The Interpersonal Theory of Psychiatry* (New York: W.W. Norton, 1953); Gerald Handel, ed., *The Psychosocial Interior of the Family: A Sourcebook for Study*

of Whole Families (Chicago: Aldine, 1972); Fred M. Sander, *Individual and Family Therapy: Toward an Integration* (New York: Jason Aronson, 1979); and George Vaillant, *Adaptation to Life* (Boston: Little, Brown, 1977).

22. See James H.S. Bossard and Eleanor S. Boll, *Family Situations* (Philadelphia: University of Pennsylvania Press, 1943); Lowell J. Carr, *Situational Analysis: An Observational Approach to Introductory Sociology* (New York: Harper and Brothers, 1948); Robert O. Blood, Jr., "A Situational Approach to the Study of Permissiveness in Child-Rearing," *American Sociological Review* 18 (February 1953): 84–87; James H.S. Bossard and Eleanor S. Boll, *Large Family Systems* (Philadelphia: University of Pennsylvania Press, 1956); E.M. Rallings, "A Conceptual Framework for Studying the Family: The Situational Approach," in *Emerging Conceptual Frameworks*, ed., Nye and Berardo; Max Siporin, "Situational Assessment and Intervention," *Social Casework* 53 (February 1972): 91–109; Gordon Hamilton, *Theory and Practice of Social Case Work* (New York: Columbia University Press, 1940); Florence Hollis, *Casework: A Psychosocial Therapy*, 2d ed. (New York: Random House, 1972); William I. Thomas and Florian Zaniecki, *The Polish Peasant in America* (New York: Alfred A. Knopf, 1927); William I. Thomas and Dorothy S. Thomas, *The Child in America* (New York: Alfred A. Knopf, 1928); Donald A. Hansen and Rueben Hill, "Families Under Stress" in *Handbook of Marriage and the Family*, ed. Harold T. Christenson (Chicago: Rand McNally, 1964), 782–819; and Peter McHugh, *Defining the Situation* (Indianapolis: Bobbs-Merrill, 1968).

23. See Kenneth Boulding, "General Systems Theory: The Skeletons of Science," in *Modern Systems Research for the Behavioral Scientist*, ed. Walter Buckley (Chicago: Aldine, 1968); Kenneth F. Berrien, *General and Social Systems* (New Brunswick, N.J.: Rutgers University Press, 1968); C. West Churchman, *The Systems Approach* (New York: Delta, 1968); David Freeman, "Social Work with Families: A Systems Approach to a Unified Theoretical Model" (doctoral diss., University of Southern California, 1973); Ludwig von Bertalanffy, *General Systems Theory* (New York: George Braziller, 1968); Robert Chin, "The Utility of Systems Models and Developmental Models for Practitioners," in *The Planning of Change*, ed. Warren Bennis, Kenneth Benns, and Robert Chin (New York: Holt, Rinehart and Winston, 1961); Carel B. Germain, "Social Study: Past, Present and Future," *Social Casework* 49 (July 1968); 403–409; Sister Mary Paul Janchill, "Systems Concepts in Casework Theory," *Social Casework* 50 (February 1969): 74–82; Roy R. Grinker, Sr., ed., *Toward a Unified Theory of Human Behavior*, 2d ed. (New York: Basic Books, 1967); James K. Whitaker, *Social Treatment: An Approach to Interpersonal Helping* (Chicago: Aldine, 1974); Ralph E. Anderson and Ira Carter, *Human Behavior in the Social Environment: A Social Systems Approach* (Chicago: Aldine, 1978); and Gordon Hearn, ed., *The General Systems Approach: Contributions Toward an Holistic Conception of Social Work* (New York: Council on Social Work Education, 1970).

4

HISTORY, SYMBOL, AND METAPHOR

A cumulative process of continuity and change over time has shaped the present social and cultural status of the remarried family. The past is embedded in present views of this family situation, and both present and past have implications for the problems, processes, and position of the remarried family in the future. This process of social change—crucial to an understanding of all family systems—is an objective reality and one of the basic tenets of history. The present visibility and increased numbers of remarried family are aspects of the family's institutional response to social change.

This chapter examines the social-historical and cultural dimensions of the schema for study of the remarried family as an institution through time. It focuses on some of the social-historical norms and patterns that have evolved and have relevance for present tensions in the family and the remarried family phenomenon. Further, it examines the cultural mold in which the step relationship has been cast by culture and tradition. The step relationship is explored as it is described in fairy tales and folklore, and some theories are offered to explain the meanings of the step theme and its crystallization in the metaphor that "step is less."

SOCIAL-HISTORICAL PERSPECTIVES

EVOLUTION OF MEANINGS OF STEP

Because current social-cultural orientations toward the remarried family have derived from human experience that shaped the earliest meanings and connotations of *step*, it is important to trace continuity and change in these interpretations through the centuries. *Step* is derived from Old German and Old English terms, the early meanings of which were tied to experiences of bereavement and deprivation. The Old English term, *stoep*, meant related by deprivation of a blood relationship; an orphan. The earliest designations then referred specifically to the child. Later, the term was broadened to refer also to the replacement parent, whether stepmother or stepfather, for the stepchild. Thus, the step relationship was comprised of a replacement parent and the bereaved, orphaned child. The concept replacement is illustrated in the comparison recorded in 1567 of a stepmother as a "bird that hatches another bird's eggs."[1] Between 1400 and 1800 the term *in-law* was used as an alternative for *step*. It is possible that because of the negative connotations the term *step* had acquired by this time, an effort may have been made to introduce *in-law* as a less pejorative substitute term. In addition, it identified the similarity of the step relationship to that of the in-law. However, this usage is no longer applicable to steppersons or the step relationship.

Today, *step* describes a relationship established by the remarriage of a widowed or divorced parent to someone with whom the child of the prior marriage has no blood or legal tie. The term has, thus, been expanded from the more restricted use denoting replacement after death to a usage that now includes an additional parent after divorce. However, the negative connotations that have long been ascribed to the parent who has replaced the deceased biological parent have been carried over and are now also attached to the parent acquired after divorce. For the term *stepchild*, a secondary definition in current use is "one that fails to receive proper care and attention."[2] The term *stepfamily*, increasingly found in lay and professional use, designates a family in which there is a steprelationship between a parent and a child and which often includes stepsiblings. It reflects a further broadening of the concept *step* to an entire family unit, and is not limited to the specification of particular family members. The term, however, is not included in standard lexicons or genealogical reference texts. Thus, four basic aspects of the human experience of the step situation are encapsulated in step: bereavement, replacement, negative connotations, and the lack of institutionalization of this family in the constellation of families.

EARLIEST FAMILIES

Little is known about how and when the family began, nor is there unanimity about the processes and stages by which the family has evolved over time. Some believe that the family was established at a particular time and in a particular place by Divine Law; others have advanced a theory of "straight line" evolution, in which the family passes through a progression of "single uniform series of stages" from the "less" to the "more" advanced. Still others suggest that the family has evolved through a process whose stages are not necessarily uniform, nor is a later chronological stage necessarily more advanced than its predecessor.[3]

Despite variation in theory about the origin and processes of the family, there is widespread agreement that the family is among the oldest institutions of the human race. It is both responsive to and stimulating of social change. Although family functions have changed over thousands of years according to environmental demands and the various economic and social needs of the time, the family, in its many diverse and meaningful forms and across many cultures, has achieved the position of a viable, significant, adaptive, and still-evolving institution—the cornerstone of civilization.

At some undetermined time in the history of the family, rituals were developed that began to define male-female relationships. A complex of customs emerged that regulated sexual attachments and legitimated the procreation of children. These customs often included prescriptions about the terms and conditions, other than death, under which ritual arrangements could be dissolved and new affiliations established. By the time of recorded history, marriage was a recognized aspect of the family concept. A pattern of norms and expectations had evolved about systems of family organization, power hierarchies, social roles within the family, and rules governing the circumstances for marital dissolution and remarriage. These patterns and practices, reflective of the circumstances and ideologies of their times, have continued through the centuries in processes of continuity and change. It is, therefore, important to explore some of the early patterns of family life within these areas that continue to influence the contemporary family and contribute to current tensions that result in marital dissolution and remarriage.

Study of the early families of Western civilization provides some understanding of the foundations of the modern family. These families were organized around a patriarchal, male-dominated extended kinship system that regulated social roles of men, women, and children, determined the power hierarchy in the family, and defined the rules for marital dissolution and remarriage. Only husbands had legal status and wives and children were paternal property. Husbands were the authority and wives were responsible for children and the home. Marriage for children was arranged by consenting fathers for the purposes of continuity of the family line and the preservation and continued acquisition of property. These patterns of patriarchal family organization, male domination, stereotyped sex roles, and little or no expectation of marital happiness have slowly undergone changes over the centuries, but they continue to represent significant areas of present-day family conflict.

Because of the harshness of life combined with a lack of medical knowledge in early times, death occurred early in the life cycle and was a major cause of marital dissolution. When families were broken by death, the surviving spouse and children were absorbed into the extended kinship network. Remarriage for both men and women was encouraged, particularly when there were young children who still needed care. At the same time, divorce was usually a privilege of men, rarely of women. Although a divorced man automatically retained custody of his children and generally could remarry easily, the social stigma attached to a woman whose husband had divorced her, and norms about remarriage for women, made it difficult, almost impossible, for them to remarry.[4] Remarriages, then, would appear to have been between divorced or widowed men and widows, each bringing their children of prior marriages into the family. Little is known about the emotional quality of life in these early families after remarriage, because records do not appear to differentiate between families that resulted from remarriage and those that did not.

Ancient family structures and norms about divorce and remarriage remained stable for many centuries, until weakened by repeated wars that took place at the time of the emergence of Christianity. Family disorganization was rampant and divorce and experimental lifestyles were the norm. Because family kinship systems were no longer able to regulate the family, the State assumed the power to control marriage and divorce through civil law. With the rise of Christianity, the Church gained the power to regulate the family, and reaffirmed the ancient principles of family organization along patriarchal lines and male domination. However, divorce was forbidden for both men and women of all social classes, and remarriage, even after death of a spouse, was discouraged.[5] One of the few records that documents the Church view toward remarriage is illustrated in a letter written by St. Jerome (circa 400 A.D.) to a widow contemplating remarriage. He writes:

> A mother sets over a child not a stepfather, but an enemy; not a parent, but a tyrant. . . . You will not be allowed to love your own children, or to look kindly on those to whom you gave birth. . . . If he, for his part, has issue by a former wife, when he brings you into his house, then even though you have a heart of gold you will be the cruel stepmother.[6]

Despite these dire forecasts about the emotional texture of life in the remarried family, the Church eventually accepted remarriage after the death of a spouse as a suitable alternative to widowhood, but continued to forbid divorce. The power of the Church to regulate the family continued through medieval times. By then, however, both the power of the extended family network and the Church to control internal family affairs had weakened, and family organization moved in the direction of increasing autonomy for the core nuclear family unit. Although children were still considered property, the concept of romantic love and marriage by personal choice was gaining acceptance. In the sixteenth century, the Reformation brought an end to the Church's absolute power to determine rules regarding marriage, divorce, and remarriage for all families, and this function was once again assumed by the State. Marriage became a civil-religious contract for many.[7] Nevertheless, issues of divorce and remarriage after divorce still remain a critical religious issue for large numbers of families.

THE IDEALIZED NUCLEAR FAMILY

When the colonists came to America, they carried with them many of the ideas of patriarchal family organization, male domination, and children as property. The hardships of the country encouraged them to live together in mutual support groups composed of the core nuclear family, unmarried relatives, boarders, widows, and orphans, likened to extended or surrogate families. All members of the family worked together as an interdependent economic unit, but the husband was the authority. Although marriages were no longer arranged by parents, parental consent was the norm. Legal marriage was the expectation, but social or common-law marriages were valid. Overall, families, although stable, were often broken by death. Remarriage for the surviving spouse was encouraged and frequently occurred soon after the death of a spouse. Divorce, however, continued to be more easily obtained by men, who also retained custody of the children. A few colonies gave women the right to divorce, but this option was rarely used by them during the early colonial period.[8] As the country industrialized and expanded during the nineteenth century, the core nuclear family individuated from the extended family structure of the preindustrial agricultural economy, and was characterized by greater mobility, urbanization, and isolation.

By the turn of the century, the core nuclear family became the predominant family unit. It had, thus, evolved from its early foundation of a male-dominated, patriarchal extended family system to a modernized male-dominated, patriarchal nuclear family unit. Social roles for men and women were clearly defined with husband as provider and wife as homemaker. One of the most significant changes that occurred was in the role of children, from early perpetuators of kinship lines and links in the economic network to valued individuals in their own right. Values and goals were child centered and family oriented and affectional ties within the family unit became an increasing expectation.[9] Most families remained intact, but death continued to be the primary cause of marital dissolution. Divorce was an option for both men and women if grounds could be proven, and custody was no longer the husband's automatic right. When families were broken by divorce, they continued to bear the social stigma of earlier times. However, whether they were broken by death or divorce, remarriage was encouraged. Although these families were not differentiated in the records from the nuclear family, they bore the weight of negative connotations associated with the step relationship. The core nuclear family was the model and the ideal of this time in the history of the family.

SHIFTING TRENDS

Not until recently did this outlook began to change dramatically. The idealized patriarchal, male-dominated family structure and stereotyped social roles were questioned by those who sought more egalitarian family forms and social roles. This ideological shift was fostered by an advanced industrial and medical technology that contributed to accelerated social change and redefinitions of the traditional roles of men and women at home and in the marketplace. An emergent philosophy of greater equality and entitlement, made explicit by the rights groups of many minority populations, the women's movement, and the youth culture, became the mode of the times. It challenged and made deep inroads into traditional orientations toward the patriarchal, idealized nuclear family. The interplay of these social forces and ideologies-in-transition contributed to accelerated social change within the context of political and social unrest. These converged in the 1960s to open up a broad range of alternative lifestyles for those who were dissatisfied with the status quo. A heightened sense of the right of self-actualization, greater economic opportunities for women, and changes in attitudes toward divorce contributed to increased numbers of men and women who were willing to consider divorce as a preferred alternative to remaining in an unhappy marital situation.[10]

Therapists now find that many of these divorcing parents are caught in the struggle of achieving a balance between two primary functions of the family—the socialization and needs of their children and their adult needs for companionate marriage, emotional gratification, and self-actualization. It would seem that this is a period of time in the history of the family when still another function must be clarified and integrated with those already identified—establishing a balance between the needs of parent and children so that all may have an opportunity for growth and gratification. Such a function is needed so that children's rights and parents' rights are harmonized in an appropriate balance of family relationships.[11]

Today, divorce has replaced death as the primary cause of marital dissolution. During the past few decades, the single-parent family has become an important area for study and social programs. However, the high rate of remarriage soon after marital dissolution, whether the original union was broken by death or by divorce, indicates that the single-parent family is a transitional family unit en route to remarriage. This suggests that the institution of marriage is still encouraged and valued and that both individual and societal needs that have traditionally encouraged and placed a positive value on remarriage continue. Paradoxically, cultural orientations toward the step relationship have been negative.

These orientations do not derive from historical documents, but are inferred from such rare documents as St. Jerome's letter, previously mentioned, folklore, and the literary works of novelists, dramatists, and poets. Although all of these sources illuminate important aspects of the step theme, the remainder of this chapter will focus on folklore.

Because an historical and continuing function of the family is to confer status, the paradox created by societal encouragement of remarriage and negative cultural orientations to the step relationship is significant for the social position and status of the remarried family. These entrenched attitudes have not only shaped current negative perspectives of the remarried family by larger society through time, but actively continue to influence views that remarried family members hold about themselves. Thus, a significant issue for consideration relates to the cultural origins of this negative perception, its meanings and enduring continuance in today's culture, and its implications for the future social status of the remarried family.

CULTURAL ORIENTATIONS

THE STEP THEME
IN FOLKLORE

Folklore, and the fairy tale in particular, has been a major wellspring for the development of current social and emotional perceptions about stepparents and their children. In its broadest sense, folklore includes all of the customs, beliefs, and traditions that people have handed down from generation to generation, first by word of mouth and later in written form. Myths, proverbs, nursery rhymes, legends, fables, and fairy tales comprise this body of knowledge.

Since the turn of the century, folklore has been an important data source for increasing numbers of historians, social scientists, psychologists, and linguists, as well as literary critics. An important focus of research of scholars in these multiple disciplines has been the extraction of meanings in folklore so that past cultures can be better understood and links with the present demonstrated. It is believed that an integration of folklore knowledge with historical, social, and religious documents adds authenticity to the portrayal of the values, customs, thinking, and feeling of earlier times and deepens our understanding of current values and belief systems.[12]

Therapists, as well, find that an understanding of folklore as it pertains to specific cultural groups enriches understanding of their values, needs, feelings, and beliefs. This is especially true in work with remarried families, because the step theme has left an indelible print on societal perceptions of the remarried family.

The origins and paths of dissemination of the fairy tale are said to be at least three or four thousand years old. They probably began as stories told by peasants in gathering places to entertain each other. Later, these stories were told by parents to their children, bards and minstrels carried the tales through the villages to court, and medieval priests used them to point a lesson. Over generations, each oral narrator, whether peasant or parent, bard or priest, may have embellished or changed the stories according to his or her views. However, many folklorists believe that, despite changes that may have transpired in the telling, fairy tales, marchen, or magic tales, as they were sometimes called, have preserved much of their original content and meaning, flavor and integrity.[13]

These early unwritten stories not only entertained, but also provided the listener with guidelines and rules to govern behavior. They helped people to know how to express joy and sorrow, how to tell right from wrong, and how to know what was safe and what was dangerous. Fairy tales had their roots in basic human feelings and wishes. They survived and had universal acceptance because they told people what they wanted to hear and were often vehicles for wish fulfillment and redress of social injustice.[14] Tale tellers expressed these feelings through symbols in the form of witches and goblins, dwarfs and giants, and fairy godmothers and evil stepmothers. Through the special language of symbols, imagination was stimulated and strong feelings were marshalled.

In his analysis of children's favorite fairy tales, Brian Sutton-Smith found that bears and wolves, giants and ogres, and witches and stepmothers were the most frequent representations of evil. The stepmother was the only mortal who shared the stage with dangerous animals and supernatural enemies.[15] In his search of motifs in the fairy tale, Stith Thompson found that "of all cruel relatives in the folktale, the stepmother appears more often than any other," and no motifs appear that identify a cruel stepfather.[16] In the same vein, Bruno Bettelheim comments that "replacement of an original 'good' father by a 'bad' father is as rare in fairy tales as the evil stepmother is frequent."[17]

MOST POPULAR FAIRY TALES

A recent content analysis of the motifs found in fairy tale anthologies from five leading publishers found that about one out of six of the stories had the motif of unnatural cruelty of stepmothers to stepchildren. Variations of this theme were found in several stories that dealt with mother-in-law mistreatment of a daughter-in-law. (Significantly, the cruelty in both situations appears to be related to the lack of blood ties.) The stories that appeared most frequently in these collections were "Hansel and Gretel," "Cinderella," and "Snow White." All deal with issues of bereavement for the child, who is deprived of a biological mother, and the relationship with the replacement stepparent. Thus, the step theme is central in all three of these tales. Other fairy tales in the anthologies that dealt with the cruel stepmother motif were "Six Swans," "The Almond Tree," "Ash Maiden," "Twelve Brothers," "Rapunzel," and "Mother Holle." It can be assumed that publishers choose to include in such anthologies those stories that are the ones most frequently read. The inclusion of so many stories with a step motif indicates the continued popularity of these particular tales, and the continued reinforcement of themes of unnatural cruelty of stepmothers to stepchildren from generation to generation.[18]

Further evidence of the popularity of these tales is documented by empirical studies. In one study, for example, parents in both Japan and the United States were asked to identify the fairy tales that they most commonly told to their preschool children. As in the anthologies, "Hansel and Gretel," "Cinderella," and "Snow White" were chosen most frequently.[19] Additional studies asking fourth-grade children in the United States their favorite fairy tales also found these stories to be among those selected most often.[20] Still another study sought to identify fairy tale recollections among professional participants in workshops on the remarried family. Participants were asked to list five fairy tales that immediately came to mind and to specify the themes they associated with each one. "Cinderella," "Snow White," and "Hansel and Gretel" were consistently included in the lists, and the themes most frequently specified were mistreatment of a stepchild by a stepmother and victory of good over evil.[21] Thus, it is apparent that parents, children, and professionals have been immersed in a culture that promotes the idea that stepmothers mistreat their stepchildren.

These three most popular fairy tales have been identified in all parts of the world. For example, "Cinderella" has been traced to ninth-century China in much the same form as it is known today. It has also been known for many hundreds of years throughout Europe, from Spain as "Ciencienta," from Greece as "Stactopcita," and from Italy as "Cennerentola." Cinderella has also been identified in Portugal and Brazil as "Barralheira."[22] Variations of "Hansel and Gretel" go back many centuries to early cultures in Africa and the West Indies, and among American Indian tribes, and "Snow White" has been traced to Renaissance Italy.[23] Although there is some debate about whether certain stories originated in one locale and diffused throughout the world or whether they developed independently in many different sites, there is no debate about their universal appeal.

The step-theme fairy tales, like all others, have an identifiable structure and a predictable sequence of events. They begin in an undefined faraway place and "once upon a time." They tell of a father who takes a second wife after his first wife dies. For a variety of reasons, including a stepmother's unwillingness to share meager provisions, feelings of jealousy toward a beautiful young stepdaughter, or resentment of a child who is more beautiful than the stepmother's own daughters, the stepmother mistreats the stepchildren and, indeed, devises ways to expel them from the home with no interference from the biological father. The children, thus, cannot rely on their natural fathers, who are helpless or absent and unable to halt the abuse. After many encounters with adversaries and misfortunes that test physical and emotional endurance, the stepchildren, either through their own wit or through supernatural helpers, are victors. The evil stepmothers, likened to witches, are punished, while the children are rewarded to "live happily ever after."

This theme of a cruel stepmother, a helpless stepchild, and an absent or passive father has continued to shape the current negative perceptions of the step situation. Its pervasive influence in today's culture has stimulated therapists to search for and identify those aspects of the step theme that are universal and relevant to the current step situation. Such a process facilitates therapeutic interventions that are more appropriately responsive to the inherent realities of the step situation.

SOME MEANINGS
OF THE STEP THEME

Although scholars in many disciplines have searched to discover the meaning of fairy tales, folklorists, in particular, have focused on this need. They have drawn heavily from anthropological and psychoanalytic interpretations. Many folklorists have urged that interpretations from these two approaches be integrated into a psychosocial approach. Still others have suggested that this focus should be broadened to include relevant understandings from history, religion, sociology, and psychocultural relationships. They emphasize that while each specific approach is valid and adds to the accumulated wisdom of links of the past with the present, each alone is incomplete. To overcome this limitation, it has been suggested that an interdisciplinary contextual field be constructed that integrates and begins to explain the recurrent themes and symbols of folktales.[24]

Richard Dorsen has said that ". . . fairy tales constitute a fantasy world constructed from cultural realities. They take the raw materials of life and interpret them through symbols that express man's conflicts, dilemmas, feelings and beliefs."[25] These symbols are powerful instruments for conveying direct lessons of wisdom and translating something in the real world into an imaginary world. In a similar vein, Erich Fromm has said that fairy tales link external and internal reality and must be understood and integrated at both obvious and hidden levels of meaning in order to arrive at a fuller understanding of the theme.[26] Thus, fairy tale themes and symbols cannot be separated from the context in which they appear.

At its most obvious level, the step-theme fairy tale, like all fairy tales, is a medium for relaxation and entertainment. It is a vehicle to transport the reader and listener to their own fantasy world and reduce the tensions of the day. It is a context in which parent and child can join for some period of time in a shared journey to consider the human condition. The fairy tale can provide a respite from the pressures of the real world and is restorative without necessarily resonating to ancient rituals or deep psychological conflicts.

From an historical perspective, the external reality of the times during which the fairy tale originated was one of physical hardship and deprivation, deep religiosity, and superstition. Life was short and the bereaved child was a common phenomenon, as were both remarriage and the replacement of the deceased biological parent with a stepparent. Although it may be assumed that stepfathers were as numerous as stepmothers, the focus of attention on the stepmother, indicated earlier, may be explained in terms of concepts of social roles. Families were organized along patriarchal lines of male domination, but men were out of the home for long periods of time in the performance of their role of provider. Meanwhile, women were the sole authority figures in charge of the home and children. In this role, stepmothers were in close contact with their stepchildren, and stepfathers because they were away, had little contact with their stepchildren. Explanations in terms of social roles provide some additional understanding of the context in which step themes took root, but they still do not explain stepmother mistreatment of stepchildren. Later chapters in this book elaborate on some of the inherent realities of the step situation that have been constants through time and may suggest some of the built-in tensions and dilemmas of the step role that were as true in ancient times as they are today.

Anthropologists have suggested that at an obvious level of interpretation the fairy tale is a cautionary moral story to both adults and children, warning that those who are selfish and jealous will be punished. This is made clear, for example, in the "African Ghost Tale" when the stepmother returns to life to warn other stepmothers: "Tell all of the other wives that I died because I mistreated the twins. Tell the other women that when they are given stepchildren as orphans to care for they must love them and treat them as their own so that they do not meet the same fate that I did."[27] It may be speculated that, in a world of early death, mothers in telling these tales to their children reinforced their own feelings that they were important to their children. At the same time, they warned stepmothers that, even after death, the natural mother continues to protect her children by taking on supernatural powers. Additionally, the fairy tale is a warning and moral lesson to children about unacceptable behavior. Another interpretation offered by anthropologists is that the fairy tale is a story of initiation or rites of passage. The child is perceived as struggling with universal psychological feelings that are unacceptable—jealousy, selfishness, and rivalry. In order to gain entry into the adult world, the child seeks to overcome these feelings by projecting them onto an outsider, often the stepmother, who symbolically represents the evil within the child that must be exorcised. The ordeals through which children must pass to save themselves from the wicked stepmother or witch are representative of the internal struggles to be won. Successful mastery of these trials represents the purging of unacceptable feelings within the child, who then becomes ready to enter the adult world.[28]

Anthropologists have also interpreted the fairy tale from a religious perspective, symbolic of the eternal struggle within man between good and evil forces. Supernatural representations of good (the fairy godmother) and evil (the wicked stepmother) are pitted against each other. Good is infinitely more powerful than evil and, in the end, prevails. "Fairy tales thus function to reaffirm the ultimate religious significance of life and the real possibility of a happy ending."[29]

Psychoanalytic interpretations of fairy tales have focused on the symbolic meanings at levels of the individual or collective unconscious. Those who have focused on the individual unconscious have interpreted folklore as a direct expression of unconscious fantasies of human beings. In the analysis of these tales from a Freudian perspective, confirmation is found of the concepts of individual unconscious efforts to deal with conflicts of existent unresolved oedipal feelings and the splitting of good and bad images.

In *Uses of Enchantment*, Bettelheim cites many examples to emphasize the value and meanings of fairy tales in pointing out important moral lessons to children, providing understanding of internal struggles related to unconscious oedipal conflicts, and the polarization of good versus bad as universal dilemmas for all children.[30] Helene Deutsch, writing more specifically about the stepmother theme in a psychoanalytic framework, suggests the importance of integrating these theoretical orientations with the reality of the step situation. She explains that the wicked step-mother story is a direct expression of hostile destructive aspects present in every parent-child relationship, but adds that it is made more intense by the step relationship. Although many who have drawn from the psychoanalytic perspective have not identified the specific factors of the step situation that intensify the parent-child conflict, Deutsch has been careful to point out that a focus on the step relationship within a format of psychoanalytic theory must take into account some of these factors. She explains the child's difficulties in the step relationship in the following manner. When the father remarries, the child loses an exclusive relationship with him that is often established after the death of the mother. After the remarriage, the child must share the father with the stepmother. Although the father was originally shared with the natural mother, the prior positive nurturing of the mother toward the child and the child's wish to maintain this relationship led to a positive identification with the mother, thus facilitating sharing the father. Because this store of love and nurturance is not present when the stepmother comes on the scene, the child has greater difficulty in sharing the parent with the stepparent. Deutsch further says that the sexual nature of the relationship between the father and the new wife stirs up "hate impulses" of children of both sexes against the stepmother. The child in the step situation has greater difficulty in resolving the oedipal conflict than is true with regard to the natural mother.[31]

Deutsch also believes that the presence of the stepmother activates the splitting of good and bad images of the mother.[32] The child, unable to express anger at the deceased mother who is perceived to have abandoned him or her, can displace this anger onto the stepmother. The inability to encompass both good and bad images within the same parent results in the child's splitting his or her feelings, assigning all of the bad feelings to the stepmother and all the good feelings to the natural mother. The natural mother continues to be "good" and is idealized, as the stepmother is cast in the role of the "bad" mother and is vilified. These unconscious phenomena feed the negative symbols and images of the "wicked stepmother" even when the behavior of the stepmother is not consistent with the image. Stepmother difficulties in relating to the stepchild are explained in terms of problems in overcoming the child's rejection and of her own motivations for the marriage. Both the concepts of unresolved oedipal conflicts and splitting of good and bad images have been useful to therapists in work with children in the remarried family.

In contrast to psychoanalytic interpretations based on the individual unconscious, many folklorists focus on theories of the collective unconscious and universal archetypes. Many believe that this focus makes more understandable shared symbols and themes of folklore that have been constant over time and great geographical distances. According to Carl Jung, the collective unconscious is the deepest and most inaccessible level of the mind. It is the primitive part of human beings that becomes the primary

base of a person's psyche and directs and influences current behavior. This theory postulates that just as the individual accu-
mulates and stores all of his or her past experiences in the personal
unconscious, so mankind collectively stores the accumulated experiences of humanity as part of a collective unconscious transmitted to every individual born. Through the collective unconscious,
man inherits the potentiality or predisposition to feel and behave
in certain ways that have been the same for people throughout
time in all parts of the world. Thus, each person is not only linked
with his or her own childhood, but with the history of entire
species. The central point of this theory is that the entire chronicle
of human evolution is imprinted on each person at birth and
repeated relatively unchanged for generation after generation. This
becomes part of the universal human experience and of each person's individual potential to feel and act in similar ways, awaiting
life circumstances to stimulate and activate these potentialities in
the present. The memories of the collective unconscious and potential for feeling and behavior are expressed through universal
archetypes.

An archetype is a pattern or model from which all other things
of the same type are made. It derives from primordial, ancestral
images. Archetypes encompass predispositions within the person
that await an actual experience in the person's present life before
the content becomes clear. The mother-child relationship is considered a basic human experience that has characterized every
generation throughout the history of mankind. This universality
is expressed in the form of the mother archetype. However, there
are many variations of this archetype depending on whether the
natural mother, grandmother, mother-in-law, or stepmother is
portrayed. Each reflects either a positive or a negative meaning,
but never both. Qualities associated with the positive mother archetype are maternal solicitude, sympathy, wisdom, and help.
Grandmother and natural mother are in the mold of the positive
archetype. On the negative side are mother-in-law and stepmother,
cast in the mold of secret, dark, and hidden qualities.[33] The lack
of a mother archetype that combines both positive and negative
qualities is consistent with positive and negative images of the
anthropological and the Freudian psychoanalytic interpretations.
If the concept of the collective unconscious is accepted, it suggests
that the potential for negative stepmother behavior is imprinted
on the psyche of every woman, awaiting the mix of appropriate
circumstances to make the content visible. The congruence of the

concept of the collective unconscious with that of the fairy tale is apparent in Linda Degh's definition of the folktale. She writes: "The folktale is a storehouse of survivals of ancient religion and ancient society. The marchen is a precious document of human history. Like the zone rings of a very old tree trunk, important events in cultural evolution can be traced through the fairy tale."[34]

Variations of the mother archetype reflected in the folktale have evolved into a belief system about the step situation. It begins with the choice of the stepmother from the symbolic representations of evil, the dark side of the mother. This has been said to reflect the "need to have the villain be an outsider in the family circle."[35] The expectation is that the natural mother is better able than the stepmother to deal with her feelings of jealousy, competition, and selfishness for the sake of her children.

The belief system about the step situation enunciates a cultural family doctrine that natural mothers are good and that stepmothers are treacherous and stepchildren are endangered by them. This doctrine, rooted in absolute values of motherhood, is consistent with concepts that split mother images as in the archetypal representations. Although the folktale limits this belief system to the stepmother and stepchild, it has the potential for transferability to stepfathers. Natural fathers can be perceived as all good, and stepfathers as all bad. In this event, stepchildren can be endangered by both stepmothers and stepfathers.

A new cultural family doctrine is needed that is more consistent with changing values of society and unique aspects of the step situation, as well as psychological theories that stress integration of positive and negative images of human beings. Thus, step feelings and behaviors can be understood as a potential mix of both positive and negative aspects that vary according to the general and specific elements of each remarried family situation. Such a belief system would facilitate a more balanced assessment of the remarried family situation.

Meanwhile, the ominous portrayal of the stepmother as dangerous often creates high levels of anxiety in many who live in step situations today. The scene set in a faraway land of "once upon a time" is not sufficiently reassuring for those who perceive that the events of the fairy tale, in less dramatic form, could happen to them. For example, following a children's story hour, a librarian asked a group of five-year-olds to discuss the fairy tale of "Snow White," which they had just heard. Many of the children were angry at the stepmother for mistreating the heroine and were happy about the turn of events, but some were subdued. One child commented tearfully that she had a stepmother. She was frightened that either she too might be mistreated or the security of her home would be disrupted if her stepmother were sent away. Another child wondered why the father had allowed all these terrible things to happen to Snow White. Not only was there fear because of what the stepmother could do, but there was also anxiety because, as in many fairy tales, the father had not acted as a protector.

Although children usually identify with the victory of the hero or heroine in a fairy tale and are comforted by this, the reality for many children today is that they *are* stepchildren; they *have* stepparents; they *live* in step situations. This reality often means that stepchildren are unable to differentiate the story from their life situation, and are fearful that they too may be harmed. Stepparents, too, may labor under the handicap of these images.

THE METAPHOR—"STEP IS LESS"

The obvious content of the fairy tale, the symbolic representation of the stepmother as evil, and the belief system espoused have all contributed to the view that "step is less." So widely accepted is this belief that the metaphor has evolved to indicate that anything that is of lesser value is "like a stepchild," while mistreatment is characterized in the phrase "like a stepmother." Many are familiar with this verbal shorthand and apply it to describe any situation that is perceived as "less good" or "less valued." It is also common to see the expression "like a Cinderella" used to denote mistreatment or neglect. One teacher, wishing to designate a boy in his class as an abused stepchild, described him as "Cinderfella," thus expanding this metaphor to specifically denote the male child. Anna Freud, searching for a way to comment on the status of adolescence, commented that "adolescence is a neglected period . . . a stepchild."[36] Conversely, there are the spontaneous accusations of enraged children who cry out against their natural mothers when angry or frustrated, "You are a stepmother!"[37] The frequency of such applications of the concept "step is less" are not isolated instances, but are representative of the pervasive acceptance of this metaphor. A letter from a teacher that appeared in a school publication emphasizes this point:

> In a recent issue you refer to science fiction as having been a
> "literary stepchild." I can find no excuse for perpetuating this

negative reference to the step relationship.

I believe that more than half of my 130 eighth grade students are involved in a step relationship of some form. To imply that this stepchild is of lesser value than one who is not "step" is offensive.

You should correct the impression you have fostered and emphasize the positive aspects of being a stepchild or stepparent.[38]

This letter reflects a popular culture that seeks to change the negative orientation toward the remarried family. Other examples that attempt to promote a more positive outlook on the step situation are evident in a growing body of literature written by stepparents and professionals.[39] In addition, a growing number of children's stories describe the stepchild's world without the terror of the evil stepmother or idealized and unrealistic expectations of quick and easy happiness for all.[40] The emergent belief system of many who write about the step situation today is that "step is not less; step is different."

Folklorists have recognized the importance of understanding the fairy tale in a broad contextual field. Within this field, prelogical and dysfunctional images of folklore that constrict contemporary functioning must be identified. When these beliefs are clarified and understood from a variety of perspectives they should be replaced with rational and constructive images that are more liberating and functional.[41] This process is now underway in the popular culture. Practitioners can also facilitate this process through specification of the inherent realities that underlie the step situation, those that have remained constant through time and those that are specific to current times. These realities can then be synthesized with relevant symbolic understandings, so that a balanced assessment of the step situation results that is congruent with social change and current society. Although the metaphor that "step is less" is not likely to disappear quickly, new images are in the making.

NOTES

1. See *Oxford Universal English Dictionary*, 3rd ed. (Oxford: Oxford University Press, 1955), p. 2014.

2. *Webster's New International Dictionary of the English Language* (Springfield, Mass.: G. and C. Merriam, 1950), p. 2470.

3. See Robert W. Habenstein and Stuart A. Queen, *The Family in Various Cultures*, 4th ed. (New York: J.B. Lippincott, 1974), pp. 5–13.

4. See William M. Kephart, *The Family, Society and the Individual*, 3rd ed.

The Remarried Family

(Boston: Houghton Mifflin, 1972), pp. 82–117; and Gerald R. Leslie, *The Family In Social Context*, 3rd ed. (London: Oxford University Press, 1976), pp. 4–27.

5. Kephart, *Family, Society and the Individual*, pp. 92–117.
6. Habenstein and Queen, *Family in Various Cultures*, p. 213.
7. Leslie, *Family in Social Context*, pp. 184–210.
8. Nancy F. Cott, "Divorce and the Changing Status of Women in Eighteenth Century Massachusetts," in *The American Family in Historical Perspective*, ed. Michael Gordon (New York: St. Martin's Press, 1978), pp. 115–39.
9. See Sidney M. Greenfield, "Industrialization and the Family in Sociological Theory," in *Marriage and the Family*, ed. Meyer Barash and Alice Scourby (New York: Random House, 1970), pp. 9–15; and Joan Berg Victor and Joelle Sander, *The Family* (Indianapolis: Bobbs Merrill, 1978).
10. For elaboration on shifting outlooks, see William O'Neill, "Divorce and the Progressive Era," in *American Family in Perspective*, ed. Gordon, pp. 140–51; Carl N. Degler, "Revolution Without Ideology: The Changing Place of Women in America," in *Marriage and the Family*, ed. Barash and Scourby, pp. 310–29; Alice S. Rossi, "Equality Between the Sexes: An Immodest Proposal," in *Marriage and the Family*, ed. Barash and Scourby, pp. 263–309; Daniel Scott Smith, "The Dating of the American Sexual Revolution: Evidence and Interpretation," in *American Family in Perspective*, ed. Gordon, pp. 426–38; Margaret Mead, *Culture and Commitment* (New York: Doubleday, 1978), pp. 95–121; Kenneth Kenniston, "Social Change and Youth in America," *Daedalus* 91, no. 1 (Winter 1962): 145–71; Judith L. Lyness et al., "Living Together: An Alternative to Marriage," in *Selected Studies in Marriage and the Family*, 4th ed., ed. Robert Winch and Graham B. Spanier (New York: Holt, Rinehart and Winston, 1974), pp. 490-97; John Scanzioni, "A Historical Perspective on Husband-Wife Bargaining Power and Marital Dissolution," in *Divorce and Separation: Causes, Context and Consequences*, ed., George Levinger and Oliver Moles (New York: Basic Books, 1978), pp. 20–36; Arthur J. Norton and Paul C. Glick, "Marital Instability in America: Past, Present and Future," in *Divorce and Separation*, ed. Levinger and Moles, pp. 6–19; and Robert F. Winch, "Permanence and Change in the History of the American Family and Some Speculations as to its Future," in *Selected Studies in Marriage*, ed. Winch and Spanier, pp. 480–89.
11. Esther Wald, "The Non-Nuclear Family," in *The Many Dimensions of Family Practice: Proceedings of the North American Symposium on Family Practice, 1978* (New York: Family Service Association of America, 1980), pp. 31–41.
12. Clifford Geertz, "Blurred Genres," *The American Scholar* 49, no. 2 (Spring 1980): 165–79.
13. Stith Thompson, *The Folktale* (Berkeley, Calif.: The University of California Press, 1977), p. 306.
14. Linda Degh, "The Oral Narrative," in *Folkways and Folklife*, ed. Richard Dorsen (Chicago: University of Chicago Press, 1972), p. 63.
15. Brian Sutton-Smith, "The Expressive Profile," in *Toward New Perspectives in Folklore*, ed. Americo Paredes and Richard Bauman (Austin, Texas: University of Texas Press, 1971).
16. Thompson, *Folktale*, p. 116.
17. Bruno Bettelheim, *The Uses of Enchantment: The Meaning and Importance of Fairy Tales* (New York: Alfred A. Knopf, 1976), p. 114.

18. Esther Wald, "Analysis of Motifs in Fairy Tale Anthologies," unpublished study, 1974.
19. Sutton-Smith, "Expressive Profile," pp. 84–85.
20. Ibid., p. 85.
21. Esther Wald, "Practitioner Perceptions of Fairy Tale Recollections and Themes," unpublished study, 1980.
22. Paulo de Cavalho-Neto, Folklore and Psychoanalysis, trans. Jacques M. P. Wilson (Coral Gables, Fla.: University of Miami Press, 1972), p. 162.
23. Thompson, Folktale, p. 36.
24. Richard Dorsen, ed., Folkways and Folklife (Chicago: University of Chicago Press, 1972), pp. 45–59.
25. Ibid., p. 21.
26. Erich Fromm, The Forgotten Language: An Introduction to the Meanings of Dreams, Fairy Tales and Myths (New York: Grove Press, 1957), pp. 11–29.
27. Barbara Stanford and Gene Stanford, "The African Ghost Tale," Myths and Modern Man (New York: Simon and Schuster, 1972), p. 349.
28. N.J. Girardot, "Initiation and Meaning in the Tale of Snow White and the Seven Dwarfs," Journal of American Folklore 357 (July-September 1977): 278.
29. Ibid., pp. 280–300.
30. Bettelheim, Uses of Enchantment, pp. 3–116.
31. Helene Deutsch, The Psychology of Women: Motherhood, A Psychoanalytic Interpretation (New York: Bantam, 1973), pp. 451–75.
32. Ibid., p. 456.
33. See Carl Jung, The Archetypes and the Collective Unconscious (Princeton, N.J.: Princeton University Press, 1959), pp. 3–25, 105–10; and Duane Schultz, Theories of Personality, (Monterey, Calif.: Brooks Cole Publishing, 1976), pp. 118–28.
34. Degh, "The Oral Narrative," p. 63.
35. Girardot, "Initiation and Meaning," p. 287.
36. See Anna Freud, quoted in John E. Horrocks, The Psychology of Adolescence (Boston: Houghton Mifflin, 1969), p. 30.
37. See Erik H. Erikson, Childhood and Society, 2d. ed. (New York: W.W. Norton, 1963), p. 29.
38. Jane D. Bucknam in "Letters to the Editor," Scholastic Voice 64 (April 1980): 18.
39. See, for example, Jean and Veryl Rosenbaum, Stepparenting (Corte Madera, Calif.: Chandler and Sharp, 1977); Joel D. Block, To Marry Again (New York: Grosset and Dunlap, 1979); and June Noble and William Noble, How to Live with Other People's Children (New York: Hawthorne Books, 1977).
40. Evan Hunter, Me and Mr. Stenner (Philadelphia: J.B. Lippincott, 1976); and Janet Sinberg Stinson, Now I have a Stepparent and It's Kind of Confusing (New York: Avon, 1979).
41. de Cavalho-Neto, Folklore, p. 200.

5

⁓

OLD IMAGES AND
NEW MYTHS

When the remarried client and therapist work together in the therapeutic context, they bring with them their views of the step situation. It may be assumed that the remarried family client, the practitioner, and others who interact with the remarried family, like the general population, have not escaped the traditional negative cultural orientations toward this family. These views combine with each person's individual life experience to result in a statement about his or her own belief system about this family situation. How the views of remarried family members intermesh among themselves as well as how those of client and therapist join in the clinical context has implications for issues of engagement, diagnostic assessment, and the therapeutic process. As the clinical interview unfolds, the belief systems of client and practitioner reflect some common dimensions. Assuming that the belief systems uncovered in the clinical interview mirror those of larger society, this process makes possible a beginning identification of current cultural orientations toward the remarried family—the new lore or popular culture.

This chapter examines the dimension of the schema for study of the remarried family that focuses on current cultural orientations that family members have toward their own family situation. These are reflected in tension points that arise around the mix of old and new images and myths, terms of self-referral and address, and issues of lifestyle and acculturation to the new family system.

Despite changing ideologies about roles of men and women in the family, a philosophy of self-actualization, and more enlightened perspectives about divorce as a resolution for marital conflict, negative orientations about the step situation have continued. These orientations have cast a shadow on remarriage as a restorative measure for many families broken by death or divorce. However, as indicated in the previous chapter, an increasing amount of literature on the remarried family population has as its purpose redress from the archaic images and stigmatized stereotypes. This literature illustrates a movement away from the old images to a more accurate reflection of the step situation. Largely autobiographical, this literature reflects attitudes that the remarried family has unique problems and a unique identity. As Ruth Roosevelt and Jeanette Lofas (both of whom are stepparents) write:

> Neither parents, nor children, nor society is prepared to acknowledge troubles endemic to the step situation. The new family will be just like the original one, only better. The old problems will disappear. That they will continue or that new problems will arise is not an idea that is easily tolerated.[1]

In contrast, the clinical interview documents that many of the clients who seek professional help have accepted the traditional stereotypes or have fashioned new myths that deny any difference between the nuclear and remarried family. Orientations are needed that recognize similarities and inherent differences between nuclear and remarried families.

Current cultural orientations toward the remarried family are a mix of old images and new myths. For some, traditional perceptions of the stepmother have been internalized. They are ever-present as residual symbols of the past, barriers to the development of trusting relationships within the family. These beliefs exist outside of the conscious awareness of the holder and emerge as surprises to those who have them. Others have been acculturated to perceptions of the remarried family as a less valued family than the nuclear. The only reference group they have by which to establish expectations are the stepfamilies of folklore. Still others have judged remarried families by standards established for nuclear families and, thus, have found remarried families wanting. They have accepted the metaphor that "step is less" and accord the remarried family less status than the nuclear family. These beliefs are often accompanied by feelings of diminished self-worth and depreciated family identity because they are members of re-married family systems.

Still others have created new myths that do not recognize the remarried family as a family with its own unique identity. These perceptions are based on wishful thinking and attempt to force reality into some predetermined mold of "what should and ought to be." Sometimes the new mold is formed in a reaction to the step position in folklore and, instead, takes the view that the step situation is "no different" from the nuclear family. These percep-tions are regarded as fact, yet they distort the reality they are intended to describe.

Other myths that expect instant love and role performance that exceeds that of the natural parent are also part of the new my-thology of some remarried families. The new myths, based on denial and unrealistic expectations of self and others, fail to ad-dress the inherent realities of the remarried family situation. The general population, remarried family members, therapists, and significant others are all vulnerable to the fallacies embedded in the old images and new myths.

It is especially important in therapeutic intervention to identify differences in cultural orientations among remarried family mem-bers in the family. Each spouse may have a different belief system about the remarried family, or spouses may agree with each other, but differ with their children. These differences contribute to prob-lems in individual and family identity as well as to different kinds of self and other expectations, perceptions of family status, and goals for family functioning. Clarification of the cultural orien-tations of remarried family members toward this family constel-lation is an early task of therapeutic intervention often overlooked by practitioners.

FAMILY MIXES
OF IMAGES AND MYTHS

One kind of family mix of cultural orientations toward the re-married family involves the interaction of one spouse, who is open and spontaneous in welcoming the new step relationship, with the other spouse, who has internalized the negative stereotypes about the stepparent. This spouse-parent perceives his or her role to be that of protector of his or her child of the prior marriage from the stepparent. Although the verbalized wish is that the new spouse-stepparent and the child develop a meaningful relationship, the behavior of the biological or adoptive parent actually inhibits this process. (For purposes of simplification, the terms biological and adoptive will not be differentiated. Natural parent will at times serve as an alternative term to reflect a parent who has been a biological or adoptive parent of a child of a prior marriage.)

THE BATESON FAMILY

When the Batesons had been married less than a year, Mrs. Bateson applied to the family service agency that had helped her though a painful divorce and a number of crises during the two-year period when she and her two daughters lived as a single-parent family unit. At the time of her remarriage, the older daughter, Ann, eighteen, was away at college and fourteen-year-old Ruth was at home.

Mr. Bateson, a successful businessman, also had been divorced. His only son, Paul, thirteen, lived with his mother for three years after the divorce, but decided to live with his father when he remarried. At the time of the application, the family comprised Mr. and Mrs. Bateson, one of her children and one of his children all the time, and Ann, who came home for holidays and vacations.

Both Mr. and Mrs. Bateson said they had felt prepared to handle the adjustments involved in blending the two families. However, they identified a pervasive sense of discomfort that all was not right in the family. As the definition of the problem was sharpened, Mr. and Mrs. Bateson specified that the discomfort they experienced appeared to be centered in their relationships to their children.

Mr. Bateson was satisfied with the relationship his wife had established with Paul and his own relationship with Ruth. Although Mrs. Bateson felt that her husband and Ruth had a warm and loving relationship, she was troubled that her husband was not as relaxed with Paul. More than that, she was puzzled by the "surface" quality of her relationship with Paul, because she felt that she had a genuine affection for him and thought that he reciprocated these feelings for her. She felt that the family as a unit was not achieving a sense of closeness.

As the possible barriers to the achievement of greater closeness between Mrs. Bateson and Paul were probed, she reflected that she never seemed to have private time with Paul, in contrast to Ruth and her husband, who seemed to manage this with no difficulty. As she reconstructed her interactions with Paul, she recognized that whenever she was disciplining Paul or planning some activity that would give them private time together, her husband suddenly appeared to interrupt the discipline or the activity.

It was not until several months of therapy had passed that the meaning of this pattern was dramatized in a episode that Mrs. Bateson brought *for discussion. She reported that she and Paul were talking about some aspect of his need to take better care of his clothing, when Mr. Bateson appeared. He justified Paul's behavior and negated the rules that Mrs. Bateson was trying to establish. As the impact of this transaction was examined, Mr. Bateson suddenly blurted out, "But you are his stepmother!" This remark brought into focus Mr. Bateson's deeply repressed anxiety that his wife, as stepmother, could harm his son. His many appearances when Mrs. Bateson and Paul were together reflected his constant watchfulness to make sure that he offered protection to his son, unlike the fathers in fairy tales who were rarely, if ever, present.*

The Bateson family situation dramatizes the repressed internalized cultural expectations of the "wicked stepmother" that lurk as ghosts to haunt families who are committed to moving beyond their earlier trauma and to forming new relationships. It is an example of Margaret Mead's observation that "fear of stepparents permeated fairy tales, and still dominates the life stories of many older people."[2] These families need help in making explicit the cultural issues that are interfering with effective family functioning. During the therapeutic process, Mr. Bateson was in touch for the first time with his internalized negative image of the stepmother as one who could not be trusted with a stepchild. Thus, he could not trust his wife with Paul and had to be constantly alert so that she would not act out the archetypal evil behavior seen in fairy tales. Once the myth was identified in his current behavior, Mr. Bateson worked to differentiate Mrs. Bateson from the folkloric stepmother. Later work helped him to achieve a more relaxed relationship with Paul, as he had been able to do with Ruth. Mrs. Bateson, now able to establish herself as a caring and giving stepmother, developed the closer bond with Paul that she sought. The pervasive discomfort described at the outset of therapy was replaced with greater family spontaneity, as distrust gave way to trust.

The image of the wicked stepmother has, in many cases, also extended to apply to stepfathers, as in the case of the Morgan family.

THE MORGAN FAMILY

The Morgans sought professional help from a family service agency after six years of unsuccessful effort to bring about a cohesive family unit. The presenting problem, in Mr. Morgan's words, was, "No matter how much I try to do for Art, he accuses me of not doing enough. I always end up feeling like the wicked stepfather."

The family interview revealed that Art had deep feelings of deprivation about the loss of his earlier family structures: he felt that his mother and stepfather had to compensate him for these losses. His mother, guilty that Art was so unhappy, turned to her new husband to make things "come out all right for her son." When Mr. Morgan found himself unable to fulfill his wife's and Art's expectations of him, he came to believe that there was something wrong with him, that he was indeed no different from the stepparent in the folktale. The underlying issues of Art's deprivation, his mother's guilt, and his stepfather's feelings of inadequacy in the context of inappropriate stepparent images became the focus of therapeutic intervention.

In cases such as the Morgans, therapist and family are often involved in shaping new images of the stepparent based on current realities.

Another frequently observed family mix of cultural orientations toward the remarried family is that of one spouse expecting that the new spouse will feel instant love for his or her child and the other experiencing this expectation as asking too much of him or her. The Gray family situation reflects these dynamics. Ellen Gray's belief reflected expectations that all in the family who loved her would love each other. Her reasoning went something like this:

I love my husband.
My husband loves me.
I love my child.
My child loves me.
Therefore, my husband and my child will love each other.

This expectation is related to a belief that all family members feel positively and the same toward each other. Such an expectation of instant love by affiliation is understandable if one's prior nuclear family was organized around the dynamic of a closely knit family unit, as it had been for Ellen Gray before she was widowed, and if, in addition, there is little knowledge of the inherent realities of the remarried family situation. Jim Gray, on the other hand, had been unmarried and did not have a background of close family ties with a former spouse and children. In contrast to some unmarried men who become stepfathers and welcome a "ready-made" family, he was reserved and distant from his stepdaughter. In such cases, the myth of instant love by affiliation is on a collision course with stepparent behaviors that do not fulfill the expectation of mutually shared love among all family members. Those who hold this view have not differentiated their new family from their earlier nuclear family. They believe that the expectations of natural parents can and should be held of stepparents. For many natural parents who hold this belief, it is inconceivable that a spouse-stepparent would not share their feelings for their children. This was the situation for Greg and Janet Ronson.

Greg expected that Janet would accept and love his children as her own. The marital difficulties they experienced were, in part, because she could not see his children as a substitute for those she wished to have. Greg had a belief that his children should become Janet's, just as they were his. He had replaced the myth that the stepmother is evil with one that said she was no different from the natural mother and, therefore, should love her stepchildren as her own. In both the Gray and the Ronson families, each spouse had different perceptions of what was possible; the spouse-natural parent expected instant love by affiliation and the spouse-stepparent rejected this expectation as unrealistic.

Conversely, many stepparents assume the myth of instant love as valid. Their belief system says that stepparents should feel no differently toward a stepchild then one would feel toward a natural child. These stepparents do not reject the negative images and archetypes of the wicked stepmother, but, rather, the images act as reminders of what one should not be. Many have constructed for themselves an idealized self-image or ego ideal that rigidly specifies expectations and behaviors for stepparents that are more exacting and demanding than those they have for themselves as natural parents. The ego ideal, that part of the personality integrating many images that portray the person at his best, becomes the organizing framework and standard by which the stepparent behavior is evaluated.

Images that comprise an individual's ego ideal are created in the course of one's development in response to mythological, historical, or living examples. The idealized self-image is the self-conception one strives to be, and it requires that there be a standard of comparison.[3] It would, seem, therefore, that a stepparent who has chosen to develop an ego ideal or idealized self-image of appropriate stepparent behavior has selected the wicked stepmother or the near-perfect mother as the comparative parameter. Stepfathers, too, may adopt this myth and equate less than idealized paternal behavior to be a counterpart of the evil stepmother.

The new myth developed by the modern stepparent sets rigorous standards of parenting behavior that include demands of unreserved positive feelings toward one's stepchild. It is an idealized image that leaves no room for common human errors, emotions, or inadequacies. It enjoins the stepparent to be "better than" a natural parent; the ego ideal is that of "super parent." Spontaneous behaviors are repressed in the service of this ideal. Joan Peters told such a story.

THE PETERS FAMILY

Joan and Bert, both in their early thirties, had been married about one year when Joan applied for professional help. She and Bert married a year after he had been widowed. Mark, Bert's son, was five years old when his mother died. After his mother's death, Bert and Mark went to live with Bert's parents, where they remained until Bert and Joan were married. Joan did not have any children. She had been married for seven years and divorced for three. At age thirty-two, she felt ready to help Bert and Mark rebuild their lives. In the process, she expected to find resolution of her own loneliness and fulfillment of her wish for a happy home life.

When Joan sought help from a local mental health clinic, she felt under constant tension to perform in the role of the "super parent" for her seven-year-old stepson, Mark. This problem was compounded because her husband and Mark's grandparents were quick to criticize any aspect of her behavior that they considered "unmotherly." Even so, she reported, she knew she did everything she "should do." She read to him, played games with him, and watched television with him. She had special treats and outings arranged when he came home from school. She made efforts to dovetail many of her activities to fit his routine. Yet, in the climate of the Peters family, where so much was expected of her, Joan found herself afraid of her own spontaneous reactions. She became very controlled in her activities with Mark, only doing and saying things for which she knew she could not be criticized.

Although the details of Joan's story may vary from family to family, the dynamics they dramatize are true for many remarried families when the myth of "super parent" is upheld by the stepparent. If other family members also subscribe to this expectation, the stepparent has no support systems to help him or her develop and accept realistic standards for role performance. Such families are locked into a network that generates constraint and inhibits genuine feelings. In such cases, the stepparent may become immobilized by the anxiety of not measuring up to his or her own idealized standards of stepparent behavior and feelings, as well as those of significant others. Feelings of diminished individual identity and self-worth frequently result.

The critical issue for therapeutic intervention is the clarification of discrepancies between normal expected behaviors and myths of "super parent" performance. In addition, it is important to find ways to help other family members consider how their unrealistic expectations reinforce myths that inhibit the development of authentic relationships between stepparent and stepchild. Issues of identity must be addressed so that the stepparent's sense of worth derives from realistic expectations. (See Ginny Blake, chapter ten.)

Another family mix frequently observed in clinical practice is reflected in the Brent family situation. In this case, the crucial issue was one of family identity. The differing perceptions of the status of the remarried family became a generational issue, with the parents subscribing to the belief that there was no difference between nuclear and remarried families, while the children adhered to the belief that "step is less."

When such polarization is observed in clinical practice, those who adhere to the myth of no difference strive to project an identity by making such rationalizations as "all families have difficulties," or "it all depends on the individuals involved," or "all kids fight." These observations, although true, ignore or underestimate the stress factors induced by the step situation itself that are in addition to the individual, familial, and external adjustments to the new life situation that are required of all persons involved. They deny the reality of objective differences that make this family a special case of family and give it a unique identity. Similarly, adherence to the "step is less" myth denies current strengths in remarried families and the opportunities that are potentially available for meaningful family relationships in this family structure. Ultimately, a family identity must be achieved that neither idealizes nor depreciates the remarried family, but recognizes its inherent realities and worth.

BY WHAT NAME?

A major gain toward achieving a new family identity is understanding and resolving the dilemmas that exist in regard to terms of reference and address. However, society has not yet given the remarried family a name it can carry without the negative derivations that diminish and are not congruent with its current status. The lack of a commonly accepted term to describe this family situation, as described in chapter three, speaks to the uncertain status of this family constellation that permeates to the core of individual and family identity. Because there is no generally accepted term by which this family is known, each family is left to choose a name for itself. Its choices often reflect confused identity, split loyalties, and conflicts about affiliation and distance. Therapists can gain access to an understanding of the cultural orientations of the remarried family with whom they are working by giving attention to how families identify themselves to the outside world and the terms of address they use for each other.

Many remarried families who come for professional help prefer not to differentiate themselves from the nuclear family, and this information may not become apparent until some time after the application for service. Some, on the other hand, have adopted the term stepfamily. Others, not able to identify themselves as stepfamilies but wishing to differentiate themselves from nuclear families, describe themselves with humor as "we're a yours, mine, and ours family," or "we're a recycled or second-time-around family." Still others, recently remarried, may describe themselves simply as a "new" family. Most remarried families are eager for a term to describe themselves that is nonjudgmental and accurately descriptive. Many have welcomed the term remarried family as such a designation.

Another way in which remarried families identify themselves to the outside world is in the choice of surname. In the nuclear family, all family members are known by one surname, unless the wife chooses to retain usage of her maiden name. In the remarried family there are often two surnames when children of a wife's prior marriage retain the surname of their biological or legal father. The difference in surname makes public the fact that this family is different. This is seen by some as an intrusion into their family privacy; yet, legal rights of an absent father and institutional policies about the use of legal names often prevent the use of the same surname for all members of the remarried family.

Although the use of the same surname for all family members is frequently desirable and a measure of the wish of all family members to belong to the same family unit, at times it is an implementation of a strategy to deny the differences between the nuclear and remarried families. It thus resonates to myths of "no difference." When this is the case, the surname is an imposed one rather than a natural consequence of family cohesion. It is an aspect of denial of difference and the reality of the new family status. It may reflect the effort, because of shame and feelings of depreciation about membership in this family system, to keep the public from knowing that this is a remarried family. Or, it may simply be a matter of convenience. One mother told of the confusion her child experienced in school because he bore a surname different from the rest of the family. In order to reduce this confusion, she decided to enroll him the next year under her name.

Different surnames within the same family contribute to maintaining separate identities and loyalties when the family goal is one of joining and cohesion. To the extent that nomenclature can preserve the "no difference" myth, many remarried families press for this solution to the issue of choice of surname. Yet, it sometimes happens that a child identified with the new surname may at adolescence seek to reestablish his or her earlier identity and return to the earlier surname.

Sometimes a child may wish to be known by the stepfather's surname, but the stepfather has difficulty sharing his name with a child who is not his own. A mother told of her husband's generosity in supporting her child, giving freely of his time and energy, yet he was unable to allow the child to assume his surname. Conversely, a stepparent may be eager to have the entire family adopt his name, only to find a child does not wish to or a child may be eager to do so, but the absent father may not allow it. When the absent parent is deceased, this issue is not as difficult and many of these families do adopt the surname of the new husband for the entire family unless deference to grandparents or school policy does not permit this.

One fourteen-year-old boy whose parents were divorced resented the fact that his name was different from that of his stepsiblings. He wanted to belong to both families. Finally, he conceived of the idea of a hyphenated name and became known as John Smith-Jones. Many families have solved the problem of different surnames by using the name of the marital couple as the family name, but encouraging children of a prior marriage who have a different legal name from the family name to use a hyphenated name. In this way, these children can retain their old identity but also be identified as a part of the new family system.

On still another level, the issue of terms of address among family members reflects cultural orientation. In the nuclear family, specific role names such as mother and father designate family position and status. In the remarried family, the appropriate designation requires the addition of the prefix *step* to differentiate the nuclear and remarried parent status. Yet, many parents are disturbed by the terms stepmother or stepfather and seek to influence their children to use terms associated with the natural parent. Elizabeth Gaskell, writing in Victorian England in 1864, focused on the issue of name as one of the complexities of the step situation. In her book, *Wives and Daughters*,[4] the father, on bringing his new wife into the home says to his daughter:

> "Molly, my dear, show—your mama to her room." Mr. Gibson had hesitated, because the question of the name by which Molly was to call her new relation had never occurred to him before. The color flashed in Molly's face. Was she to call her 'mama'?—the name long appropriated in her mind to someone else—her own dead mother. The rebellious heart rose against it, but she said nothing.

Later in the evening, Molly asks her father: "Oh, papa! Must I call her mama!" Her father replies:

> I should like it. . . . Why shouldn't you call her mama? I'm sure she means to do the duty of a mother to you. We all make mistakes and her ways may not be quite all at once our ways; but at any rate let us start with a family bond between us.

Finally, Molly agrees: "Papa, I will call her mama." Her father answers: "You won't be sorry for it."

However, not all children are as compliant as Molly and the issue of name is not so easily resolved. Mead has suggested that a new nomenclature is needed to specify remarried family positions so that negative images of the past are not embedded in these terms.[5]

Although some children are able to use a parental role name for a stepparent, others may wish to differentiate their natural parent and stepparent by using an alternative role term. Thus, one parent is "mother" and the other "mom." Or, in some families "aunt" or "uncle" are used as substitutes for maternal and paternal role names. Some children are unable to accept any of these alternatives and employ a strategy of avoidance; they simply do not call a stepparent anything or, at best, the stepparent is "he" or "she." David Schneider, in a discussion of names for in-law parents of husband and wife, describes an analogous situation when daughters and sons-in-law are unable to resolve this dilemma and resort to a no-name status for their in-law relatives.[6]

The use of first names for stepparents is a solution for many remarried family members. It is one of the predominant terms of address used by older children who still have ties with absent parents and wish to preserve a separate status for parent and stepparent. Younger children often resolve this difficulty by combining the role name with the first name, such as Daddy Jim or Mommy Sue. Difficult as this situation is, most remarried families resolve these problems through a process of discussion and shared decision making, in which the comfort level of all family members is considered. However, at times, disagreement among family members about terms of address may be the presenting problem in an application for professional help. When the Donahues applied for help, they stated that their problems concerned "What to call each other."

THE DONAHUE FAMILY

Mrs. Donahue applied for service because she felt that Leah, her stepdaughter, was disruptive to family unity and morale. Leah had decided to live with her father and stepmother after her parents' divorce because her mother worked and had an active social life, leaving little time for family life. Her father, on the other hand, had remarried and had a wife who was very home-oriented, with two children of a prior marriage.

Mrs. Donahue complained that she had anticipated that Leah would call her "mother," since she had so clearly come to live with them because she wanted more of a "family." Besides, she felt she was more of a mother to Leah than Leah's mother was to her. Yet, Leah did not introduce her to her friends as "mother." Instead she said, "This is my father's wife," or "This is Maggie." In such circumstances, there was no way that this family could be seen by the community as a nuclear family. The issue of names was further compounded because Mrs. Donahue's first husband was refusing to allow his son to take his mother's new last name. Thus, the school called her by her former name, so she was constantly reminded of her former status. Besides, it once again made evident that this was not the original family unit.

In family interviews Leah acknowledged that she did not want to call her stepmother "mom" or any other name she might use for her own mother. Despite her recognition of her mother's inability to provide the kind of home for her that she wanted, she loved her mother and did not want to blur the importance of that relationship by using the term for her stepmother. On the other hand, she did admit that she felt uncomfortable introducing her stepmother by her first name. Nor had her earlier solution of a "no-name" status been satisfactory.

Mrs. Donahue felt that the refusal of Leah to use a traditional role name to address her was an erosion of her authority as a parent. Moreover, she was fearful that the younger children would also call her by her first name if Leah did. Mr. Donahue had also hoped that his daughter would be able to fit into the family as though she had always been there.

He was also disappointed that she would not call his wife "mother," but, unlike his wife, could accept that Leah was not able to make this adaptation and that, indeed, she had a right to preserve her relationship with her mother even it was only in name.

Matt, Mrs. Donahue's younger son, was angry at Leah because she did not call his mother "mom." After all, he said, he called his stepfather "dad." Moreover, he was locked in a battle with his natural father because he wanted to be able to use his stepfather's last name in school and his father would not permit it. Matt said, "I never see him, just like you never see your mother, so why should I keep his name?"

The Donahue family situation mirrors the practical and concrete choices that must be made by all remarried families in order to facilitate communication and carry out the routines of day-to-day activities. Yet, this issue brings to the surface the pain of many deeply buried issues of affiliation and attachment to a parent no longer living under one roof with the child. At the same time, it highlights the feelings of parents who are providing daily parental care and nurturance and their wish to be acknowledged in this role. Moreover, for Mrs. Donahue this was a jarring note, a constant reminder that the earlier family had been broken.

Many stepchildren, whether the antecedent to their parent's remarriage was death or divorce, see their choice of surname and term of address as a declaration of loyalty that has implications for a sense of continuity and affirmation of belonging. Many stepparents, and natural parents as well, believe that the visible difference in name inhibits the bonding process. Thus, they are advocates for the process of denial that underlies the myth of no difference.

During the therapeutic process with the Donahue family, the focus was on helping each family member become more empathic to the plight of the other. Feelings were examined not as a rejection of the parent, but as reflections of internal psychological needs for recognition of prior ties as well as recognition of parental roles. Mrs. Donahue's cultural orientation toward the remarried family as a system was related to the acceptance of her associations of her family with the step situation of folklore. She demonstrated that "personal identity is meshed with group identity, which itself rests on an historical past."[7] With work on the inappropriate connotations of the archaic image for many remarried families today, and hers in particular, Mrs. Donahue became better able to tolerate the differences in step and nuclear family designations. Leah became more empathic to her stepmother's feelings, as she could understand the basis of these feelings and no longer needed to interpret them as a denial of her right of self-determination or depreciation of her mother. Mr. Donahue no longer was the "person in the middle," and Matt no longer needed to be his mother's ally and spokesman. The alliances and power struggle in the family shifted with new understandings, and alternative role names were worked out so that, while the step designation was not used, Mrs. Donahue was able to accept that Leah would call her "mom" while "mother" was reserved for her natural mother.

ACCULTURATION TO THE REMARRIED FAMILY

In addition to the cultural issues embedded in old images, new myths, and terms of address, the remarried family must negotiate potential differences in lifestyle of prior single-parent status and the new remarried family status. At times, one family has been accustomed to a flexible and unstructured lifestyle, while the new spouse and his or her children may have been accustomed to a more rigid and structured lifestyle. Values and priorities must often be blended as family units acculturate to each other. (See the Brent Family, chapter ten.)

A problem frequently brought for therapeutic consideration is that of differences in socialization patterns and child-rearing practices between the spouses in their roles as parents. The problem is frequently described as "he (or she) is too lenient with his (or her) children and too harsh with mine." Differences in parenting style related to cultural orientation, values, and priorities are interpreted as favoritism for biological or legal children and rejection of stepchildren. In such cases, what may begin as differences in cultural orientation toward how children should be socialized to become adults are translated into psychological terms of rejection and lead to marital and parent-child difficulties.

THE LEWIS FAMILY

Mary and Ben Lewis, in a family life education meeting, talked about the intense marital disagreements they were experiencing only a few months after remarriage because Mary thought Ben was too harsh with her children. He felt that unless Mary became tougher with her children, they would never be able to get along in the world. In group discussions, Ben revealed his strong belief that children who were not helped to tolerate frustration simply could not make it in the adult world. For example, Ben was troubled that his wife had no expectations that her seventeen-year-old daughter, Shari, should take care of her own room and help with household tasks. Mrs. Lewis, however, felt that because Shari was an outstanding student and was preparing for college, she should not have the pressures of household tasks.

Mr. Lewis said that he genuinely loved his "new" children and wanted to give them his guidance in the best way he knew. When Mary was able to accept that Ben's intentions were positive and he was not the male counterpart of the bad stepparent, but rather, had a different cultural orientation to child rearing than she did, she welcomed his help in parenting. Instead of seeing Ben as a harsh and rejecting parent, she began to see him as a parent who could help her set appropriate limits and boundaries for her children—something she had not been able to do in the past.

Attention to cultural orientation in child-rearing practices and the ability to work for a balance acceptable to both spouses is essential if the blending process is to take place. This same process is applicable when differences in values and priorities about the distribution of time, money, and space are at issue. The way in which these issues are approached is frequently apparent in family rules and regulations.

Rules and regulations, outward evidence of cultural orientation and family lifestyle, are among the most frequently identified problems in all family systems. In the remarried family, where one family that has had a history of rules and regulations that have evolved over many years joins with another family that has had a different set of rules and regulations, tensions are inevitable. Working out rules and regulations all can accept is often one of the first tasks on which the therapist and family must work. This requires sensitive awareness of the values and priorities of each family system and recognition that there must be adjustment to reflect the values of both prior family orientations.

The mutual work of all family members in arriving at rules for the new family provides the family with an opportunity for learning about each other's communication patterns and the basis for their values and priorities. Further, it begins the process of building feelings of belonging through task bonds established in the process of shared work. Often, this is a necessary prelude to the formation of emotional bonds. The therapeutic focus must facilitate the process of acculturation by encouraging the establishment of rules and regulations that do not subordinate one part of the family to another but, rather, focus on the welfare of the family unit as a whole, so that the needs of all are served. Basic to the therapeutic process is the practitioner's task of helping family members build empathic bonds with each other through understanding of differences in cultural orientation that preceded the formation of the remarried family.

CLIENT-FAMILY-PRACTITIONER MIXES

Client and therapist cultural orientations come together in the clinical interview. The importance of the therapist's self-awareness of his or her own belief systems in relationship to work with individuals and families of different social, economic, and ethnic backgrounds is well documented in the literature.[8] Some of these same principles are relevant in work with remarried families, so that practitioners do not reinforce negative orientations toward the remarried family nor encourage unrealistic self and other expectations. Therapists immersed in a culture that is moving toward, but has not yet transcended, the archaic images develop an array of responses to the remarried family situation, similar to those of remarried family members themselves. How these interrelate with remarried family clients on the issue of remarried family status and identity has implications for the therapeutic process.

Therapists who are uninformed about the built-in realities of the remarried family situation often assume that the remarried family is no different from any other two-parent, two-generation family. They approach this family without sufficient attention to its cultural heritage, current structure, family developmental history, and legal constraints. When this occurs, therapists, like many of the remarried families with whom they work, assume expectations in role performance and bonding capacities that are relevant to the nuclear family. These therapists have not appropriately differentiated the generic aspects of the nuclear and remarried families from the specific built-in realities unique to the remarried family. Other therapists believe it is necessary to avoid focusing on the differences, so that these families will feel just like other two-parent, two-generation families. In an effort to separate this family from archaic negative images, they seek to minimize the differences and consider the issues of this family to be the same as that of the nuclear family.

When practitioner and client share the view of no difference, either through lack of knowledge or through myths based on denial of realistic differences, there is a mutual reinforcement of unrealistic expectations and goals. In clinical interviews marked by such a mix of client-therapist perceptions, there is usually a process of repetitious content with no new ground broken or problems resolved.

Another client-practitioner mix that is equally unproductive occurs when there is a discrepancy between the client's and therapist's awareness of differences in remarried and nuclear families. Clients are often emotionally aware of the differences between the remarried and nuclear family situations, but are unable to articulate the basis of their feelings. When these clients work with practitioners who believe this family to be no different from the nuclear, the empathic bond between client and therapist that is so essential to a positive working alliance is more difficult to establish. Therapists in this situation may work from the premise that the real problem is within the person and may ignore the immediate situational and reality concerns of the remarried family. Instead, therapists may focus on internal psychological states as they pursue an agenda that is their own rather than that of the client. Other therapists, committed to a focus on the family, may apply concepts of normative family behavior relevant to the nuclear family without attention to a specific body of knowledge relevant to remarried families. Either approach assumes the myth of no difference. The client is not engaged because empathic bonds based on mutuality of problem definition have not been established. The working alliance does not mature, and early termination often follows.

Another client-practitioner mix is encountered when the therapist is pessimistic that anything can be done to improve this family situation. The remarried family is perceived as "one of those multiproblem families," with many complex and intertwining problems. This orientation may reinforce attitudes the client may have of the hopelessness of the situation, or it may diminish feelings of confidence that therapeutic intervention can improve the situation. The therapist's pessimism, based on response to the multiproblem aspects of this family situation, discounts such remarried family member characteristics as high motivation, investment in the new family, and capacity for self-observation. When these resources are discounted, the clients' own doubts are reinforced, and the therapist's pessimism may be accepted as a true measure of their situation. The therapist has reinforced the despair aspect of the hope-despair continuum and once again failed to build empathic bridges based on realistic understanding of the remarried family situation.

It also happens that, at times, a practitioner, steeped in the folklore of the neglected and abused stepchild, identifies with the child and minimizes the impact of the child's behavior on the family situation. It can and does happen that the syndrome of the wicked stepmother, abused stepchild, and passive father is not operative. Indeed, a new syndrome has been identified—that of a helpless stepparent, provocative stepchild, and advocate natural parent. Practitioners in such cases often join forces with the advocate parent, thus reinforcing the stepparent's sense of despair and helplessness. Another identified syndrome constitutes a misunderstood stepparent, a manipulative stepchild, and a natural parent caught between spouse and child. The tendency to perceive the child as scapegoated and abused, consistent with folklore and classical literature, often obscures the reality that the stepparent rather than the stepchild is the scapegoat. When the practitioner fails to recognize this, the dysfunctional patterns of the family are ignored and maladaptive family systems are strengthened.

The therapeutic approach in work with the remarried family that appears to have the greatest potential for successful intervention includes the recognition that both therapist and client come with preconceived cultural orientations toward the remarried family. Both carry with them the legacy of the past and the individual ways in which they have adapted it to the present. These predispose client and therapist alike to a range of biases and misperceptions that interfere with the objective assessment of the remarried family situation. Only as therapists increase their attention to the risks of the assumption of dysfunctional myths of the past and the present can they be in charge of this aspect of the "mix" between the client and themselves.

Systematic study of the cultural orientations of the larger society toward the remarried family and understanding of how these are reflected in client and practitioner cultural orientations is a first essential task in work with remarried families. Knowledge of the curious mix of old images that derive from folklore, new myths that comprise the popular culture, terms of address, and issues of acculturation to the remarried family suggest some beginning answers to the client who asks, "Why is a remarriage where there are children of a prior marriage so difficult?"

NOTES

1. Ruth Roosevelt and Jeanette Lofas, *Living in Step* (New York: Stein and Day, 1976), p. 16.
2. Margaret Mead, "Anomalies in American Post Divorce Relationships," in *Divorce and After*, ed. Paul Bohannan (Garden City, N.Y.: Doubleday/Anchor Books, 1971), p. 114.
3. See Theodore Lidz, *The Person: His Development Throughout the Life Cycle* (New York: Basic Books, 1968), p. 244; and Ralph Turner, *Family Interaction* (New York: John Wiley, 1970), p. 30.
4. Elizabeth Gaskell, *Wives and Daughters*, 1864. Reprinted (New York: Penguin Books, 1979).
5. Mead, "American Post Divorce Relationships," p. 124.
6. David M. Schneider, *American Kinship: A Cultural Account* (Englewood Cliffs, N.J.: Prentice-Hall, 1973), pp. 83–89.
7. A.L. Strauss, *Mirrors and Masks*, quoted in Edward E. Sampson, *Social Psychology and Contemporary Society*, 2d ed. (New York: John Wiley, 1976), p. 295.
8. Alfred Kadushin, *The Social Work Interview* (New York: Columbia University Press, 1972), pp. 219–41.

6

~~~~~

YOURS, MINE, OURS, AND MORE

As in work with any client or family system, practitioners working with remarried family members must gather information about who is involved in what problem, with whom, and how. But, unlike the nuclear or more traditional two-parent, two-generational family unit, the remarried family comprises individuals in family positions, roles, and statuses that are different from and more uncertain than those of the nuclear family. These new familial arrangements introduce significant role transitions and strains.

Most practitioners who have worked with remarried families are intuitively aware of the greater complexity of the remarried family system compared with the nuclear. Yet, they have applied intervention approaches based on understandings of the structural role positions and expectations of the nuclear family. Remarried family clients have often responded to these interventions with expressions of frustration like, "You just don't understand how complicated our family is!"

If practitioners are to intervene more appropriately with remarried family members, they need to have a system for classifying new familial arrangements so that the remarried family may be more appropriately differentiated from the nuclear family. The meanings of new familial arrangements could then be more accurately assessed as these have relevance for recurrent problems in remarried family system's, and interventions would be more precise.

This chapter will focus on the structural dimension of the schema for study of the remarried family. This discussion provides a foundation for understanding recurrent problems that derive from cultural orientations as explored in chapter five, developmental issues as examined in chapter seven, and legal aspects of this family system as explained in chapter eight. The greater structural complexity of the remarried family inextricably linked to all these dimensions will be made explicit through specification of variations in subsystems and structural ties, role positions and role complexity, and some examples of frequent structural configurations unique to the remarried family. Complexity is integral to an understanding of the remarried family structural components, but also has applicability to other dimensions discussed throughout this book.

DEFINING COMPLEXITY

Complexity, an important orientation in the analysis of systems, emphasizes that qualitative changes occur in systems as they move beyond a simple state to one that is more complex. By definition, a simple system is one that is unmixed and uniform. Conversely, a complex system is involved and a mixture of many dimensions. It has been suggested that "complexity arises from the number of ways in which we are able to (or desire to) interact with a system."[1] Analysis of such systems requires categorization of simpler subsystems within the larger system so that characteristic modes of interaction can be studied.

This kind of analysis provides a view of the totality of the system and its component subsystems. As this process of analysis takes place, emergent characteristics that do not appear in simple subsystems but are unique to the more complex system are identified. It has been argued that the emergence of new behaviors in interacting complex systems will always be a puzzle if the rationale is sought through application of what is known about simple systems.[2] The implication is that the nuclear family, a simple system compared with the remarried family, does not provide an accurate model for understanding interaction in the remarried family. Recurrent problems unique to the remarried family suggest qualitative changes and emergent behaviors in this system that are not known to the nuclear family. The remarried family must be understood as a system in its own right.

COMPARING NUCLEAR AND REMARRIED FAMILY SYSTEM STRUCTURES

All family systems are made up of interrelated parts that form a whole and can be analyzed in terms of their unique structures. Structure describes the organization of parts of the whole system; structural delineation of each part of the family system makes possible the differentiation of each person in terms of two basic kinship ties or connections: the biological and the marital. Biological or blood ties signify descent from a common ancestor. These ties are enduring and are basic to man's continuity. Marital ties derive from relationships established between persons connected through marriage. Further ties are formed as marriage introduces the relative-in-law relationship for persons previously unrelated. Biological and marital ties are reinforced by legal sanctions and are the basis for developmental, psychological, and social ties.[3] Through cultural and legal practice, the parent-child adoption tie is considered in this same category.

Biological and marital ties establish positions in the family of husband-father, wife-mother, son-brother, and daughter-sister. Each of these positions carries clearly defined roles and is the basis for three major formal subsystems in the family: marital, parent-child, and sibling. Informal subsystems evolve as individuals from each of the various subsystems form alliances, coalitions, and triangulations. In contrast to the relative stability of the formal subsystems, informal subsystems change and evolve as the values and needs of individuals change.

The remarried family, unlike the nuclear family, does not maintain all three of the formal subsystems over time. Marital and two-parent units have been broken by death or divorce before all of the children are grown. This initiates the transitional single-parent structure. If divorce has occurred, an absent parent-child subsystem also exists. A later marital affiliation reestablishes the husband-wife position and the marital subsystem. In addition, a two-parent, two-generational family system is reestablished. The step position, introduced for parent-child and sibling subsystems, is central to the new kinship group. In contrast to the nuclear family, where roles for each kinship position are well-defined, step role expectations are ambiguous and often contradictory.

The comparative analysis of structural aspects of nuclear and remarried families that makes up the balance of this chapter highlights the internal differences between these two kinds of families. For purposes of this discussion, the remarried family includes the remarried couple, his or her children of prior marriages who may live with them or live elsewhere, absent parents of children who live in the remarried family, and children born to this union. Reference is also made to extended family member systems.

MARITAL SUBSYSTEMS

In most cultures, the marital subsystem has been considered to be the heart and security of the family. Husband and wife are the architects of the family, adults in charge of the parenting and socialization of children. They are responsible for decision making, power alignments, nurture, and safety. The parents are the role models for the children and provide them with their earliest sense of identity and belonging.

Over 90 percent of nuclear families are composed of a husband and a wife who have never been married before.[4] In contrast, in the remarried family, at least one of the spouses has been married, then widowed or divorced, and subsequently remarried to someone who was single, widowed, or divorced. This yields eight possible marital status combinations: divorced man-single woman, divorced woman-single man, divorced man-divorced woman, widowed man-single woman, widowed woman-single man, widowed man-widowed woman, widowed man-divorced woman, and widowed woman-divorced man.

This information has clinical importance because it informs the practitioner about the marital history of each spouse and the subsystem to which each marital couple belongs. For example, in the Brent family both spouses had been divorced and could empathize with each other about the difficulties of that experience. In contrast, Greg Ronson, who had been divorced, and Janet, who had been single, seemed unable to understand each other's feelings. Although individual personality differences play a significant role in these responses, analysis of prior marital status combinations among remarried couples indicates a selection factor: most frequent combinations are between persons of similar prior marital status, followed by divorced persons to single persons, and widowed persons to divorced persons.[5] An assumption that derives from similarity in prior marital status may contribute to an underlying empathy between spouses and may be an important re-source in working with remarried couples; dissimilarity may contribute to tensions based on the lack of a shared experience. Additionally, the differences in husband-wife ties to children of a prior marriage may have significance for recurrent problems in role performance and emotional bonding (see chapter seven).

PARENT-CHILD SUBSYSTEMS

In the nuclear family, the marital tie has preceded the parent-child tie, and neither parent has children of a prior marriage. All children belong to the marital couple through birth or adoption and all generally live together until the children are grown. In contrast, in the remarried family a parent-child tie, for at least one parent, precedes the marital tie. Remarriage introduces a new spouse who assumes the marital position formerly held by the deceased or divorced spouse, and a stepparent position vis-à-vis the spouse's children of the prior marriage. This situation, which results in differing kinds of ties between husband and wife for the children they parent, is illustrated in Table I. Nuclear (biological and adoptive) families are compared with remarried families in terms of four specific ties—biological, legal, developmental, and social. Differences in ties held by a biological or adoptive parent and a stepparent begin to delineate structural aspects unique to the step position.

In the nuclear biological family, biological and legal ties are simultaneous and the same for husband and wife. Although a

TABLE I. Comparison of Ties Between Parents and Children in Nuclear and Re-married Families

Types of ties between Parents and Children	NUCLEAR		REMARRIED	
	Biological Resident H = W	Adoptive Resident H = W	Biological Resident H = W	Adoptive Resident H = W
Biological	× ×	– –	× – or – ×	– –
Legal	× ×	× ×	× – or – ×	× – or – ×
Developmental (Shared time and space)	× ×	× ×	× – or – ×	× – or – ×
Social (Parents-in-charge)	× ×	× ×	× ×	× ×

× = marital tie exists – = tie does not exist

91

husband and wife who are adoptive parents do not have biological ties to their adopted children, they have the same or symmetrical legal ties to their adopted children. Husband and wife also share developmental ties as nuclear adoptive and biological parents, beginning with the birth or adoption of children. This tie, which is discussed more fully in chapter seven, consists of the shared role of husband and wife in the processes of socialization of and psychological bonding with their mutual children. At the same time that children become a part of the nuclear household, husband and wife are the parents-in-charge of the family unit. Clearly, the husband and wife in the nuclear family are in a symmetrical position with each other vis-à-vis the ties to their mutual children in all four dimensions: biological, legal, developmental, and social.

In the event of marital dissolution by death, all of these ties are broken. However, if divorce has occurred, biological and legal ties are retained by the absent parent. Developmental and social ties between one biological-legal parent and the child(ren) have been broken and may or may not be reestablished on an absent-parent basis. The resident single parent continues to hold all four ties, with the developmental and social ties open for sharing with a new spouse in the event of remarriage.

When there has been a remarriage, the remarried couple does not begin at the same point in time with children who live in the household. The new step position introduces imbalances in the structural arrangement of ties husband and wife share toward the children they parent. Thus, in contrast to the nuclear marital couple, husband and wife in the remarried family will never share symmetrical biological ties to children of prior marriages. They can share a symmetrical biological tie with each other only if they have children in the new marriage, establishing a nuclear family within the remarried family unit. The remarried husband and wife do not share legal ties in regard to children of prior marriages unless a stepparent adopts a child of a spouse's prior marriage—because of the legal complexities involved when there is a living absent parent, this is not common (see chapter eight). In addition, the husband and wife in the remarried family do not at first share developmental ties with children of a prior family marriage. (The developmental complexities this generates for socialization and psychological bonding processes is the subject of chapter seven.)

The remarried couple do share the social tie that comes into being at the time of remarriage. This tie makes possible the initiation of a future shared developmental tie left open by the now absent biological-legal parent. Thus, at the time of the remarriage, unless legal adoption has preceded the remarriage, husband and wife are in symmetrical positions vis-à-vis children of a spouse's prior marriage in only one of the four dimensions analyzed—the social tie. This, then, is the nature of the parent unit around which parent-child subsystems are organized in the remarried family.

In addition to the new step position, parent-child structures in the remarried family must be considered in terms of the prior parental status of each spouse, the children of the absent parents, and the birth of children to the remarried couple. By definition, at least one of the spouses has some or all of his or her children of a prior marriage living in the remarried family so that a two-parent, two-generation household is established. A variation of this arrangement is the remarried household in which the children do not live on a day-to-day basis but are actively involved with the remarried couple through a joint custody arrangement or frequent visitation. Because this arrangement is becoming more frequent, it is important to include this variation, although it is a more limited kind of two-parent, two-generation family structure than those in which parents and children live in a sole custody arrangement. Table II describes a total of fifteen possible parent-child subsystems. In twelve of these, all or some of one or both of the spouse's children of a prior marriage live with the remarried couple on a sustained daily basis, and in three subsystems, children of a prior union live elsewhere but interact with the marital couple in ways that establish a more limited, but nevertheless functional two-parent, two-generation family system.

Examples of many of these parent-child combinations have been reflected in the case discussions. In both the Gray and the Peters families, one spouse had a child of a prior marriage and the other spouse had none. In both cases, the nuclear family had been dissolved by death so that no alternative parent-child arrangement was possible.

If a widowed parent who has children of the earlier marriage remarries a divorced spouse who has retained custody of all children of a prior marriage, the parent-child configuration is established in which both parents have all children of prior marriages living together under one roof. This was the situation for the Carr family, while in the Brent and Bateson families this parent-child subsystem configuration obtained for two formerly divorced

TABLE II. Parent-Child Subsystem Combinations of Children from Prior Unions in the Remarried Family

Children of Prior Unions	
Husband	Wife
All	None
All	Some/some elsewhere
All	All elsewhere
All	All
None	All
Some/some elsewhere	All
All elsewhere	All
Some/some elsewhere	Some/some elsewhere
Some/some elsewhere	None
All elsewhere	Some/some elsewhere
None	Some/some elsewhere
Some/some elsewhere	All elsewhere
All elsewhere	None
None	All elsewhere
All elsewhere	All elsewhere

None = marital partner has no children from prior marriage(s)

All = marital partner has children of a prior marriage, all of whom live with him or her in the remarried family household.

Some/some elsewhere = marital partner has children of a prior marriage, some of whom live with him or her in the remarried family household and others who live elsewhere.

All elsewhere = marital partner has children of a prior marriage, none of whom live with him or her in the remarried family household.

spouses, each of whom had all of his or her children from prior marriages living with them under the same roof.

When all of the children of each spouse's prior marriage do not live with the remarried couple, parent-child arrangements become more complex. This is related to parent-child subsystems wherein one partner may have all children of a prior marriage living in the remarried household and the other may have all children of a prior marriage living elsewhere. In the Dean family, Mr. Dean was the resident stepparent for his wife's children and an absent parent for his children of a prior marriage. Even more complex are parent-child arrangements in which one parent may have all children of a prior marriage residing with him or her and the other may have some who reside with him or her and some who reside elsewhere, as with the Maynors. In this kind of situation, a parent is a resident parent for some of his or her children of a prior marriage and an absent parent for his or her children who live elsewhere, and a resident stepparent for the spouse's children. Further, as in the Ronson family, one spouse may have no children of a prior marriage, but the other may have children who live elsewhere but are integrally involved with the remarried family through frequent visitation arrangements.

Still another variation of absent parent-child subsystems is one that derives from children who live with the remarried family but maintain ties with an absent parent. Thus, either husband or wife or both may have children of prior marriage(s) who maintain ties with an absent parent. Questions such as Nellie's, "How can I love two fathers at the same time?" or fantasy like Billie's of parental reunion of his divorced parents highlight the tensions many children experience in these circumstances. Children in the remarried family who have been a part of an earlier nuclear family structure that dissolved have had three parents, two of whom are the same sex. In the case of an absent divorced parent who remarries, the child has four parents; two biological parents, who now live apart, and two stepparents.

If the remarried couple have children of their own, fifteen more parent-child subsystem possibilities are added to those already identified. Resulting parent-child subsystems would then include children of the husband's prior marriage, the wife's prior marriage, and the remarriage. This kind of family has popularly been called a "yours, mine and ours" family (see the Allen family described later in this chapter). Knowledge of the range of parent-child subsystems that exist in the remarried family offers explanations of the structural basis for many of the issues of identity discussed in chapter five, as well as psychological problems of split loyalties, grief and mourning, fantasies of parent reunion, and barriers to the formation of emotional bonds between stepparent and stepchild, discussed in later chapters.

SIBLING SUBSYSTEMS

Sibling subsystems are equally complex in the remarried family. In the nuclear family all of the siblings have the same two parents. In the remarried family there may be siblings who share the same mother, but not the same father, siblings who have the same father but not the same mother, or siblings born to this marriage who share the same two parents: maternal siblings only, paternal siblings only, stepsiblings if both maternal and paternal siblings reside under the same roof, half-sibling(s) if children are born to the new union, nuclear siblings of the current marital union if more than one child is born to this marital couple, absent stepsiblings if the absent parent has remarried and has stepchildren, and absent half-siblings if the absent parent has remarried and has children in the new union.

Thus, if a child lives in a remarried family, he or she may potentially experience many of these possible sibship ties because of variation in the parent-child arrangements, in contrast to a child in the nuclear family who has only the nuclear sibship tie because all children share the same ties with the same father and mother. The increased number of sibling subsystems and different kinds of kinship ties is clinically significant because ordinal positions of children in the sibship may change as children come into or leave the remarried family system, and children do not share the same ties with parents and each other. Sibling rivalry, a problem in many families, is exacerbated and changes in alliances and coalitions that intensify interpersonal stress are commonly identified as difficulties. The Brent, Maynor, and Carr families demonstrate some of the problems that are related to the increased number and complexity of sibship subsystems in the remarried family.

EXTENDED FAMILY SUBSYSTEMS

At the time of a first marriage, the kinship network of each spouse expands to include the kinship network of his or her spouse and becomes a nuclear in-law extended family subsystem. Children born of this first marriage in the nuclear family thus have maternal and paternal extended kinship family networks to which they are related. If nuclear families are broken by death or divorce, the marital tie is terminated but the maternal and paternal kinship extended family ties continue. When the widowed or divorced parent remarries, a step extended kinship subsystem is also established. In remarried families in which both spouses have children of a prior marriage, two step extended kinship subsystems are established because each child in the family has both a biological parent and a stepparent. If, in addition, the absent parent is divorced and remarried, then step kinship subsystems exist in terms of the absent parent and his or her new spouse. Eight extended family kinship subsystems forming four combinations are possible in the remarried family: resident paternal/resident stepmaternal, resident steppaternal/resident maternal, absent paternal/absent stepmaternal, and absent steppaternal/absent maternal.

Obviously, remarried family households potentially include

many more extended family subsystems than the nuclear because of the addition of the stepparent. Although this often requires still another adjustment for family members, the addition of a step extended family network can be an enriching experience. In one family, for example, the young daughter, who had never known a grandmother, said, "At last, I can have a Nana like my best friend does." However, if grandparents cannot integrate new family members, tensions result, as described in the Peters family.

It is clear that sheer numbers of new persons who become a part of a remarried family system, as well as the ways in which they combine in formal subsystems, have implications for shifting alliances, triangulations, and coalitions. These, in turn, have implications for family interactions and problems that come to the attention of the therapist, and will be further discussed later.

MAPPING THE FAMILY

The greater number of family positions, subsystems, and role complexities in the remarried family compared with the nuclear family is often confusing to both therapist and remarried family members. It is, therefore, helpful to employ a systematic way to clarify or "map" the structural organization of each specific remarried family with whom one works. Mapping, a technique often used by family therapists to trace family of origin kinship affiliations and to organize complex systems data,[6] is also useful in clarification of the structural components of the remarried family system. This technique provides a quick visual conceptualization of who belongs to whom, age and sex of each family member, extended family relationships, and visitation patterns in and out of the family system. If absent parents have remarried and children are involved with the absent remarried family, these structural subsystems may also be shown. As the map takes form, persons who have joined the remarried family after its inception and those who have left are both designated. Thus, the ways in which a family has expanded, contracted, or remained the same are evident. Formal marital, parent-child, and sibling subsystems are clear, and informal alliances, coalitions, and triangulations are quickly discerned. Figure 1 shows the symbols that are used to denote residence, sex, marital status, kinship ties, and direction of visitation.

The Remarried Family

Figure 1: Glossary of Mapping Symbols (from the Perspective of the Remarried Family as Client)

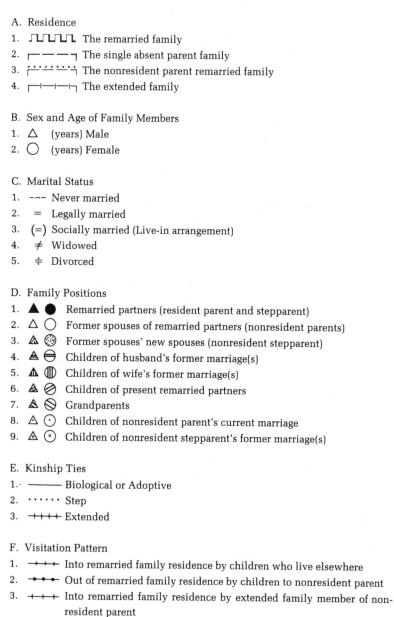

A. Residence

1. ЛЛЛЛ The remarried family
2. ┌ — — ┐ The single absent parent family
3. ┌··_··_··┐ The nonresident parent remarried family
4. ┌─┼─┼─┐ The extended family

B. Sex and Age of Family Members

1. △ (years) Male
2. ○ (years) Female

C. Marital Status

1. --- Never married
2. = Legally married
3. (=) Socially married (Live-in arrangement)
4. ≠ Widowed
5. ÷ Divorced

D. Family Positions

1. ▲ ● Remarried partners (resident parent and stepparent)
2. △ ○ Former spouses of remarried partners (nonresident parents)
3. ▲ ⊛ Former spouses' new spouses (nonresident stepparent)
4. ▲ ⊖ Children of husband's former marriage(s)
5. ▲ ⦀ Children of wife's former marriage(s)
6. ▲ ⊘ Children of present remarried partners
7. ▲ ⊗ Grandparents
8. △ ⊙ Children of nonresident parent's current marriage
9. ▲ ⊙ Children of nonresident stepparent's former marriage(s)

E. Kinship Ties

1. ——— Biological or Adoptive
2. ······ Step
3. ++++ Extended

F. Visitation Pattern

1. →→→ Into remarried family residence by children who live elsewhere
2. ●→●→ Out of remarried family residence by children to nonresident parent
3. +++ Into remarried family residence by extended family member of nonresident parent

Working with these symbols allows the therapist to map complex family structures that occur with considerable frequency so that the subsystem structure, family positions, and role complexities are immediately visible. The "yours, mine, and ours" family system of the Allen family is an example of a complex family structure made more understandable by mapping, but this technique is useful with other family systems as well.

THE ALLEN FAMILY

The request for service to a local mental health association was made by Mrs. Allen. She said that she was in a state of constant turmoil and confusion, as though she were "falling apart."

The Allens were a remarried family, in which the husband, age thirty-nine, and the wife, age thirty-two, had each been divorced. Each had children of a prior marital union. At the time of their divorces it was agreed that each of the divorcing parents would have custody of some of the children. Both Mr. and Mrs. Allen said that their ex-spouses had been good parents and they wished to preserve these influences. Mr. Allen retained custody of his two sons, who were nine and five at the time, while his ex-wife kept their two daughters, who were then eight and three. In a similar fashion, Mrs. Allen retained custody of her two daughters, five and four, while her seven-year-old son remained with his father. Mrs. Allen's daughters retained the legal name of their biological father, Jackson.

Mr. Allen lived as a single parent with his two sons for one year and then remarried. During the period as a single parent, he saw his daughters regularly, and his sons maintained an active relationship with their mother. Mr. Allen said that all of the children appeared to thrive when they were removed from the conflictual marital situation. The present Mrs. Allen lived as a single parent for three years. During this time, a harmonious coparenting relationship with her former husband was maintained, and children continued to be involved with the nonresident parent through frequent visitation.

When Mr. Allen remarried, his former wife was still single. However, she remarried about a year later. His children then acquired two stepparents within two years after their parents' divorce. In addition, they acquired stepsiblings because each of the new spouses also had children of prior marriages who were living with them. Mrs. Allen's husband had remarried a few months before she did, so that her children were also adjusting to two stepparents and other stepsiblings. Within three years, two daughters were born to Mr. and Mrs. Allen. Thus, there, were two daughters of the current marital union, two sons from Mr. Allen's prior marriage, and two daughters from Mrs. Allen's prior marriage living in the Allen household. Mrs. Allen reported that her former husband and his new wife had also had a child in their current marriage, so that her

Figure 2: The Allen Family at the Inception of the Remarriage

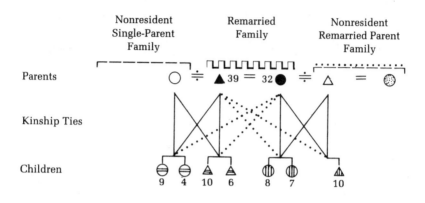

Figure 3: The Allen Family Four Years Later (at the Time of Application for Service)

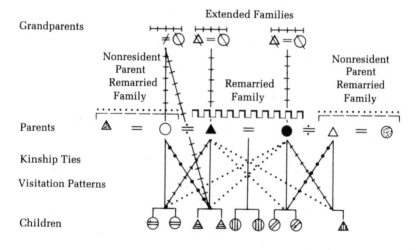

*Not shown in Figures 2 and 3 are six children of nonresident parents' new spouses: four of Mr. Allen's ex-wife and two of Mr. Jackson's new wife.

children had acquired three half-siblings in three years. All three of the remarried families lived in the same community. In addition to the multiple parent-child and sibling subsystems, the active participation of grandparents with differing patterns of inclusion and exclusion of step grandchildren contributed to sibling rivalries. In working with the Allens, the therapist mapped their family structure to help them to understand how the structural complexity contributed to the feelings of confusion and constant turmoil they had identified as the presenting problem.

Figures 2 and 3 reflect the residence, marital status, age, and sex of each family member, the nature of the kinship bond, and the visitation arrangements as children either visit into the Allen family or depart to visit absent parent families. In addition, the contacts with grandparents are shown in figure 3, because tension surrounding these relationships for the children and for Mr. and Mrs. Allen was identified as a problem in this family situation.

Analysis of the structural aspects of this family reflects prior divorce status for each partner, and the multiple kinds of parent-child subsystems—his children, her children, their children, and children who live with former spouses. Role complexities are apparent, in that each spouse has several parent positions: a natural parent to some of his or her children of a prior marriage who live in the remarried family, an absent parent to some who live with a former spouse, a resident stepparent to children of the present spouse's former marriage, and an absent stepparent to children of the present spouse's former marriage who live elsewhere. In addition, both husband and wife are symmetrical biological-legal parents to children born in this marriage. Further, there are sibling subsystems that include maternal, paternal, step, half, and nuclear siblings living under one roof. This complexity is compounded by the remarriages of absent parents, so that there are absent biological and stepparent positions in absent remarried family households, as well as sibling subsystems in that remarried family, similar to those of the Allen household. Finally, there are significant relationships with parent-in-law structures for each spouse and with new grandparents for each child.

James H. Bossard and Eleanor S. Boll, in their study of large family systems, found that the greater the number of possible dyads in a family, the greater the potential for stress. Their formula is derived from the number of possible interpersonal relationships in the family at any point in time, based on the number of its members. The number of dyadic relations in a family can be determined by the following, in which y stands for the number of family members and x stands for the number of dyadic subsystems that result:[7]

$$\frac{Y^2 - Y}{2} = X.$$

Applying the Bossard and Boll formula, according to the boundaries defined for the remarried family,[8] the number of interpersonal relationships (dyadic only), based on five grandparents, Mr. and Mrs. Allen, two absent parents and their spouses, and fifteen children of prior and current marriages, all of whom regularly interact with each other, is 325. It is small wonder that Mrs. Allen described herself as feeling "confused and falling apart." This was indeed a Yours, Mine, Ours, and More Family. The situation is also true, however, for many remarried families and will, probably become more widespread as longevity increases and grandparents continue to be involved in the lives of their children and grandchildren. Moreover, fathers are increasingly acquiring custody of their children, so that the phenomenon of divorced parents sharing custody arrangements may be expected to increase. In addition, many couples seek to solidify their remarriage by having children of their own. Thus, the experience of the Allens is unlikely to be an isolated one. Indeed, it may herald another kind of extended family system.

Although the existence of many different subsystems in the remarried family is often confusing and problematic, it is possible to view them as potential resources that can become parts of a mutual support network. Ultimately, this was true with the Allens. The cooperative relationship between the former spouses about their mutual children permitted joint family interviews focused on clarification of shared time and parental roles. This reduced the chaos that Mr. and Mrs. Allen originally described. In addition, an intergenerational focus that included some limited interviews with grandparents promoted discussion of grandparent roles and worked toward helping them expand their boundaries to include their stepgrandchildren. Although such therapeutic efforts are not always appropriate or achievable, therapists can recognize the potential resource in the multiple subsystems within the remarried family, and engage in exploring ways to develop mutual support systems in this new kind of extended family unit.

ROLE COMPLEXITY AND
ROLE STRAIN

The increased number of subsystem combinations and persons in the remarried family that derive from the unique step position are also reflected in the increased numbers of role positions and have implications for clinical practice. In contrast to the large body of instruction for nuclear parents, the stepparent role has no clearly defined guidelines. This lack often results in expectations that role performance be the same for both biological parents and stepparents. However, when the asymmetrical ties between husband and wife and the many variations in the parent-child subsystems are considered, expectations that there can be no difference in biological parenting and stepparenting are unrealistic. The lack of definition about appropriate step role behavior has been identified as a major source of dysfunction in remarried families.[9]

In the absence of culturally defined expectations about step roles, one of the earliest tasks for remarried families becomes learning new roles. Essential to this process is the exploration of workable role behaviors, and achievement of consensus among family members of reciprocal rights and duties is an early aspect of this process. In working out definitions of appropriate stepparent role behaviors, the imbalance between husband and wife in ties they share toward children must be harmonized, with a focus on defining realistic normative expectations to strengthen the social-parent tie. If there is also an absent parent, step role behavior must be defined in ways that are cognizant of the child's earlier ties to this parent. If, in addition, the stepparent has never had children, the step role definition must be worked out, usually with an older child, without the benefits that accrue from the more gradual process of learning the parent role from birth onward.

The lack of clarity about step role behavior becomes even more complex if the same person is both a biological parent and a stepparent or if a child is both a biological and a stepsib. The combined or hybrid role is still another new position in the remarried family that is often fraught with role strain as differences in feeling are associated with differences in biological and step ties. The combined biological-step role becomes even more complicated if a parent has biological children of a former marriage living in the remarried family household and others living with the former spouse, and, in addition, is a resident stepparent to his or her spouse's children of a prior marriage. Internal tensions

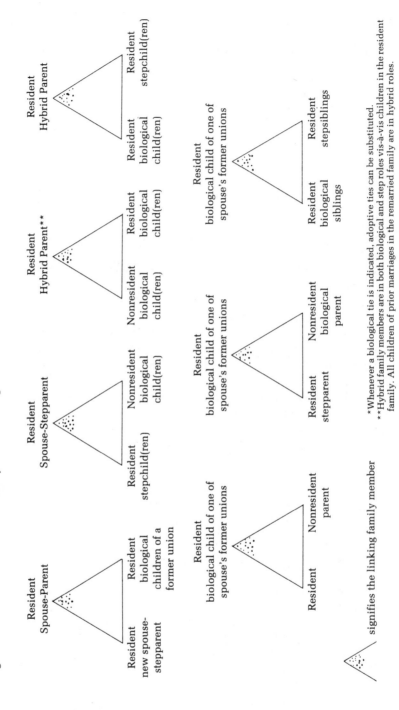

Figure 4: *Some Resident Remarried Family Member Triangulations*

Resident
Spouse-Parent

Resident
new spouse-
stepparent

Resident
biological
children of a
former union

Resident
Spouse-Stepparent

Resident
stepchild(ren)

Nonresident
biological
child(ren)

Resident
Hybrid Parent**

Nonresident
biological
child(ren)

Resident
biological
child(ren)

Resident
Hybrid Parent

Resident
biological
child(ren)

Resident
stepchild(ren)

Resident
biological child of one of
spouse's former unions

Resident
Nonresident
parent

Resident
biological child of one of
spouse's former unions

Resident
stepparent

Nonresident
biological
parent

Resident
biological child of one of
spouse's former unions

Resident
biological
siblings

Resident
stepsiblings

*Whenever a biological tie is indicated, adoptive ties can be substituted.
**Hybrid family members are in both biological and step roles vis-à-vis children in the resident family. All children of prior marriages in the remarried family are in hybrid roles.

signifies the linking family member

104

following disappointment in step role performance and interpersonal tensions in marital and parent-child relationships that center on unresolved differences in reciprocal step role expectations are common.

Another source of role complexity and role strain is associated with the linking position. This position exists for persons who connect old and new family systems and ties. The triangulations shown in figure 4 demonstrate some of these linking positions.

A common denominator in all the triangulations shown is the fact that the linking person is pulled in two directions. Role strains in these situations are related to the tensions that arise out of conflicting loyalties. Helping the linking person resolve some of the tensions related to his or her position is a frequent therapeutic focus of clinical intervention. Therapeutic interventions sensitive to these role complexities and strains can begin to develop a body of norms about appropriate step role behavior that can guide families in a search for realistic expectations. As consensus is achieved on what contributes to stepparent role adequacy, remarried families can stabilize and move toward a workable family balance.

GENERATIONAL BOUNDARIES IN THE REMARRIED FAMILY

Role strain related to the maintenance of generational boundaries, a potential problem in any family, is intensified in the remarried family because of the lack of definition of appropriate step role behavior. This is especially true when a parent remarries a spouse who is within the same generation as one or more children of a prior marriage who live in the home. In this structural configuration, the lack of age generational boundaries between stepparent and stepchild compounds the issue of appropriate step role definition. This was a problem for Jennifer Warren, referred by the police department to a youth center after an unsuccessful runaway attempt. Up to that time, Jennifer, a senior in high school, had been a conscientious and excellent college-bound student.

JENNIFER WARREN
When Jennifer was first seen at the youth center, she explained that she had run away from home with a plan to find a job and set up an apartment for herself and her sister, Teri, who was thirteen, away from her father and her stepmother. The precipitant to Jennifer's running away had been

a quarrel with her stepmother, because the stepmother felt that Jennifer would not obey her as "a mother." Jennifer related angrily that her stepmother was only a few years older than she and had no right to tell her what to do. Jennifer specified that she wanted help from the agency in finding an apartment and in getting a job. She would postpone college until her sister was old enough to take care of herself. Because Jennifer was seventeen, she did not think there should be any question of her right to make the decision to live as an emancipated juvenile.

After several interviews, Jennifer related that her mother and father had been divorced for three years and that prior to the divorce there had been many periods when her parents had been separated. During these periods, Jennifer was in charge. After her parents divorced, Jennifer continued in the role of parent surrogate to her younger sister, Teri, and spouse surrogate and companion to her father for two years. She enjoyed the relationship with her father and welcomed his praise and appreciation of her efforts in "keeping the home together." Her mother had remarried during this period, but Jennifer rarely saw her because she did not like her mother's husband. Jennifer had not anticipated that her father might also remarry. When he did, he chose a never-before-married woman of twenty-four. Jennifer resented giving up her position in the household and resented even more the authority that her stepmother assumed in relating to her and Teri. Suddenly, Jennifer felt demoted from being in charge and responsible to being a "kid" who was "bossed" by someone not much older than she.

Demographic studies of age differentials indicate that when men remarry, frequently their wives are significantly younger than they are. A study of recent population trends found that in 27 percent of the widowed or divorced men who remarried, their new wives had never before been married and were at least ten years younger.[10]

Structurally, Jennifer and her stepmother were more in a sibling position to each other than a parent-child position. Competition between the stepmother and Jennifer for the husband and father as well as for significant family roles was made more intense by the lack of a generational boundary. The lack of this boundary between stepparent and stepchild becomes even more complex when the stepchild is a male adolescent with a stepmother.

DAVID LYND
David Lynd, seventeen years old, and a senior in high school, ran away from home three months after his forty-four-year-old father, Alvin, a widower, remarried twenty-seven-year-old Susan. Mr. Lynd had been widowed two years earlier, when David was fifteen and David's sister,

Bonnie, was ten. Susan Lynd had also been widowed, and had a three-year-old son, Eddie, who had been adopted by her husband.

When David voluntarily returned to his father's home, he asked for help so that he could better understand the urgency of the feelings that had prompted him to run away. In therapy, he described his stepmother as warm, responsive, and fun—very different from his mother who had been more distant and restrained. During the months of intensive therapy that followed with David, he recognized that the feelings of agitation that had preceded his running away were related to his heightened anxiety because of the close relationship that was developing between him and his stepmother. He recognized that she was the kind of person he hoped he would marry.

Alvin and Susan Lynd were seen in conjoint therapy. Mrs. Lynd explained that her intense efforts to establish a relationship with David grew out of her empathy for him because he had lost his mother. She thought that in her new role she could in some way compensate to him for his loss as her husband was doing for her son, Eddie. She explained that if ever something happened to her and Eddie had a stepmother, she hoped that the stepmother would treat him as she did David.

The therapeutic issue of defining appropriate step role behavior in the context of the lack of age generational boundaries was compounded for the Lynds by their lack of knowledge about normal adolescent developmental issues, as well as by the reduced strength of the incest taboo presumed in the step situation.

INCEST ISSUES IN
REMARRIED FAMILIES

The reduced strength of the incest taboo in the remarried family is presumed to be related to the structural nature of the step position, which is nonbiological, nonlegal, and, typically, has not involved proximity or developmental ties between step-related persons over the years of growth and development of family relationships. Indeed, the only tie that step-related persons share is the social tie with its potential for emotional attachments to grow over time. When children grow up in a nuclear family with parents and siblings whom they have known all of their lives, they learn to deal with their own sexual drives in ways that are usually within the prescribed norms and expectations of society. The intensity of sexual drives are diluted and directed outward from the immediate household. The incest taboo, with its ban on intrafamilial sexual relationships between blood or primary relatives and some extended relationships is near-universal and enforced by legal sanctions in almost all parts of the world.

There has long been debate about the origins and persistence of the incest taboo. Some have argued that there is an innate biological aversion to sexual relationships between blood-related persons associated with the dangers of inbreeding; others have argued that the taboo is culturally imposed and reflects man's transition to humanity. They believe that sexual attraction between blood relatives is repressed in order to preserve the continuity of mankind, appropriate role differentiation, and stability of the family.[11] Robin Fox proposes that the incest taboo is most likely to break down when family members have not shared close emotional ties and "are as strangers to each other" before children have reached adolescence.[12] By extension, this proposition would be applicable to the step relationship, where ties are tenuous and steppersons often describe feelings of being strangers to each other. At the present time, no definitive answers can be found. However, the frequency of the incest theme in step relationships, as reflected in drama and novels, attests to the interest of society in this phenomenon over many centuries.[13] For purposes of this analysis of intrafamilial sexual relationships between step-related persons, it is assumed that the structural arrangements associated with the step position, the lack of appropriate step role definition, and the frequent stranger phenomenon among step-related persons contribute to the reduced strength of the incest taboo in remarried families.

Recent studies indicate that incest is a problem of increasing proportions in the general population and that it occurs in parent-child (particularly father-daughter) and sibling subsystems.[14] More definitive information is needed on the incidence of incest in remarried families. Recent publications on the step situation, however, comment on the tensions and anxieties experienced by remarried family members about this possibility.[15]

Homer Clarke suggests that there is need to differentiate between "real" incest between primary blood relatives and "technical" incest between secondary step or extended family relationships.[16] Despite such differentiation, abhorrence and disorder result when step-related persons are sexually involved. This activity often precipitates family crisis and brings remarried families to social agencies. Although more study is needed of these situations, it appears that the remarried family is less likely to reinforce incestuous relationships through the conspiracy of silence and unconscious collusion that are true in the nuclear family. With increasing numbers of remarried families in the general population, practitioners may work with many variations of "technical" incest.

Some problems that therapists might encounter with clients in the remarried family are related to the often highly erotic climate in the home as the new couple express their positive sexual feelings toward each other. The heightened sexuality in the remarried household stimulates children's curiosity, sexuality, and feelings about their parent's sexual involvement with a new partner. If, in addition, these children are adolescent and have only recently met each other, their own sexual drives are exacerbated and sexual acting out between them may occur. Mr. and Mrs. Roberts sought help from a social agency for such a problem.

THE ROBERTS FAMILY

When Mr. and Mrs. Roberts came to a local youth guidance clinic they were extremely agitated, angry, and frustrated. They had just learned that Mr. Roberts' sixteen-year-old son, Stan, and Mrs. Roberts' sixteen-year-old daughter, Tracy Anderson, were sexually active with each other.

Stan had joined the Roberts household three months ago. Previously, he had lived with his mother in a different state. His father and mother had been divorced since he was twelve. At the time of the divorce, his father had taken a job in another part of the country, but had maintained contact with his children through business trips and vacations. Stan's father and mother had each remarried within the past year. When Stan found that he could not get along with his stepfather he asked to come and live with his father.

Mrs. Roberts was widowed five years ago when her first husband died following many months of illness. She and her daughters, then eleven and seven, went to live with Mrs. Roberts' mother, who supervised the girls while their mother went to work. When Mr. and Mrs. Roberts remarried, they had no thought that any of Mr. Roberts' children would come to live with them. They established a household, and were just beginning to feel like a "real" family when Stan asked to live with his father. Because of the distance between the two households and Mr. Roberts' ability to see his children on business trips, neither Mrs. Roberts nor her children had ever met Stan before he joined the household.

Mr. and Mrs. Roberts were pleased that Tracy, her older daughter, appeared to take Stan over and included him in her activities. Indeed, they ruefully acknowledged that they were so involved in their own marital relationship they had not noticed how intense the relationship between Stan and Tracy had become. It was only while attending a school function that they learned that Tracy and Stan were considered boyfriend and girlfriend and not brother and sister. This was easily understood because they had different last names, were the same age, and were in the same class in school.

In their efforts to put an end to this relationship, Mrs. Roberts felt that Stan should return to live with his mother; Mr. Roberts thought that Tracy should go to live with her grandmother. Both parents were outraged that the "other's" child should do this to "his" and to "her" child. Neither seemed willing to consider any other alternatives.

The problems in this case highlight some of the difficulties involved when a remarried family unit is disrupted by the addition of a child who has made a parent-switch. This issue was compounded in the Roberts' household because the new family structure now included a male and a female adolescent, each sixteen, who had not known each other until three months ago. Developmentally, each was vulnerable to his or her own heightened sexuality in a climate which was already eroticized because of the newness of the remarriage and the parents' own immersion in the marital relationship. The "stranger" phenomenon was present because Tracy and Stan had not grown up together. Thus, structure, developmental aspects of each individual child, and the recency of the parental remarriage were intertwined.

The questions facing the family and the therapist were whether expulsion of one of the adolescents was the way to handle this problem and, if so, who would go? Or, what other options were possible? In the nuclear family, if siblings become sexually involved, both parents are in the same structural position to the children and there is no parent in the wings to whom the child can be sent. In the Roberts family, each parent became the ally to his or her child, felt anger toward the stepchild, and bitterly defended the territorial prerogative to keep his or her child in the home. Expulsion of one of the children is often seen as the only alternative; however, a frequent aftermath of this kind of decision is marital conflict and resentment for the parent who has given up his or her child. At times, it may be possible to work toward a more appropriately supervised environment to reduce the potential for sexual acting out between stepsiblings. This is often best done before families with adolescent children of different sexes join the household. At that time, some of the normal developmental aspects of sexual interest between stepsiblings can be discussed in the context of a newly formed marital unit, with a focus on prevention of sexual activity between stepsiblings.

The dilution of the incest taboo observed between stepsiblings is also present for stepparent and stepchild. This may be manifest in frank stepparent-stepchild sexual relationships or may be masked in provocative and angry behavior between stepparent and stepchild, as a way of discharging yet denying sexual attraction. It is assumed that as families are better able to articulate their concerns in this area and to define appropriate step role behavior, generational boundaries will be strengthened and the potential for intrafamilial step sexual relationships will be reduced. At best, the possibility of "technical" incest between step-related persons is a difficult situation for remarried families, but one that must be recognized as a potential reality by both families and therapists.

SUMMARY

The cases that have been selected for this chapter suggest only a few of the unique structural configurations that are possible in the remarried family. Variation in the structures, role positions, and role complexities exist for legally remarried as well as for live-in or socially remarried families. These structures become even more complex if there are redivorces or a series of live-in partners. Because there is a higher rate of divorce among remarried than among nuclear families, many of these children know multiple stepparents and stepsiblings.

The greater structural complexity of the remarried family over the nuclear family is evident from a structural analysis of each of the three major family subsystems and of the position and role of family members. Although this analysis is academically interesting, its greater importance for the practitioner is that it provides a systematic way of analyzing kinship affiliations in the remarried family. This information can then shed light on the relationship of the structural kinship arrangements and the recurrent problems for which remarried families seek help. The following chapters explore the interrelationship of the structural complexity of the remarried family and the developmental and legal issues in the formation of step relationship attachments and the achievement of a workable family balance.

NOTES

1. Robert Rosen, "Complexity as a System Property," *International Journal of General Systems* 3 (April 1977) :229.
2. Ibid., p. 227.

3. Robin Fox, *Kinship and Marriage: An Anthropological Perspective* (Harmondsworth, Middx.: Penguin Books, 1971), pp. 33–36.
4. United States Bureau of the Census, "Number, Timing and Duration of Marriages and Divorces in the United States, June 1975," *Current Population Reports,* Series P–20, no. 287 (Washington, D.C.: U.S. Government Printing Office, 1976), p. 2.
5. Kristen M. Williams, "Remarriages, United States," (Rockville, Md.: National Center for Health Statistics, 1973), pp. 10–11.
6. Ann Hartman, "Diagrammatic Assessment of Family Relationships," *Social Casework* 59 (October 1978):465–76.
7. James H. Bossard and Eleanor S. Boll, *Large Family Systems,* quoted in Joan Aldous, *Family Careers* (New York: John Wiley, 1978), p. 341.
8. Ibid.
9. Irene Fast and Albert C. Cain, "The Stepparent Role: Potential for Disturbance in Family Functioning," *American Journal of Orthopsychiatry* 36 (1966): 485–91.
10. Williams, "Remarriages," p. 10.
11. Fox, *Kinship and Marriage,* pp. 55–76.
12. Ibid., p. 74.
13. See, for example, the classical Greek tragedy, Euripides' "Hippolytus," Guiseppi Verdi's "Don Carlo", and Henrik Ibsen's "Little Eyolf"; also see Eugene O'Neill's "Desire Under the Elms."
14. See Karin C. Meiselman, *Incest* (San Francisco: Jossey-Bass, 1978); Blair Justice and Rita Justice, *The Broken Taboo* (New York: Human Sciences Press, 1979); and Herbert Maisch, *Incest,* trans. C. Bearne (New York: Stein and Day, 1972).
15. See *Stepparent News* 1, no. 5 (September 1980). Entire issue.
16. Homer H. Clarke, Jr. *Law of Domestic Relations* (Minnesota: West Publishing, 1968), pp. 70–73.

7

SO MUCH, SO FAST

As the therapist works with the remarried family, the therapeutic focus moves beyond the initial processes of identification of the problem, clarification of cultural orientations, and specification of structural arrangements. Events, discontinuities, and processes that are inherent in and unique to the remarried family situation are disclosed as the client's story unfolds. These realities are integrally related to the problems of the remarried family and have implications for the normal development of individual members as well as for the family as a whole.

This chapter explores the developmental dimension of the schema for study of the remarried family from a psychosocial perspective. Nuclear and remarried family developmental life cycle stages and developmental tasks related to each stage are compared, with special attention to the bonding processes involved. Therapeutic interventions that deal with some of the critical issues and problems generated in each stage are suggested. Although developmental aspects of remarried families are examined discretely for purposes of analysis of their situation, it must be remembered that structural and developmental issues are inextricably intertwined in the real life experience of remarried families.

THE DEVELOPMENTAL PERSPECTIVE

The developmental approach to the study of individual personality and behavior has long been an important clinical tool. Practitioners are, therefore, well schooled in developmental theory of the individual. More recent are therapeutic applications of psychosocial developmental theory focused on the nuclear family. However, formulations about the developmental life cycle of the remarried family are lacking. Indeed, many family theorists have commented on the need for a developmental frame of reference that identifies "normative" regularities in nonnuclear families.[1] The principles and concepts described below have guided the formulation of the remarried family developmental perspective presented in this chapter.

The developmental perspective is a conceptual framework for understanding some aspect of change through time. Three key concepts that are central to the psychosocial developmental perspective are life cycle stages, developmental tasks, and emotional bonds. The life cycle serves as a longitudinal time frame in which universal and predictable natural sequences of critical events and changes in individual and family life are marked off as stages. Entry into and exit from a stage is variable because the life cycle model is intended to reflect the natural sequence and process of transition. At times, stages are overlapping or coexist; at other times a specific event may mark the initiation or ending of a stage. Biological or social readiness of the persons or families involved and the cultural matrix within which they function are significant factors affecting the timing and duration of each stage. At best, each stage is a guide or an approximation. This lack of precision has presented difficulties for use of this perspective in empirical studies.[2] However, the flexibility of the developmental model has provided a useful approach for clinical application.

Traditionally, individual developmental life cycle approaches begin at birth and stages are marked by chronological age divisions that may reflect biological, psychological, social, and intellectual maturation through the life span. They also consider the impact of life experience that disrupts or facilitates normal growth processes in one or more areas. Individual developmental perspectives have, for the most part, emphasized the stages from birth through adolescence with scant attention to the stages of adulthood. More recently, adult stages of the life cycle have been explored in greater depth.[3] This knowledge has provided a useful bridge in the study of family psychosocial theory.

Family developmental approaches begin with young adulthood, when a new family unit is established. The family is perceived as a small primary group social system composed of individuals in a kinship network of biological and legal ties. The psychosocial adaptations of husband and wife intermesh with the growth and development of their mutual children, thus integrating individual and family theory. Stages are specified according to such criteria as changes in marital status and parental relationships, gain or loss of family members, role transitions, education and developmental status of children, and occupational status of adult family members. Each of the events or stages designated in individual and family developmental approaches is assumed to have descriptive and predictive powers to identify problems and issues associated with each stage. Central issues within each stage are designated as developmental tasks. Many of these issues continue into later stages and must be integrated with new developmental tasks throughout individual and family life cycle stages.

Developmental tasks represent psychosocial and cultural demands on individuals or families to master tensions and problems associated with each stage. These tasks are often presented as polarities, "a" versus "b," with "a" representing the idealized positive outcome and "b" the undesired negative outcome. This polarity has often been referred to as a "universal culturally defined crisis."[4] The level of mastery for most individuals and families is on a continuum somewhere between the idealized and the undesired result. The expectation is that mastery of the task or crisis results in the acquisition of skills, knowledge, or attitudes that facilitate movement into the next developmental stage. Each stage has its roots in an earlier stage and builds a bridge to the next. Although each stage has its own irregularities, a basic process of tension at entry into a stage, stabilization as new skills are learned and implemented, and emergent tension as the next stage is anticipated are recognized.

Bonding is a central process examined in each stage of individual and family developmental life cycles. This process involves the continuous selective and reciprocal building of connections between individuals and the family as a group and is integral to the social roles of each member as determined by the culture. The existence of a bond denotes a relatedness, an attachment, between persons. The process of bonding for each individual begins with birth and normally takes place in the context of one's family of origin. For the family, the process begins with the marital relationship and expands to include children of this union through their growth and maturation. It is assumed that the fewer the discontinuities and stressful events there are in the predictable sequential process of individual and family development, the greater the potential for normal growth and development for all family members.

The optimal developmental situation is one in which mastery of the task assigned to a stage occurs while the individual or family is in that stage. This mastery is assumed to result in higher levels of functioning for those individuals and families in that stage and in subsequent ones. Incomplete mastery or failure of mastery is believed to inhibit later effective functioning and makes the acquisition of skills and knowledge in later stages more difficult. The individual or family then carries forward residuals of these unresolved issues as unfinished business for potential mastery in later stages. Thus, the developmental perspective implies a "second" or "later" chance to resolve tensions or acquire skills not achieved earlier. This perspective is particularly useful in therapeutic intervention with remarried families because of the orientation toward normal transitions and growth and the possibility that later stages provide opportunities to heal or correct feelings and behaviors that have resulted from earlier trauma and discontinuity.

COMPARING NUCLEAR AND REMARRIED FAMILY LIFE CYCLES

Nuclear family developmental life cycle models indicate that four core stages can be identified,* although different theorists may add to these to specify greater differentiation within each stage.[5]

Stage I: Establishment of the nuclear family unit through marriage.

---

*These four stages represent a compression of Duvall's eight-stage life cycle model: (1) marriage, (2) childbearing years, (3) preschool children, (4) school-age children, (5) adolescent children, (6) family as launching center, (7) marital pair without children and (8) marital pair in postretirement years, until death of one spouse ends the marital relationship.

Stage II: Expansion and stabilization of the nuclear two-parent, two-generational unit through birth or adoption of children and stabilization of this unit through childrearing years. (Infancy through adolescence.)

Stage III: Contraction of the family unit as young adult children leave home to establish independent living arrangements.

Stage IV: Reestablishment of the marital unit without children at home.

Nuclear family developmental models assume that the marital unit remains intact until all of the children have been launched. They therefore do not reflect accurately the life cycle of families in which there has been a dissolution of the marriage by death or divorce before all of the children are grown, and a remarriage while one child or more is still in the home. Because a death-divorce-remarriage cycle has significance for developmental processes of the individuals and families involved that are not true for nuclear families, it is important to formulate a model that does reflect these events and consider their meaning for the bonding process.

Although a broad body of literature exists on the formation of bonds between parents, particularly the mother and children, in the earliest years of life in the nuclear family little attention has been paid to the formation of bonds between steppersons in the remarried family. The focus of analysis within each stage of the remarried family life cycle is, therefore, on the normal aspects of the bonding process in each stage and implications of disruptions to this process for the maintenance of existent bonds and the formation of new ones between steppersons.

Seven developmental life cycle stages have been identified for the remarried family: four are the same as those described above for the nuclear family, and three are additional and unique to the remarried family. These additional stages are: (1) dissolution of the nuclear family through death or divorce, (2) contraction and reorganization as a single-parent family, and (3) expansion and reconstitution as a remarried family. Dissolution occurs at some time after the birth of the last child to the nuclear couple, and remarriage must take place before all children have been launched. Developmental tasks involve the mastery of interrelated individual and family developmental tasks for each family member. The developmental tasks specific to the remarried family are expected to facilitate healing so that trauma related to earlier losses can be

mastered and subsequent bonding and the achievement of a workable family balance can occur (see Table III).

STAGE I: ESTABLISHMENT OF
THE NUCLEAR FAMILY MARITAL UNIT

Families begin with the establishment of the nuclear family unit
through marriage or cohabitation arrangements. Although there
is some variation as to when individuals marry, depending on
socioeconomic and educational factors, 90 percent of the population of the United States marry at least once, with the average
age at marriage being twenty-four for men and twenty-two for
women.[6]

The cultural expectation is that young adults separate and individuate from their families of origin when they marry. Husband
and wife are expected to shift their predominant commitment
from their family of origin to the new family unit and to define
marital roles. Individual developmental tasks of young adulthood
must be integrated with the new family status. The developmental
task for this stage is the balance of marital interest versus self-
interest, so that the marital unit becomes a complementary and
viable working relationship where accommodation, mutually supportive interactions, and positive bonding prevail. Relationships
with extended family members must be balanced with the new
marital relationship. Although the developmental task of marital
interest versus self-interest arises in and dominates stage one, it
continues to exist as a task for integration with other tasks during
all subsequent stages in the nuclear family. The assumption is that
most couples who later divorce have not mastered this developmental task with the nuclear marital partner.

STAGE II: EXPANSION AND STABILIZATION
OF THE NUCLEAR FAMILY STRUCTURE

The birth or adoption of the first child marks the entry of the
nuclear married couple into stage two. On the average, a first child
is born after approximately two years of marriage and a second
child almost three years later, thus establishing parent-child and
sibling subsystems.[7] These changes require that the marital couple
expand their boundaries to include children, surrender the space
and privacy enjoyed as a two-person family unit, and take on the
roles of parents to their mutual children. During this stage, parents
and children progress through normal individual developmental
processes and milestones. Childrearing and socialization patterns

are established, and husband and wife must integrate their individual needs and goals so that they are harmonious with marital and parental roles and the individual developmental needs of all of their children. Bonds and attachments among family members are strengthened and a family identity is forged as social networks and mutual support systems with relatives, friends, and community are solidified.

The overarching family developmental task of this stage is stabilization as a two-parent, two-generation nuclear family unit versus dissolution. Interlocking with this task are two additional developmental tasks related to the bonding process between parent and child: (1) the inclusion of new children who are born or adopted versus exclusion, and (2) mutual separation and individuation of parents and children versus enmeshment as the children mature. In the nuclear family, this stage continues through children's adolescence and until the first child is launched in stage three.

Although all two-parent, two-generation families enter into this stage, those that are broken by death or divorce do not remain in this stage until their children have completed adolescence. At some point after the birth of the last child to the nuclear couple, a dissolution process is initiated that disrupts the normal sequential transitions within this stage. (Although in some families dissolution begins before the birth of the last child, for purposes of this discussion it is assumed that the birth of a child represents the expectation that the nuclear family will continue.) Developmental tasks of inclusion versus exclusion of children of this union and appropriate separation and individuation of children versus enmeshment may be achieved, but the overarching developmental task of stabilization versus dissolution has not been achieved. The remarried family diverges from the nuclear family at some time during stage two and begins the three remarried family stages that differentiate this family from the nuclear. These three stages must be completed before the last child is launched so that the two-generational aspect of the family is present at the time of remarriage.

STAGE III: DISSOLUTION OF THE
NUCLEAR MARRIAGE AND FAMILY STRUCTURE

This stage occurs while the nuclear family structure is still physically intact, but the marital unit is undergoing a process of dissolution. The nature, duration, and developmental tasks of this stage vary depending on whether death or divorce is the cause of marital dissolution. In addition, ages of children and the period of time during which the family was stable prior to dissolution have implications for later adjustment in the remarried family. This stage terminates in dissolution by death or divorce. The increased number of families in which the original marriage was terminated by divorce reflects changing cultural norms and legal processes that facilitate the decision to divorce. The average duration of marriage ended by divorce is seven years.[8]

For those families broken by death, the dissolution and termination of the nuclear family may be simultaneous because of accidental or sudden death, as with Ellen Gray. On the other hand, a long period of terminal illness may precede death, as in the Carr family. The developmental task for families broken by death is the initiation of a process of mourning versus denial.

Dissolution of the nuclear family by divorce is the predominant process for those who later remarry. The beginning and duration of this process are seldom clear. For many who divorce, this stage is often punctuated by repeated separations and reconciliations as ambivalences about marriage are considered. On the other hand, despite multiple separations and reconciliations, ambivalences about marital partners, and marital conflict, many couples continue to live together and remain as intact nuclear families. It is the termination of the marriage that differentiates remarried from nuclear families. George Levinger has provided a useful conceptualization for analysis of the differences between those who divorce and those who do not.[9]

The developmental task of this stage for those who undergo the dissolution process that terminates in divorce is decision versus ambivalence. The marital couple concerned with this decision is, at the same time, continuing to be involved in developmental tasks related to socialization of children and parent-child relationships. The intertwining of developmental tasks specific to this stage and those general to any parent-child subsystem often contribute to children's assumption of blame for marital tension.

Inherent in the marital task of decision versus ambivalence is the expectation that the spouses who divorce will have achieved emotional as well as physical separation—an expectation that is not always realized. Instead, there is sometimes a residual task of emotional separation for mastery at a later stage in the developmental life cycle. The cultural and legal expectation for children, in contrast with that for marital partners, is that parents and children will continue to maintain emotional bonds despite physical separation.

Many couples seek professional help during this stage of marital dissolution. Therapists find that increasing numbers of men and women are asking more of their marital partners and accepting less of what they do not like. At such times, therapists are often confronted with the tensions produced by the conflicting goals of the marital partners; one may wish to remain in the marriage, the other may not. Or, in some cases, the parents have made the decision and children are opposed to and resentful of their decision. At such times, practitioners become acutely aware of the opposing needs of individuals and the family and find that their own biases are brought to the fore and most sorely challenged. The difficulty couples experience in maintaining a workable balance between individual, marital, and children's interests is a critical issue that practitioners must explore during this phase. The therapeutic issue is to help the marital couple clarify if the nuclear marriage can be stabilized and, if not, to help the family traverse the dissolution process with the least possible damage for all concerned.[10] Whether a dissolution process terminates in death or divorce, the losses of significant persons, the marriage, and an idealized family structure must be recognized and mourned. Then, the developmental task for all family members becomes the initiation of a process of grief and mourning versus denial of losses. This process continues into the next remarried family stage.

STAGE IV: CONTRACTION-REORGANIZATION AS A SINGLE-PARENT FAMILY STRUCTURE

This stage is initiated by the death of or divorce from a spouse and the ensuing loss of marital status. The time of entry is specific and the family is highly visible because of the structural change that involves contraction from a two-parent to a one-parent family system. The stage ends with the social or legal remarriage of the single parent. Its duration is, however, highly variable. If remarriage follows immediately after divorce, as it did for Mr. Maynor's first wife, it is almost nonexistent. Alternatively, it may extend for many years, as it did for Ellen Gray. Despite variations, on the average, for those who divorce this stage begins before or soon after the oldest child begins school.[11] In the event of dissolution because of death, the children are usually older because of reduction in death rates of men and women in childrearing years. For most single parents, whether widowed or divorced, the average duration of this phase is about three years.[12] However, increasing numbers of single parents establish social remarriage units before they legally remarry.[13] For these families the effective duration of this stage may, therefore, be considerably less than three years.

When the single parent and his or her children of the former marriage enter this stage they carry with them all of the parent-child developmental tasks that would have continued had the nuclear family not been broken. These tasks then coexist with the new developmental tasks relevant to the single-parent family that were not known to the nuclear family.

The new developmental task for all family members at this time is coping versus disorganization. At the most immediate level of reorganization are issues of adapting to a new lifestyle, establishing new rules and daily routines, and coping with frequent problems related to financial stress. All must now adjust to the single-parent stage in a culture in which the nuclear two-parent, two-generation family is the model and the ideal. In the new role of single parent, the divorced are often stigmatized and do not enjoy societal empathy. The widowed parent, on the other hand, is helped through this stage with institutionalized support systems, such as social security survivors insurance, and societal empathy. For the single parent, widowed or divorced, who previously had never worked, there are the added tasks of making adjustments to the work world while integrating new responsibilities at home. For children who have not had to make the adjustment earlier, this additional separation parallels the separation from an absent or deceased parent.

On an interpersonal level, the critical issue that confronts the single parent is the assumption of roles formerly carried by the deceased or divorced spouse. Also, children may assume roles of parent surrogates. Although this is often a necessary aspect of family reorganization, the appropriate distinctions between parent and child roles may be obscured. In addition, a child may become a spouse surrogate, increasing the risks of enmeshment and contributing to further role confusion. These risks exist in any family, but they present a higher risk in the single-parent family. The child's heightened apprehensions about parent loss combine with parental guilt and often result in enmeshment rather than appropriate generational separation.

Another aspect of the problems of the divorced single parent revolves around coparenting. Power struggles and marital conflicts surrounding issues of visitation, child support, and custody continue to be played out through children. Resolution of these issues is best dealt with during this stage so that residuals are less likely to surface and interfere with adjustments in later stages. Recent studies document the need for attention to these issues and suggest the importance for children to retain contact with the absent parent.[14]

On a psychological level, the single parent must continue to confront the critical issues of the loss of primary relationships, significant family structure, marital status, and self-esteem whether the dissolution was caused by death or divorce. Children, too, must deal with issues of loss of significant persons and family structure, as well as with feelings of responsibility for the parental divorce and fantasies of parental reunion. The developmental task of mourning versus denial, initiated during the dissolution stage, continues into the single-parent stage because grief and mourning cannot be assumed to be mastered in a short period of time.[15] Moreover, the mourning process ebbs and flows so that as new crises or events occur, feelings of loss resurface and call for further work during this and later stages. These losses must be appropriately mourned so that psychological healing can take place. The freedom to share feelings of grief with close family members facilitates appropriate mourning, but many single-parent families feel unable to share these feelings with each other. Children whose parents have been divorced often feel unable to talk with the parent with whom they are now living about their feelings of loss for the absent parent, and children who have lost a parent in death are often fearful of burdening the surviving parent with their feelings. Similarly, parents often believe it would be harmful to the children if they, as parents, reveal their feelings of loss. In such situations, parents and children do not share their grief and build bonds through appropriate recognition of losses that are mutual.

At times, the successful resolution of feelings about the loss are facilitated by the availability of mutual support systems, social networks, and self-help groups as well as social agencies. Therapists who are involved in work with single-parent families have the opportunity to help these families during this transitional period so that later tasks of the remarried family may build on a foundation of the resolution of as many of these problems as possible. Therapeutic tasks include helping families identify and deal with the issues of loss and grief so that they may be free to form later meaningful relationships. In this process, issues related to loss of self-esteem and children's fantasies of parental reunion can be addressed. In addition, it is important to help single parents establish appropriate generational boundaries with children and avoid enmeshment. Finally, issues related to parenting with a former spouse and the resolution of power struggles over children are areas of therapeutic intervention during this stage. Ultimately, most single parents form new relationships preparatory to social or legal remarriage. Children's responses to these new relationships vary; some welcome the greater involvement of their parent while others perceive it as a further loss. Entry into the next stage may reawaken issues, quieted in earlier stages, for integration and mastery in a new context with new persons when single parents establish social or legal remarriage units.

STAGE V: EXPANSION AND RECONSTITUTION AS A REMARRIED FAMILY STRUCTURE

The remarriage of the single parent initiates still another stage unique to the remarried family and represents still another discontinuity. Entry into this phase introduces the step relationship and expands and reconstitutes the single-parent family as a socially or legally remarried two-parent, two-generation family unit. The social expectation is that the new family unit will remain intact through the old age of the marital couple and that remarried family members will form emotional bonds and attachments similar to those in other two-parent, two-generation family structures. This latter expectation is, however, often frustrated because of the greater developmental complexity of the remarried family.

Reasons for this greater developmental complexity include the existence of the prior parent-child attachment, step role ambiguity, and devaluation. Another explanation is the greater vulnerability of remarried family members because of earlier traumatic discontinuities and losses because of death or divorce, rated as two of life's most stressful events.[16] Still another factor that contributes to the developmental complexity of the remarried family is related to the lack of a shared developmental tie among all family members, because psychological bonds that grow from living together are there for some family members and not for others. Husband and wife have not shared the process of socialization and nurturance of mutual offspring. Children who have shared their earlier growing up years with a now absent parent, may perceive the new parent as an intruder and a stranger. If, in addition, each spouse has children of a prior marriage, the stepsiblings also have no shared developmental history. Many subsequent problems of territoriality for space and relationships are generated. The only tie that all remarried families share in common at the beginning is the social tie of membership in the same family system.

The remarried family is, in effect, a small group in formation working on issues of affiliation, control, and bonding intermingled with high levels of anxiety about the permanence of the new family unit and the constancy of new persons. Moreover, the parental decision to remarry is, at times, in conflict with children's wishes to have their parents reunite or remain in the single-parent unit. Losses and discontinuities specific to earlier stages must be reintegrated in this stage and often require that one or more family members return to earlier "unfinished business" of never or only partially mastered tasks for further work. These may include issues related to continued emotional attachment between former spouses, unresolved mourning of one or more family members, children's hopes for parental reunion, identity issues, and feelings of lowered self-esteem because of the dissolution of the nuclear family. Also, as was true for the single-parent family stage, parent-child developmental tasks of separation-individuation versus enmeshment that apply to any two-generation family system continue from earlier stages and are in addition to those developmental tasks identified as unique to this stage of reconstitution.

The remarried family, like the nuclear, must deal with three developmental tasks specified in stages one and two of the nuclear family: stabilization versus dissolution of the new two-parent, two-generation family structure, interrelated tasks of marital interest versus self-interest, and inclusion versus exclusion (see Table III). However, all of the tasks of unfinished business, parent-child relationships and those that are unique to the reconstitution stage must be recast as they are relevant to the developmental realities of the remarried family system. Moreover, they must be mastered in the context of negative cultural orientations (see chapters four and five), structural complexities (see chapter six), and legal contradictions (see chapter eight) not operative for the nuclear family.

The resumption of marital status reintroduces the developmental task of marital versus self-interest. However, this task is more complicated in the remarried than in the nuclear family. As noted earlier, the cultural expectation for those who marry without children is that the marital couple establish their own residence as a two-person family unit apart from other relatives. It is expected that while prior family bonds will be balanced with the new, the predominant commitment will be shifted to the marital unit. In contrast, the remarried couple does not establish a residence exclusive of other relatives. Indeed, children of a prior marriage of one or both of the spouses are immediately present. The process of balancing new and old family bonds is much more complex in the remarried family because prior bonds now include one's children and there are no cultural norms that encourage separation from one's minor children and a shift in commitment to the marital unit. The need to balance the old bonds with one's children and new bonds with one's marital partner is a critical issue with which remarried couples must deal. Mastery of the task of marital interest versus self-interest is often impeded because self-interest and prior family interest are merged.

The simultaneous assumption of marital and parental roles inherent in the remarried family situation further complicates the mastery of marital tasks because privacy, time, and energy available to couples without children present is not readily accessible to those who remarry with children immediately present. Thus, early marital adjustments must be worked out in a context in which marital and children's needs compete for the available time, space, and energy, as described by the Carrs in chapter two. These needs bring into focus the developmental task of inclusion versus exclusion. In the nuclear family, this task begins some time after the establishment of the marriage and is initially between parent and child. Only later, as children have siblings, does the task of inclusion extend to them. In the remarried family, the task of inclusion versus exclusion cuts across all of the subsystems within the family and immediately involves all of the family members. Husband and wife must expand their boundaries to include someone else's children, and children must include still another parent and often stepsiblings. The frequent ambivalences expressed by many in the step relationship about accepting the new persons in the family makes this task pivotal to the stabilization of the remarried family. In addition, the lack of established norms for appropriate step-role behavior often reinforces ambivalence in bonding. Clearly associated with the task of inclusion versus exclusion is that of role definition versus ambiguity.

Because the remarried family is structurally composed of at least one single parent and children of a prior marriage and a stepparent, or possibly two single-parent families, the risk of family schism or cleavage is high.[17] It often happens that single-parent units that have been reconstituted resist the tasks related to the stabilization of the new family unit by maintaining prior single-parent family lines. Frequent patterns that emerge are the rigid attitudes of the prior single-parent families that lead to two separate families living under one roof or to the mobilization of a prior single-parent unit to exclude the stepparent.

The overarching developmental task of this stage, stabilization versus dissolution, and other tasks more specific to marital and parent-child relationships are more likely to be mastered if two tasks relevant to this stage are added; namely, balance of old and new bonds versus schism and the task of achieving a remarried family identity versus maintenance of prior family identity. Mastery of these tasks facilitates the mastery of all the other tasks of this stage and moves the family toward the goal of the attainment of a workable family balance that reduces the risk of schism. A workable family balance is one in which reconstitution is achieved in the context of expectations based on an understanding of the situational realities of this family system, while schism reflects a division within the family so that prior family lines are hardened. The achievement of a workable family balance involves a shift away from predominant concern with the prior family unit to one that balances interest in the old with the new family system so that the rights and needs of all are recognized.

Identification of barriers to the mastery of developmental tasks is the heart of therapeutic work with many remarried families. As recurrent barriers are specified, therapists can develop some guiding principles for clinical intervention. The therapeutic focus and goal in the development of these principles is on the processes of intervention that facilitate the building of empathic bridges among all family members and move the family from a small group of strangers to one that has identified realistic goals in the service of achieving a workable family balance.

The following classification, although not exhaustive, suggests some of the recurrent issues on which therapists and remarried families must work. This list does not reflect a ranking of problems, but rather is intended to delineate problems that are related to the interaction of individual and family developmental issues. Among the many areas that might have been selected are (1) manner of induction into the remarried family, (2) ghosts of prior relationships, (3) enmeshment issues, (4) biological bond preference (5) bond shifts, (6) split loyalties, and (7) adolescent issues.

Manner of Induction into the Remarried Family System. Sometimes problems that create barriers to family bonding and the achievement of a workable family balance begin before the family is formed because of the way in which children learn of the remarriage of their parent. A group of high school sophomores, in a peer group formed to talk about remarried family issues, discussed some of their feelings of exclusion:

Soon after the formation of the group, students shared their experiences of how they learned their parent was about to be or had remarried. Some had known for some time the person who would be their stepparent and were prepared for this change in their family situation. Others had little or no advance knowledge and felt hurt and excluded. For some, this situation meant that their parent did not believe them important enough to be told in advance.

The most extreme example involved Gary, who related having been away at camp when he was eleven. On his return home, he found that his mother had remarried someone he had never before met. Another example was provided by Marcie, who inadvertently learned from a neighbor that her mother planned to remarry. The consensus of the group was that remarriage was indeed a parental decision but, they concluded, they could deal better with their new situation if their parent shared some of the planning with them along the way.

Although many parents do prepare children for the transition from the single-parent to the reconstitution stage, some parents, fearful of children's resistance to the idea, take the easy way out. Rather than go through the painful process of working through their children's resistances to the idea, they choose instead to present the child with the accomplished remarriage. Children in these circumstances feel excluded because they have not been informed of a change so vitally important to their futures. Resentment about this may smolder for years, interfering with the formation of new bonds and creating tension in the bonds with their biological parent.

Pre-remarriage counseling with all family members is often useful in examining anxieties and expectations about family reconstitution. Although each family must individualize how preparation is accomplished, the process of anticipatory socialization facilitates the achievement of a workable family balance after the family has become reconstituted.

Ghosts. Ghosts of prior marriages (idealized memories of the first spouse) sometimes interfere with marital developmental tasks and frequently lead to negative comparisons with the current spouse. In addition, when the former spouse has died, unresolved issues of mourning may stimulate guilt about accepting the new relationship. In the case of divorce, ghosts may take the form of expectations that the new spouse will behave as the old did in ways that produced tension areas in the first marriage. The second time around the spouse may decide to "protect" him or herself and set up responses as if the new spouse were the old. In situations like these, the current spouse has not been allowed to assume his or her unique identity. When such situations come to the attention of the practitioner, the therapeutic task is to facilitate a process of appropriate differentiation between the new and the old spouse. Further, barriers to marital bonding may occur because of intrapsychic ghosts if issues that were contributors to marital difficulties in the first marriage are also active in the second. In these situations, the therapeutic focus might require individual therapy to deal with internal issues and help clients make the necessary changes in their behavior.

Enmeshment. Marital bonding in remarried families is frequently inhibited by prior parent-child bonds that intrude on the successful mastery of marital tasks. Because the parent-child bond preceded the marital, role and bonding patterns have been established before the new spouse came on the scene. Many of the patterns of parent-child relationships grew out of mutual needs during the single-parent family stage and demonstrate unresolved developmental tasks of the single-parent stage carried forward into the reconstitution phase. Such bonds, often intensified by mutual need during the crises of divorce or death, may result in insufficient separation and individuation between parent and child so that they are enmeshed. In these circumstances, it is not unusual for the marital partner to feel as though he or she is an outsider and that the spouse and child of the prior marriage constitute the primary relationship. Marie Cox described her feelings of being the "other woman" in the relationship between her husband and her ten-year-old stepson.

THE COX FAMILY

Marie and Nick applied for marital therapy about nine months after their marriage. Nick was married when he was twenty-four, and his first child, Carl, was born when he was twenty-six. Three years later, a daughter, Debby, was born. Deeply involved in climbing the corporate ladder, Nick admitted that, in retrospect, he had little time for his family. After a series of separations and reconciliations, his first wife left him, taking with her their youngest child, and Nick was left to care for Carl. A divorce became final when Carl was almost seven. Nick and Carl lived in a single-parent family stage for almost three years.

As if to compensate for the years of isolation and uninvolvement, Nick took over the parenting role so that he became a "total parent," and all other interests were secondary to his investment in caring for Carl. Nick assumed all of the mother roles, including cooking, laundry, and acting as "room father" when Carl was in second grade. In explaining this process, Nick said, "We were each other's survival because we were so bereft." He said that this had worked out well until he remarried. Nick was certain that the good adjustment Carl made to school and his increasing confidence in peer relationships was because Nick had been so supportive and available to his son after his wife had left. Nick was fearful that Carl would experience his father's remarriage as a betrayal. Carl fostered these kinds of feelings by his resentment toward his stepmother. Marie, on the other hand, felt as though she was part of a triangle and compared her feelings with those she had when her first husband became involved in an extramarital affair that had resulted in the breakup of her marriage. The bonding that had helped both Carl and his father come through the difficult time after divorce was now a barrier both to marital bonding and parent-child bonding between Marie and Carl.

Therapeutic intervention involved working through some of the enmeshment issues between Carl and his father so that more appropriate parent child ties could be established. This process of deenmeshment included protecting "special" time for Carl and his father to counter feelings of still another loss. As Carl and Nick began to differentiate themselves from each other, they learned that this did not spell disaster. Nick and Marie were able to focus on marital tasks of mutual accommodation that included relating to Carl in ways to promote his individual development. As these changes took place, the marital bond was strengthened, and Marie perceived Carl as less of a rival and more a child she could mother. Slowly, Nick relinquished his overdetermined "mothering" and shared this role with his wife.

A variant of the enmeshment pattern described above is the child who becomes the spouse or parent surrogate during the single-parent family stage. When this is carried forward to the reconstitution stage, the new spouse often feels excluded. It is not easy for a child who has been in a position of close alliance and authority in a household to yield this position to a new stepparent, as demonstrated in the Carr family. The therapeutic task involves work with the family to establish appropriate generational boundaries so that the marital unit, rather than the parent and child, is the parental unit in charge of the family.

It is clear from the above discussion that marital tasks in the remarried family cannot be separated from the developmental task of inclusion versus exclusion. For many remarried family members who seek professional help, difficulty in the mastery of this task is the primary issue. Successful resolution promotes positive affiliations and emotional attachments. A survey of initial applications of remarried families at a family service agency indicated that most applications for help were made in the first three years of remarriage with the peak number of applications during the first twelve months. A recurrent problem was stress involved in bonding between steppersons.[18] This observation has been confirmed by other empirical studies indicating that step relations are the area of greatest stress even in remarried families who have not approached social agencies for help.[19] Thus, the complex issue of inclusion versus exclusion is critical in therapeutic intervention with biological, cultural, legal, and developmental aspects of the remarried family situation. The lack of attention to this problem often results in dysfunctional step relationships that continue and become firmly entrenched. Thus, therapeutic intervention around the developmental task of inclusion versus exclusion is central in work with remarried families.

Biological Preference. Still another issue that interferes with the mastery of developmental tasks is the preference for biological over step relationships. This preference is evident in frequent stepparent acknowledgements of "I know I shouldn't, but I love my own children more," as well as in children's fantasies of parental reunion. Some explanations for this recurrent preference lie in the lack of clear guidelines about the appropriate step role behavior, structural realities, and developmental realities discussed earlier. Another explanation of biological preference has emphasized that biological ties are the most enduring. Unlike contractual ties, such as the marital, which can be broken, the biological tie is a "sacred bond" that is permanent and invulnerable.[20] In addition, as has been pointed out, cultural orientations and legal doctrines reinforce biological preference.

The parent who combines both biological and step roles is often deeply anguished by the discrepancy between feelings experienced for biological children and for stepchildren. This feeling is often a problem that requires intensive therapeutic intervention (see Ginny Blake, chapter ten). Some parents believe that such biological preferences are built-in and they resent the imposition of standards that insist there should be no difference in feelings between biological and step-children. One stepfather who had been labeled the "wicked stepfather" by his wife talked about his need for autonomy and the right to decide when and how much he could, would, and should love his stepdaughter. Given the right to establish his own boundaries and his own distance-closeness ratio, this stepfather and his stepdaughter created their own social parent relationship of friendship and acceptance, rather than one based on the mother's formulation of what the stepfather should feel and do.

THE BAKER FAMILY

Mrs. Baker applied for counseling services for herself and her husband in response to some publicity she had seen about a special stepparenting project at a local agency. She saw counseling as the last hope to change her husband's attitude toward her daughter, Stacy, fourteen.

The Bakers had been married for four years. Mrs. Baker had been widowed after nine years of marriage, following a long illness of her first husband, when Stacy was six years old. Mr. Baker had been divorced after twelve years of marriage, following many separations and reconciliations. At the time of divorce, his daughter, Lee, was eleven and his son, Brian, was eight, and they continued to live with their mother. Two years later, Mr. Baker remarried.

During the course of therapy, Mrs. Baker described the major problem as the difference in her husband's attitude toward his children and Stacy. She said that he had been distant and cold toward Stacy from the first day of the marriage. In contrast, he was warm and affectionate to his two children, who visited every weekend. She thought that this kind of favoritism made him just as much a "wicked stepfather" as if he had hurt Stacy physically. For Mr. Baker, the major problem was described as his difficulty in parenting a child not his own on a day-to-day basis, while his own children were living elsewhere. He explained the differences in his feelings on the grounds that "blood is thicker than water." Moreover, he felt that he had a right to these feelings and resented his wife's efforts to tell him what he should feel and how he should act toward Stacy. He was angry at being depicted as the "wicked stepfather" when he did the best that he could do.

The therapeutic task in working with families where the presenting problem is the difference in feelings for biological and stepchildren is to help the other spouse view these feelings as understandable, given current cultural and legal orientations and possible biological predispositions. Explication of structural and developmental realities is often helpful as well. Within this context, feelings of loss and disappointment experienced by the parent for his or her child are recognized and mourned. However, the therapeutic goal is to help the marital couple reformulate expectations so that feelings do not become rigidified into power struggles within the marriage and intensify feelings of resentment toward the child for being the object of so much tension.

To begin the process of reduction of this tension it is first necessary to relabel the step relationship from one that is a poor substitute for a nuclear parent to one that is a social parent relationship, different and a relationship in its own right. Working from the premise that stepparents and children have the right to decide their own boundaries and distance-closeness ratios, therapists can help both build a social parent-child bond that is uniquely their own. These social bonds give meaning to the social tie present for all family members at the time of reconstitution.

Social bonds are emergent crescive bonds that grow from shared positive experiences over time. They are not so automatic or inevitable as biological predetermined bonds, nor are they legally enforceable. The role that participants fill in relation to one another may facilitate or limit the growth of crescive bonds. Those who experience crescive bonding gain a sense of validation of worth.[21] In this way, social bonds that do not build on biological or legal ties can be encouraged to evolve so that inclusion rather than exclusion becomes the dominant mode in the family. Marital bonds can be strengthened if husband and wife do not become immersed in hurt feelings and anger on behalf of the excluded child. The family can then move toward stabilization and the achievement of a workable family balance.

Biological preference may also be true for children who have both a stepparent and an absent parent. The principles of autonomy in decisions about timing and dosage of closeness-distance regulation described for stepparents is also valid for stepchildren. The intuitive implementation of this principle by a sensitive stepfather demonstrates how his ability made possible the formation of social parent-child bonds, which, in time, filled the emotional

void left by an absent parent and helped the child achieve a sense
of worth and positive identity.

THE LAWSON FAMILY

Alice had been married for nine years before she left Scott's father. At
that time, Scott was eight and his sister, Helen, was six. Alice described
her husband as violent and physically and verbally abusive. She finally
had the courage to seek shelter in a local center for battered wives and
never returned to the marriage. After the divorce, she returned to her
home state and had no further contact with her former husband. Two
years later, when Scott was ten, she met Wayne Lawson and, after living
together for almost six months, they decided to become legally married.
However, Scott's determination to keep his future stepfather out of his
life concerned Alice and Wayne and they decided to seek help at a child
guidance clinic. In addition, Scott was having difficulty with his peers.

In a series of family interviews, Scott talked about the wonderful times
he had enjoyed with his father. He was angry when his mother and sister
attempted to remind him of the violent episodes he had witnessed and
tried to convince him of how much better things were for all of them
now. His mother was angry at Scott because he deliberately broke things
Wayne bought for them to make together. She described a recent episode
in which Scott smashed a model airplane he and Wayne had been building together.

Wayne acted as the mediator between Alice and Scott. He seemed able
to understand and accept Scott's attachment to his father and tried to
help Alice to be less anxious about Scott's rejection of him and Scott's
need to deny the reality of his father's behavior. After several months of
combined family and individual therapy with Scott in the context of
Wayne's consistent patience and nondemanding attitude toward him,
coupled with a reduction in his mother's insistence that Scott accept
Wayne as better than his father, Scott began to recall some of his father's
erratic and unreliable behavior. He began to talk about his intense shame
at his father's behavior as well as fear that he too might become like his
father. Eventually, Scott was helped to differentiate himself from his
father and learn to assert himself appropriately with his friends without
fear of becoming violent and hurting them.

Eventually Scott learned he could love and remember his father as
someone who had both disappointed him and given him pleasure. Other
family members were helped to allow each other to have the right to own
their feelings, even if at times they were in disagreement with each other.
In family therapy, sessions work revolved around integrating the gains
Scott was making in individual therapy with general discussions that
educated the family to some of the normative issues in becoming a remarried family. Scott's repressed affection for Wayne slowly surfaced
when he was given permission to have positive feelings for his father.

He also began to see himself as a separate person who did not have to repeat the negative aspects of his father's behavior. The Lawsons felt they were on their way to becoming a "real" family when Scott and Wayne successfully finished building a model airplane.

Wayne Lawson's intuitive recognition of Scott's prior bond to his father and his need to define his own timetable and distance-closeness ratio to him were basic to the success of the formation of later positive bonds. Several basic principles emerge that have general applicability in situations in which children have difficulty in accepting the new stepparent because of idealized images of an absent parent, because of unresolved mourning, identity issues, or a combination of both. These are (1) the ability to refrain from personalizing the attachment to a prior bond as a rejection, but to understand it in the context of a normal and expectable reaction; (2) the ability to retain a nonjudgmental attitude about the child's absent parent so that defensiveness is not stimulated; and (3) the ability to help family members accept and tolerate differences in feelings and perceptions about each other. Such guidelines begin to delineate orientations toward appropriate step role behavior and are essential groundwork in the formation of new bonds in the remarried family.

Bond Shifts. In addition, bonding strains also result from bond shifts. These occur when the step role position is added to the prior biological position. The remarried family member who combines these positions sometimes deals with the tensions resulting from this hybrid status by making a shift to new relationships without maintaining appropriate emotional bonds with the old. It is likely to occur, for example, if a hybrid parent, intent on winning the love of the spouse's children, ignores the need for continued emotional bonds with his or her children of a prior marriage. Ann and Roy Harris told of such a bond shift in their household after their mother remarried.

Ann and Roy moved into their stepfather's house after their mother remarried. They described feelings of not only having lost their father, familiar surroundings, and former school, but also their relationship with their mother. Ann felt that she was overlooked by her mother and not as important to her as she had been before her mother's remarriage. She missed the shared activities and companionship that had characterized their former relationship. Roy explained, "My mother is so busy with the new kids, she never has time for us."

In a similar vein, the bond shift sometimes occurs when bonds between siblings of a prior marriage are shifted to stepsiblings. For example, Jeff complained bitterly that his older brother, who had been his friend and caretaker during the single-parent family stage, now ignored him in favor of an exclusive friendship with his stepbrother. Still another variation of this pattern occurs when a child shifts his or her attachment from the biological parent to the stepparent in an effort to gain a foothold in the family. These shifts are aspects of the structural rearrangements in the informal subsystems that take place in remarried families and demonstrate the interlocking nature of shifts in structural subsystem alliances and emotional bonds. Therapeutic intervention in these instances revolves once again around helping family members find the balance between old and new ties, so that old ties are appropriately maintained and nourished even as new ties are encouraged.

Split Loyalties. Still another source of bonding strain derives from the linking position, wherein a parent must balance ties between the marital partner and children of a prior marriage. In contrast to situations of enmeshment, where the choice is made in favor of the child of the prior marriage, or bond shifts, where new relationships are chosen, some persons experience feelings of split loyalties or cross-pressure in their linking position between old and new ties. For example, Ellen Gray felt pulled in two directions: between her love for her child and her love for her husband. Similarly, Mr. Hanley understood his wife's feelings about his children's loyalty to their mother, yet he could also understand his children's resentment of his wife's methods of discipline.

THE HANLEY FAMILY

Mr. Hanley sought help for his family when the children asked to have the custody arrangements changed so that they could live with their absent mother and her new husband. They did not get along with their stepmother and perceived her as harsh and moralistic. Their mother had left them in order to live with a man whom she subsequently married.

When the children visited their mother, they found their stepfather fun-loving and easygoing. Few demands were made on them and no questions were asked when teenaged Sara ignored the curfew. On the other hand, the stepmother with whom they lived felt compelled to correct the "loose" standards of the absent parent family. When Mr. Hanley talked about the situation, he described with great poignancy his feelings of being "cross-pressured" in his linking role between his new wife and the children of his former marriage.

Mr. Hanley's eight year old son, Stephen, also felt caught in the linking role of child to two biological parents who were now parenting apart. Perhaps his comment most vividly reflects the extent of his torment at being in a position of having to make a choice between his two parents when he said, "Saw me in half!" In the course of further work with this family, the poignancy for the father was magnified when it became clear that the children's request for a change in custodial arrangements did not reflect a choice of biological mother over biological father, but that of stepfather over stepmother.

The linking position in this situation was a difficult one for both father and children. Mr. Hanley wanted to support his wife's efforts to set limits for his children, but he could understand their perception of her standards as harsh and moralistic. Stephen, too, felt the tension of pulls from two directions. His solution—"Saw me in half"—was a child's effort to terminate the tension and be in both places at the same time. He felt powerless to make a choice. The linking positions of father and children were compounded by the parenting styles of each of the new stepparents. Stepparents were compared with each other by the children, who debated in which household they would choose to live. In such circumstances, stepparents compete with each other for winning the child just as biological parents often do.

Parents are sometimes immobilized when they identify with the feelings that are held both by persons to whom they have prior bonds and those to whom they have new bonds. The therapeutic tasks in such situations are to build on their capacity to see the whole picture and to help the cross-pressured client make objective decisions and move flexibly between new and old bonds. Decisions are made in terms of the specific issues involved, rather than on the basis of a predetermined alliance with the children of a prior marriage or a total shift to the new relationship without consideration of the issues involved for those children. The achievement of a workable family balance based on the balance of old and new bonds and on realistic goals within the context of this family continues to be a guiding principle.

Children also are frequently caught in the cross-pressures of the linking position. Emotional strains are apparent in split loyalties between an absent and a resident parent. Although such pressure is not unique to the remarried family, it is exacerbated if children are experiencing bonding strains with a stepparent. Ultimately, the goal is to help children accept membership in both the resident and the absent parent household. However, parents often need to work on their feelings about allowing and facilitating this dual membership when bitterness has run high and marital issues between the former spouses have not been resolved. These reference points in the bonding process all require that old and new bonds be balanced, and they have implications for mastery of the developmental tasks of inclusion versus exclusion and the achievement of a workable family balance.

Adolescent Issues. Analysis of reapplications of remarried families to social service agencies reveals that although the highest number of applications come during the first year of marriage, many reapplications are made when children reach adolescence.[22] The turmoil of adolescence, a difficult time in all families, propels many who had earlier achieved a workable family balance to reapply for service. Parental authority, tenuous at best during adolescence, is often vigorously rejected with comments such as, "I don't have to listen to you, you're not my real mom or dad." In addition, many adolescent reexperience earlier losses during this period as they search to clarify and establish their sense of worth and identity. Therapists report that issues of grief and mourning, even if dealt with earlier during the single-parent stage or early reconstitution, resurface for still another chance at mastery. During this period, developmental issues between parents and children related to appropriate separation and individuation continue and are often intensified when remarried parents view normal adolescent thrusts toward separation as evidence of rejection of the new family situation or of the stepparent. These issues are often carried forward into the launching stage.

STAGE VI: LAUNCHING-CONTRACTION

This stage is the same for both nuclear and remarried families, although it poses some unique issues for remarried families. It is a time for contraction, because young adult children leave home to establish independent living arrangements. The developmental task of this phase is the maintenance of connections versus detachment. For many parents, it is a particularly difficult time if their feeling of individual worth and identity are invested in parenting children. However, in the nuclear family, bonds with children forged over many years by both parents who are in a

symmetrical position to their children usually make the ambivalences of this period a shared experience. In the remarried family,
the marital partners may have differing attitudes toward the
launching, growing from the differences in their structural ties
and consequent emotional attachment to these children. These
tensions may result in marital conflict if the biological parent
perceives the launching of his or her child as a loss, while the
stepparent sees it as a gain and an opportunity to strengthen the
marital bond. If a biological parent has an intense attachment to
a child, launching may reflect feelings of loss that transcend those
that are normal to parents at this stage. A stepparent who has not
had the years of a continuing relationship through the developmental stages of the child from his or her birth may see this as an
opportunity for legitimate separation. This feeling runs counter
to the wishes and attachment pulls of the biological parent. In
such circumstances, when a child leaves home, the biological
parent may blame the stepparent and believe his or her child
would not have left home if the stepparent had not wanted to be
rid of the child. This happened with the Rossi family, who applied
for help during the launching stage.

THE ROSSI FAMILY

Mr. and Mrs. Rossi were in their middle fifties. They had been
married for three years. At the time of their marriage, Mrs. Rossi's
two daughters, aged twenty-five and twenty-three, were married
and living in a neighboring community. Mr. Rossi had two children, a married son, twenty-two, and a daughter, sixteen.

Both Mr. and Mrs. Rossi had been widowed before their remarriage;
she for nine years and he for two. They each reported stable and happy
earlier marriages. They had been able to share with each other their
feelings of loss about their deceased spouses and, in general, felt they
were sensitive to each other's needs and feelings.

The tensions around the "launching" of Mr. Rossi's daughter Jean were
thus distressing to both of them. Mr. Rossi felt that there was something
"basically wrong" with his wife for wanting to see Jean establish herself
in her own apartment. He interpreted her encouragement of Jean in this
effort to mean she wanted to "get rid of her," and as "unmotherly." Mrs.
Rossi reported that she felt entitled to her feelings. She and Jean had a
friendly and "reasonably good relationship." They appeared to like each
other and respected each other's privacy. Yet, Mrs. Rossi admitted with
much hesitation and shame that she had always looked forward to the
time when Jean would leave home. She had raised two daughters, and

had gone through the turmoil of their teenage years as a widow. When she married Mr. Rossi, she had not looked forward to going through a period with a teenager again. She had never felt free to admit this to Mr. Rossi and thought she could be patient and wait until Jean was ready to leave. She had not been prepared for Mr. Rossi's resistance to Jean's leaving, and perceived it as giving his relationship with his daughter greater priority than his relationship with her.

Mr. Rossi, on the other hand, spoke about the strong tie that had developed between him and his daughter after his wife's death and his son's marriage soon after. He believed that Jean would not be leaving if his wife had been more of a mother to her, even though he admitted that they seemed to be "good enough friends." He had always been secretly disappointed that they were not more like mother and daughter. His fantasy was that when he remarried it would be "just like it had been with his first wife."

The therapeutic task in this case was to explore what the developmental issues were for all family members and work out an appropriate balance so that the needs of all were recognized. In a flexible use of marital, family, and individual therapy, it was determined that Jean did indeed want to leave home and that it had nothing to do with her stepmother's "unmotherly" behavior. In fact, she felt appreciative of her stepmother's sensitivity in not making demands on her to be "more daughterly." Jean felt that the issue for her was her readiness to strike out on her own and become independent. She was involved in the normal processes of separation-individuation appropriate to her developmental stage. Mr. Rossi was struggling with counterpulls to keep Jean at home.

The Rossi situation is not unique. Sometimes it is the stepfather who is eager for the launching, and charges of "wicked stepfather, unable to love his stepchild" are made. The therapeutic task remains to clarify the relevant realities and developmental needs of all of the family members involved. The overriding therapeutic goal is to help families resolve these tensions so that all may grow, maintain significant bonds, and yet become autonomously functioning individuals. These issues, if resolved, prepare the way for transition into the final stage.

STAGE VII: THE MARITAL UNIT
WITHOUT CHILDREN AT HOME

The developmental task for nuclear and remarried families during this phase is renewal of the marital bond and expansion of interests so that departures of children do not result in emptiness and boredom. For remarried couples this is the first time in which there has been an opportunity to be a "couple without children." Marital tasks frequently ignored or postponed because of the press of meeting immediate needs of children often are undertaken during this stage.

DEVELOPMENTAL COMPLEXITY

The developmental complexity of the remarried family is demonstrated by the increased number of stages and developmental tasks it experiences. Shown below in Table III is a comparative

TABLE III. *Comparison of Nuclear and Remarried Family Life Cycle Stages and Developmental Tasks*

Nuclear		Remarried	
Stages	Tasks	Stages	Tasks
I. Establishment (marriage)	Marital interest v. self-interest	I. Establishment (marriage)	Marital interest v. self-interest
II. Expansion (birth or adoption of children)	Stabilization v. dissolution Inclusion v. exclusion	II. Expansion (birth or adoption of children)	Stabilization v. dissolution Inclusion v. exclusion
Begin the two-parent, two-generation nuclear family structure	Separation-individuation v. enmeshment		Separation-individuation v. enmeshment
		III. Dissolution (death or divorce)	Decision v. ambivalence (divorce) Mourning v. denial Separation-individuation v. enmeshment
		IV. Contraction (reorganize as single-parent structure)	Coping v. disorganization Separation-individuation v. enmeshment
		V. Expansion (reconstitute as a two-parent, two-generation remarried family structure)	Stabilization v. dissolution Marital interest v. self/ prior family interest Inclusion v. exclusion of step-related persons Balance of old and new bonds v. schism Separation-individuation v. enmeshment Role definition v. role ambiguity Remarried family identity v. prior family identity
III. Contraction (children launched)	Connection v. detachment Separation-individuation v. enmeshment	VI. Contraction (children launched)	Connection v. detachment Separation-individuation v. enmeshment
IV. Stabilization (marital couple without children in the home)	Renewal v. boredom	VII. Stabilization (marital couple without children in the home)	Renewal v. boredom

analysis of nuclear and remarried family life cycle stages and developmental tasks.

The central goal in the remarried family, the formation of new bonds, has been examined as it is affected by the developmental realities of the additional life cycle stages and tasks. Some common barriers to bonding between step related persons that interfere with the goal of achieving a workable family balance have been suggested. Still other barriers to the bonding process are discussed in the next chapter on legal aspects of the remarried family.

NOTES

1. Graham Spanier and William Sauer, "An Empirical Evaluation of the Family Life Cycle," *Journal of Marriage and the Family* 41, no. 1 (February 1979): 38.
2. Stephen Nock, "The Family Life Cycle," *Journal of Marriage and the Family* 41, no. 1 (February 1979): 24.
3. See Daniel J. Levinson, *The Seasons of a Man's Life* (New York: Alfred A. Knopf, 1978); Bernice L. Neugarten, ed., *Middle Age and Aging* (Chicago: University of Chicago, 1975); and George E. Valliant, *Adaptation to Life* (Boston: Little, Brown, 1977).
4. Henry W. Maier, *Three Theories of Child Development*, rev. ed. (New York: Harper and Row, 1969, p. 30; and Erik H. Erikson, *Childhood and Society*, 2d ed. (New York: W.W. Norton, 1963).
5. Joan Aldous, *Family Careers: Developmental Changes in Families* (New York: John Wiley, 1978), pp. 84–87; and Evelyn Mills Duvall, *Family Development*, 4th ed. (New York: J.B. Lippincott, 1971), pp. 121–51.
6. United States Bureau of the Census, "Marital Status and Living Arrangements: March 1979," *Current Population Reports*, Series P-20, no. 349 (Washington, D.C.: United States Government Printing Office, 1980), p. 1.
7. United States Bureau of the Census, "Perspectives on American Fertility," *Current Population Reports*, Series P-23, no. 70. (Washington, D.C.: United States Government Printing Office, 1978), p. 19.
8. United States Bureau of the Census, "Number, Timing and Duration of Marriages in the United States, June 1975," *Current Population Reports*, Series P-20, no. 297 (Washington, D.C.: United States Government Printing Office, 1976) p. 9.
9. George Levinger, "A Social Psychological Perspective on Marital Dissolution," in *Divorce and Separation: Context, Causes and Consequences*, ed. George Levinger and Oliver C. Moles (New York: Basic Books, 1979), pp. 37–61.
10. Esther Wald, "The Non-Nuclear Family," in *The Many Dimensions of Family Practice: Proceedings of the North American Symposium on Family Practice* (New York: Family Service Association of America, 1980), p. 36.
11. Joan Aldous, *Family Careers*, p. 91.
12. United States Bureau of the Census, "Number, Timing and Duration of Marriages and Divorces in the United States," p. 15.
13. United States Bureau of the Census, "Marital Status and Living Arrangements," Mar. 1979," p. 3; and Paul C. Glick and Graham Spanier, "Married and Unmarried Cohabitation in the United States," *Journal of Marriage and the Family* 42, no. 1 (February 1980): 19–30.

14. Judith Wallerstein and Joan B. Kelly, "Children and Divorce," *Social Work* 24, no. 6 (November 1979): 471.

15. John Bowlby and C. Murray Parkes, "Separation and Loss Within the Family," in *The Child in His Family*, ed. James E. Anthony and Cyrille Koupernick (New York: Wiley-Interscience, 1970), pp. 197–215.

16. See Thomas H. Holmes and Minoru Masuda, "Life Change and Illness Susceptibility," in *Stressful Life Events: Their Nature and Effects*, ed. Barbara Snell Dohrenwend and Bruce P. Dohrenwend (New York: John Wiley, 1974), p. 52.

17. Jessie Bernard, *Remarriage, A Study of Marriage*, (New York: Russell and Russell, 1971), pp. 252–65.

18. Esther Wald, "Analysis of Years of Remarriage at Time of First Application and Reapplication," unpublished study, 1977.

19. Lucille Duberman, "Step-Kin Relationships," *Journal of Marriage and the Family* 35 no. 5 (May 1973): 283–92.

20. Ralph H. Turner, *Family Interaction* (New York: John Wiley, 1970), pp. 91–92.

21. Ibid., pp. 80–87, 161.

22. Esther Wald, "Analysis of Years of Remarriage at Time of First Application and Reapplication," unpublished study, 1977.

8

~~~

SOCIAL GOALS AND
LEGAL CONTRADICTIONS

Many remarried families seek professional help with problems that are related to their legal situation. Prior divorce and the presence of children of an earlier marriage as well as the step situation present legal realities for the remarried family that are not true for the nuclear. These differences are an aspect of many of the recurrent problems for which remarried family members seek help.

Practitioners must work with each family to clarify the problem and set goals within the context of their legal reality. Thus, it is essential that practitioners have some knowledge of relevant legal aspects of the remarried family situation in order to facilitate more effective clinical intervention.

This chapter focuses on the legal dimension of the schema for study of the remarried family. It identifies some of the evolving legal doctrines and principles that have shaped current custodial options, and the legal status of the remarried family in the context of changing societal values and ideologies. Variations in child-care arrangements related to child custody, visitation, and child support are discussed. Unique legal aspects of the situation and issues and dilemmas that flow from this are explored. An analysis of the balance of rights and obligations among husbands, wives, and children at the time of divorce and the rights of biological parents, stepparents, and children in the remarried family, as specified in family law and relevant to clinical practice, is central to this discussion.

HISTORICAL INFLUENCES AND LEGAL DOCTRINES

Family law, a special branch of law that has evolved over time, determines the legal rights and obligations of husbands and wives and parents and children, and covers such matters as marriage, divorce, adoption, child custody, child support, visitation, remarriage, and incestuous relationships. Rules of conduct supporting ethical and social mandates of society are explicated and enforced by threat of punishment for violations.

Although there is an increasing number of federal uniform acts in family law that states may or may not adopt, there is no overall body of federal family law. Each state enacts its own statutes and develops its own precedents. There is, thus, considerable inconsistency among states and even within the same state on many aspects of family law, depending on the orientation of the court that hears the case. Notable are inconsistencies in decisions on divorce, child custody, and adoption—all of which are particularly relevant to the remarried family. Despite these inconsistencies, the evolution of family law has been guided by several historic, universal, and enduring values. Among these have been the right of the family to privacy, the right and obligation of parents to care for their children, and a belief in the inviolate nature of the biological tie. These values, derived from antiquity and codified in Biblical and Roman law, continue to be endorsed today.

Judicial thinking has sought to implement these values through statutes and precedents and in case-by-case decisions that have evolved into legal doctrines. A study of these doctrines demonstrates the legal institution's response to changing ideologies and practices of society, as well as its interpretation of human behavior and social interaction. Indeed, Justice Holmes' observation in 1921 that the law is a "magic mirror" and that every important social development in life has its impact on the law appears to be as true today as it was then.[1] Legal doctrines are a reference point that mark the court's interpretation of how to deal with some specific phenomenon at a particular period. They are a linking instrument between a specific family with a specific problem and related social issues in larger society.

Overall, legal doctrines have mirrored the court's changing position on when, why, and to what extent the state should intervene in family privacy and parent-child relationships. These doctrines have been responsive to changing cultural ideologies and new knowledge and, at the same time, have been influential in shaping future directions of the family. Occasionally, in a creative leap, some specific doctrine advances and recasts legal interpretations of familial rights and duties so that new and meaningful directions are set forth. Such doctrines become guiding principles for the courts, and lead society in balancing the rights of human social relationships. They grow into classics for future decision making because they have so transformed existing approaches that a greater unity exists between the phenomenon and the law. Other doctrines have limited value and die of disuse. Perhaps the greatest number began as an appropriate response at a given time but, because of societal and cultural changes, became stereotyped and outdated. Others may remain in transition and coexist or eventually blend with new and emerging views that are more responsive to the current scene.

All married families who have come through the legal process of divorce and decision making about care of their children must live by the rationale and prescription set forth under the particular doctrine that a court has applied to their situation. At times, this situation results in tensions between social goals and values for family cohesion and legal realities that inhibit or even prevent cohesion. To be helpful to remarried families whose problems involve adaptation to or change in legal decisions, the practitioner must study some of the key legal doctrines that have shaped these decisions, as well as some of the emerging new legal directions.

PATERNAL PREFERENCE

The most classic and most enduring of all doctrines in family law is that of *parens patriae* (father of the country), derived from common law and explicated in seventeenth-century England. This doctrine, carried by English settlers to America, is now the basis of state authority in local statutes. It gives the state power to protect children and act for their welfare. The early and continued rationale for this incursion into the privacy of the family and judgment of how parental responsibility toward children should be carried out derived from the assumption that children could not speak for themselves; they required protection through laws that gave the state power to intercede on their behalf under specified circumstances. The expectation was that courts would not interfere in private family matters when both parents shared the rights and duties of custody and the welfare of the child was not in jeopardy.

Custody was broadly defined as all of the rights and duties involved in the care and rearing of a child. In the event of dissolution of a family by death, the surviving spouse became the custodial parent and there was no court intervention. However, in the event of dissolution of the family by divorce, the legal termination of a marriage was involved. Because of the traditional social and religious emphasis on the indissoluble nature of marriage, divorces were at first granted by special legislation, and general divorce laws were not enacted until toward the middle of the nineteenth century. Therefore, courts made determinations about circumstances when divorce could take place and where the children of divorcing parents should reside.

Under the doctrine of *parens patriae*, early American courts supported societal patterns of power and authority in family organization. The hierarchy of male domination, female subordination, and children as paternal property was legally reinforced as a natural and rightful order in family relationships. Although some American colonies granted women the right to divorce, the predominant early presumptions of the law were that divorce was the prerogative of the husband, and custody of the children the father's right. Only men had legal status and could make determinations about property. Thus, fathers, as legal representatives of the family, were held responsible for and considered to be better able than mothers to provide for the protection, economic security, and education of their children. Financial responsibility and physical custody, with rare exception, were lodged with the father.

MATERNAL PREFERENCE

By the middle of the nineteenth century, glimmers of change from this orientation began to appear. Here and there, courts were finding that paternal custody should not be absolute and that, at times, the welfare of the child required maternal custody. These rulings came during the period of the country's growing industrialization and changing philosophic orientation toward the child, not as property but as an individual having intrinsic worth and value.

To support the broad principle of the welfare of the child embodied in the doctrine of *parens patriae*, the tender years presumption evolved. This presumption reflected a shift from the orientation that the father was the most suitable guardian of the child to one that held that the mother's influence during the first seven years of life was critical to the developing child. Implicit in this doctrine was the belief that the mother was the more nurturant parent during the child's early years, and, hence, more crucial than the father to the child's emotional and physical growth and developmental needs.

The tender years presumption provided the courts with a tangible direction, because the age of the child could be a determinant in disputes involving a custodial decision between divorcing parents. A decision applying the doctrine read as follows:

> An infant of tender years is generally left with the mother (if no objection to her is shown to exist) even when the father is without blame, merely because of his inability to bestow upon it the tender care which nature requires and which is the peculiar province of the mother to supply.[2]

The doctrine of parental culpability was another principle that developed before the turn of the century to aid the courts in the determination of the child's welfare. It gave courts the power to specify the party at fault in divorce and to refuse custody to that person. Thus, the routine procedure of awarding custody to the father could be challenged if he were found to be "at fault" for the divorce, and the mother could become the custodial parent. The rationale for awarding custody to the presumed innocent party in a divorce was based on the assumption that he or she was more likely to give the child proper care. With this doctrine, grounds for divorce became a matter of blame and fault and the adversary system in divorce was strengthened.

By the beginning of the twentieth century, women had acquired legal status separate from their husbands and the argument that the father, as legal representative of the family, was entitled to custody because children were his paternal property no longer held. With this development, one of the greatest obstacles to maternal custody was removed. In addition, maternal custody was expanded as courts ruled fathers were responsible for financial support of their children even if the children no longer lived with their father. Physical custody and financial support were no longer necessarily lodged in the same person, and courts increasingly appointed mothers as primary custodians.

Although the separation of physical custody and paternal financial responsibility gave the courts greater flexibility in ruling in favor of one or the other parent when a clear preference was possible, it did not address the court's need for guidelines in making decisions when both parents were evenly matched in custody disputes and a clear preference was not possible. The anguish faced by judges in such cases, often referred to as "Solomon Sword" situations, is well documented in the literature.[3] Some judges dealt with these difficult decisions by seeing the child involved in private chambers or by requesting social agencies to study the situation. The goal in such procedures was to determine child's preference. The rationale was that if the child had a definite custodial preference and was old enough and "capable of reason," his or her choice should be honored. Limited though they were, these instances led to later principles that espoused children's rights to speak for themselves or have their views represented in the courts.

Still another option that some courts used in custody contests when either parent was a suitable guardian was that of placement of the child with the parent of the same sex. Implicit in this practice was an advanced recognition of the psychological concept that role models developed through identification with the same-sex parent are an important aspect of the child's emotional growth. Although these options served as "tie-breakers" to relieve courts in contested custody situations when both parents were fit, the predictable and consistent pattern in custody matters by the end of the first quarter of the twentieth century was maternal preference, paternal financial support, and visitation rights for the non-custodial father. Some observers of this routine pattern concluded that the trend had been reversed from absolute paternal preference to one of absolute maternal preference—the rights of the father had given way to the rights of the mother, and, if the welfare of the child was served, it was incidental.[4]

THE BEST INTERESTS OF THE CHILD

The best interests of the child doctrine, laid down by Justice Benjamin Cardozo in 1925, addressed this issue and made explicit the court's concern for the child's welfare. It stated:

> The court acts as a *parens patriae* to do what is best for the interest of the child. . . . He is not adjudicating a controversy between adversary parties to compose their private differences . . . nor determining rights as between a parent and a child,

or as between one parent and another. Concern is for the welfare
of the child rather than rights of parents as litigants.[5]

In essence, this doctrine declared that there is no inherent custodial preference and repudiated the concept that either father or
mother has a preferential right to custody before the law. It flowed
from growing judicial dissatisfaction with "fault"-based or "sexual"-based presumptions and the difficulties courts found in de-
termining "right" or "wrong" in a divorce as the basis for custody
decisions. The best interests doctrine recognized that each child
is unique and that the needs and rights of the child should be
protected and should take precedence over parental rights between divorcing partners in contested custody cases. This doctrine
enunciated a broad philosophy that has since become one of the
guiding principles and prevailing judicial doctrines involving
children.

PARENTAL PREFERENCE
Although the increasing divorce rate has focused attention on
the resolution of custodial disputes between divorcing parties, a
significant number of custodial disputes involve contests between
a noncustodial biological-legal parent and a stepparent. These
disputes are often considered in the context of the doctrine of
parental preference, which argues that the biological parent is the
preferred parent in disputes with a third-party parent, whether a
relative, foster parent, adoptive parent, or stepparent. This emphasis is related to the ideology that the parent-child tie is "so
rooted in the traditions and conscience of our people as to be
ranked as fundamental. . . ."[6] The doctrine of parental rights or
preference has evolved as a mirror to this ideology. It declares
that:

> A natural parent, whether father or mother, who is of good char-
> acter and a proper person to have custody and reasonably able
> to provide for the child, is ordinarily entitled to custody as
> against all other persons. Under this view, the rule that the wel-
> fare or interest of the child is the paramount consideration is
> subject to the condition or qualification that a fit parent with a
> suitable home has a right to the custody of his child superior to
> the rights of others.[7]

This doctrine presumes that parental rights are inherent and
intrinsic human rights derived from the sacred nature of the bi-

ological bond and precede legal bonds that are conferred by the state. Thus, the biological bond has preference over all others and can be terminated only under extreme circumstances. However, there is considerable variation among courts in the interpretation of the circumstances under which the biological bond can be terminated. These range from a strict interpretation, which preserves parental rights unless unfitness can be proved beyond a doubt, to those in which courts determine that the best interests of the child reside in a third party, even if the parent is not unfit.[8]

RECENT LEGAL DIRECTIONS

By 1970, changing social conditions, values, and expanding psychological and sociological understandings were mirrored in laws that overturned many established doctrines. Divorce rates continued to rise and the concept of the individual's right to marital happiness became the prevalent norm. At the same time, the blurring of traditional family roles occurred so that there were increasing numbers of families with both parents working, greater parental sharing of child care, and divorced fathers' organizations demanding equalization of custodial rights and responsibilities. These changing values and ideologies were recognized in state legislation, case-by-case decisions, and a growing body of federal uniform acts dealing with child custody.

In 1970, California passed the first no-fault divorce laws and these have since been adopted by almost all states. The underlying principle of these laws reflected recognition that the complexity of marital relationships defied a finding of fault in divorce actions and that absolute criteria in the light of today's more sophisticated understandings of human relationships were not possible. Because blame no longer was attached to either partner, neither spouse had to prove that the other was at fault and the earlier standard of parental culpability on which courts had relied for custody decisions was, therefore, eroded.

In the same year, the tender years presumption, supporting maternal preference, lost its foothold when the Uniform Marriage and Divorce Act was adopted. This law provides that custody decisions be made according to the "best interests" test.[9] The widespread acceptance of this principle reflected the expanding child rights movement that sought to protect the welfare of the child and moved beyond consideration of the child as parental property to "rather as a trust imposed on the parent for the child's benefit."[10] Robert Mnookin states that "in the past two centuries, we have moved from a pattern of treating a child as a possession or a 'thing' to be owned to a much more child-centered mode of analysis."[11]

The best interests test continues to be the underlying principle applied in custody decisions. However, discretionary and contradictory rulings using this broad doctrine have led many to urge the development of specific guidelines to measure the best interest. The expectation is that such specification will facilitate decisions that minimize bias, enhance consistency and predictability, and preserve a philosophy that focuses on the welfare of the child in the context of the need to arrive at postdivorce child-care plans and possible custody modification after remarriage. Two central concepts that have been important in developing criteria to determine the child's best interest in custody situations have been the concept of the psychological parent and the concept of children's preference.

CHILDREN'S PREFERENCE

The concept of psychological parent, tenuously recognized both by the tender years presumption and by matched custody awards of children to the same-sex parent, came of age in the 1970s. In contested custody decisions between divorcing parents, courts sought to determine the child's best interests in relation to the parent who had the "more psychological" meaning for the child. This determination would be made on the basis of a fact-by-fact analysis of the child's attachment to each parent and the importance of minimizing discontinuities in the child's life.

Much debate on the role of the concept of psychological parent in custodial decision making has taken place in recent years. Joseph Goldstein, Anna Freud, and Albert J. Solnit in, *Beyond the Best Interests of the Child*, have taken a vigorous advocacy position in favor of the psychological parent principle as a critical aspect of children's rights.[12] Others have argued that such a position is untenable because of the difficulties of assessing the more psychological parent when both parents meet the psychological needs of their children in the same or in complementary ways.[13]

Many courts have dealt with this issue by making decisions about which parent is the more psychological parent in tandem with the concept of children's preference. This principle reflects the courts efforts to "receive the child's preference" in making its custody award, if the child is of "sufficient age and capacity to reason so as to form an intelligent preference."[14] Although this principle has been recognized in case law as early as 1830 it has increasingly become a factor in initial child custody awards after divorce and later custody modification, as evidenced by statutes in twenty states by 1977 calling for consideration of children's preference in custody proceedings.[15] This concept is relevant to that of the psychological parent because it may be presumed that the child's preference reflects the child's view of the parent who is the psychological parent for him or her. In custodial disputes that have involved the stepparent as the third-party parent, courts have often considered the interrelationship of the principles involved in children's preference and psychological parent with those of the doctrine of parental preference.

Although the principle of children's preference provides judges with an aid in custody decisions by making the child a participant in his or her own custody arrangement, either at the time of divorce or after remarriage, it carries with it many weighty considerations: How, for example, can courts develop reliable methods to help children know their feelings and speak openly about them? What does it mean to a child to choose between his or her parents and deal with issues of conflicting loyalties at a legal level? Under what circumstances is the child's preference in his or her own best interests and when is it not? The obvious advantage of the application of this principle in custody decisions is that children no longer need feel totally disenfranchised in custody choices and can have a voice in their own destiny. An obvious risk, however, is that courts may begin to apply this doctrine automatically, without the careful consideration of all of the necessary factors.

Among the procedures that have been suggested to deal with the risks and complex questions that are inherent in the principle of children's preference is *guardian ad litem* (guardian for the suit) representation of the child in the court through advocate lawyers, and the use of neutral mental health professionals to develop factual and objective social studies for the courts to use as a basis for their decisions. Another alternative suggested has been a team approach, in which educators, mental health professionals, and legal representatives explore the issues and make joint recommendations to the court.[16] The remarried family usually carries forward into reconstitution the child-care grid that comprises various custody options, visitation arrangements, and child-support plans. Practitioners must, therefore, have an understanding of the similarities and differences among these plans and the legal parameters within which remarried families live.

CURRENT CUSTODY, CHILD SUPPORT, AND VISITATION OPTIONS

Therapists are often involved in working with remarried families on problems that derive from legal decisions made at the time of divorce with regard to child custody, child support, and visitation. Because the range of legal options in these areas is the same after remarriage as at the time of divorce, practitioners must become familiar with the available plans and their advantages and disadvantages. This information can be used in clinical intervention when families have difficulties related to existing legal arrangements or seek to modify them after remarriage.

SOLE CUSTODY

The most familiar custody form is separate maternal or paternal custody. In this plan, one parent is designated by the court as the sole residential and custodial guardian for all the children in the family. The absent or noncustodial parent and children have visitation rights that may be specifically defined or flexibly arranged. Preference by the courts for separate and sole custody awards has been based on the values that as much of the child's environment and family structure should remain as intact as possible and that all siblings should live together. This orientation adheres to the belief that a consistent residential parental arrangement with minimal discontinuities enhances the child's opportunity for emotional growth and development. From the perspective of the parent, however, separate custody awards result in one parent becoming the ongoing daily parent while the other becomes the "outside" parent.

A variation of sole paternal or maternal custody occurs when custody of the children is divided between the parents. In divided custody, maternal and paternal custody coexist; some children are placed with the mother and others with the father. This option has long been used in cases when children in a family are divided according to sex (boys with the father and girls with the mother), age (young children with the mother and older children with the father), or children's preference. Visitation rights exist for each of the absent parents and their children who live elsewhere. However, because each parent is the sole custodian of some but not all of the children, each parent is also an "outside" parent for some but not all of the children. Such arrangements do, however, make possible a sharing of rights and responsibilities of child care, and there is potential for individualizing the needs of each child according to age, sex, and the child's preference. The concept of the psychological parent is implicitly recognized in this option, because custody may be vested in the parent with whom the child feels the stronger bond. Divided custody provides continuity for the child in the same environment; however, the family is fragmented and objections have often been raised by the courts and by practitioners about the wisdom of separating siblings.[17]

Still another variation of separate custody is the alternating or split awards. In this situation, each parent is sole custodian of the children for a specified period of the year. Such block placements are usually made when geographic distances prevent regular visitation with a child, and the parent with whom the child is residing is the primary guardian for that period of time. The split custody option reduces the issues of "outside" parent because each is an outside parent for part of the year. However, because the child is shifted from one environment to another, the issue of discontinuity for the child remains.[18]

Traditionally, in each of the variations of separate custody, child support has been assigned to the father, but emerging trends indicate that financial responsibility may be assigned to the mother or may be shared by both parents.

JOINT CUSTODY

The joint custody option is the most recent. Departing from traditional practices of custody awards to a sole parental guardian, this plan stipulates that both parents are "joint guardians with equal rights of custody and control."[19] This option usually entails joint child support, and no specific visitation rules exist because children move flexibly between households of both parents and neither parent is an "absent parent."

The joint custody option derives from the rationale that although there has been a husband-wife divorce, there has not been a parent-child divorce. Accordingly, the child should not be deprived of an ongoing relationship with both parents, even though they live under separate roofs. Moreover, both parents should share equally in all decisions concerning the child. The strength of this option lies in its attempt to protect the child-parent relationship for both parents and their children within the divorce context. Perhaps it, more than all others, requires a high level of parent cooperation if the best interests of the child are to be observed. Neither parent in this arrangement is the "outside" parent. Parents customarily live in the same community, and children may pursue their social and academic interests without dislocation. Given the growing numbers of fathers who wish to share in the ongoing parenting role, and the increasing number of states that have mandated joint custody as the preferred option, it is anticipated that this arrangement will find increasing favor with courts and parents.

Despite the increased number of custodial options available to divorcing parents and children and the increasing flexibility of the courts in making custody awards, 90 percent of today's awards at the time of divorce continue to be made to mothers as the primary guardians, with visitation rights between absent fathers and children, and fathers charged with child support for their children of prior marriages.[20]

LEGAL ASPECTS OF THE STEP SITUATION

The differences in legal characteristics between nuclear and remarried families derive from three critical legal realities: (1) the legal dissolution of the nuclear family because of death or divorce; (2) in the event of divorce, two legal parents living apart share parenting responsibilties for mutual children in one of several child-care grids; and (3) after remarriage, one legal parent and one stepparent together parent children of one or both spouse's prior marriages. These legal realities have implications for intrafamilial issues true for all remarried families and interfamilial issues specific to those remarried families in which there has been a divorce prior to remarriage. This information is relevant for clinical practice because it involves consideration of the balance of rights and obligations, legally established, among persons in the remarried family, between divorced parents, one or both of whom has remarried, and their mutual children, and among the noncustodial legal parent, his or her legal children, and the stepparent with whom they live. Moreover, problems and dilemmas in these areas are associated with many remarried family problems of identity, role performance, and bonding.

THE NETWORK OF LEGAL TIES

Legal aspects of the step situation must be examined on an intrafamilial level in relation to three basic structural family subsystems: marital, parent-child, and sibling. The balance of legal ties among these subsystems must then be considered as it has relevance to some of the tensions and dilemmas that are unique to the remarried family.

The legal status of husband and wife in legally sanctioned remarriages is the same as in the nuclear family, but live-in or socially remarried couples do not have legal status, except as courts in some states may recognize these unions as de facto marriages.[21] However, both legally remarried and live-in socially remarried families share the legal realities in parent-child and sibling subsystems that differentiate them from the nuclear family.

In nuclear families, husband and wife have symmetrical legal ties to their children, and siblings in this family have legal ties to each other because they share the same parents. Thus, all nuclear family members are legally related to each other. In remarried families, however, two different parent-child subsystems coexist; one is the legal parent-child subsystem carried forward from the prior marriage and the other is the stepparent-stepchild subsystem initiated at the time of the remarriage. The legal parent-child subsystem brings all prior legal rights and obligations into the new remarried family, but the stepparent-stepchild subsystem has no prior legal rights and obligations nor does it acquire any at the time of remarriage.

Sibling subsystems also follow two different legal lines of connection—the legal sibling subsystems, in which children have shared biological and legal parentage from their prior nuclear family, and the stepsibling subsystem established at the time of the parental remarriage. Thus, unlike nuclear families, in which all family members have a shared legal tie, some remarried family members share legal connections but others do not because of the structural and developmental realities of the step situation.

On an interfamilial level, legal ties exist between the remarried family and the divorced spouse-parent through children who have continuing ties with both biological and legal parents of the prior marriage in the context of one of the custodial arrangements discussed earlier.

THE STRANGER PHENOMENON

Although there is no overriding body of federal family law, each state specifies the reciprocal rights and duties of marital partners and biological and adoptive parents and children. However, specification of rights and duties of stepparents toward their stepchildren is notably absent. At the present time, a stepparent is not legally required to assume the same duties of child support, education, authority, inheritance, or any other parental duties to a stepchild that he or she may have toward a biological or adopted child. Exceptions to this situation are found in New York and California statutes that mandate that, if a family is receiving welfare and there is a stepparent, he or she is liable for the financial support of stepchildren as for the support of a spouse.[22]

However, the more usual legal situation is one in which neither stepparent nor stepchild has any legal obligation or responsibility toward the other. Thus, the doctrine of strangers for step-related persons is operative. Legally, a stranger is defined as "anyone who is in no event resulting from the present state of affairs liable for the other." Practitioners have observed that many stepparents frequently describe themselves as "strangers" in the new family situation, and stepchildren often remark that "they feel as strangers to their stepparents." Stepsiblings have said of each other, "we are strangers, yet we are expected to act and feel toward each other as real (biological-legal) brothers and sisters."

This legal distinction between biological and adoptive parents and stepparents results in important practical as well as psychological and cultural difficulties in the day-to-day living of remarried families. For example, stepchildren have commented that, because they are supported by their legal fathers and not their stepfathers, they do not have to accept stepfathers' authority. Stepfathers, on the other hand, have said that they are reluctant to assume a role of authority with their stepchildren when a legal parent contributes to the financial support. Stepparents have reported on the difficulties involved in making emergency medical decisions when the legal parent is not present, because they, as stepparents, do not have this right.[23] Nor do stepparents have access to school records in the same way that biological or adoptive parents do, unless some legal provision is made that gives the stepparent this privilege.[24] Neither can a stepchild inherit property from a stepparent as a legal right.[25] Unless some specific legal provision is made, an unknown blood relative is considered the rightful inheritor rather than the stepchild, even if stepchild and stepparent have lived together for many years.

Despite the complex problems and familial strains associated with the asymmetrical legal ties among remarried family members, the doctrine of parental preference, and the doctrine of strangers, many stepparents willingly assume parental obligations to their stepchildren under the doctrine of *parens in loco parentis* (in place of a parent). However, in contrast to nuclear families, these duties are not binding and can be abrogated by the stepparent with no sanctions if he or she so decides.

At the present time, two legal options are available to the stepparent; he or she may parent within the existing legal limitations or adopt the child. However, these options do not accurately reflect the wish of many stepparents to parent their stepchildren in a sensitive responsible way without adopting them, but with greater legal rights to fulfill their roles effectively. Perhaps the direction taken by England in the Children's Bill of 1975 may offer some beginning resolution to this dilemma. This bill confers guardianship and limited legal rights to stepparents without diminishing the legal rights of the biological-legal noncustodial parent.[26]

Practitioners, aware of the problems imposed on the remarried family by existing legal constraints, help many stepparents to achieve constructive and complementary parenting roles with their spouse who is the custodial legal parent and, in addition, with the noncustodial legal parent of their stepchild. However, at times it is not possible to establish such a workable family balance and tensions lead to a request for custodial modification.

CUSTODIAL MODIFICATION
AFTER REMARRIAGE

Consideration of custodial modification for children after divorce and remarriage becomes a viable option for single-parent and remarried families, because two formerly married biological and legal parents now parent apart but continue to have emotional bonds and legal ties to children of the prior marriage. Children in nuclear families who are dissatisfied with their family situation do not have the option of custodial change or "parent-switching," nor do nuclear parents have the option of sending a child to a "parent-in-the-wings" when the going gets tough.

Although some of the legal decisions about child custody, child support, and visitation made at the time of the divorce remain unaltered after remarriage, others may be changed. In some cases, problems related to these decisions date back to single-parent family days and continue unabated after a remarried family has been established. In others, decisions in these areas, implemented with little or no difficulty prior to remarriage, become problematic after remarriage. Possible reasons for post-remarriage custody modifications, either into or out of the remarried family household, are related to changes in the social and developmental needs of children as they grow and mature, and unresolved tensions associated with the step situation, described in earlier chapters. Still other reasons for custodial change predate the remarriage and reflect long-standing parent-child difficulties.

Custody modification has always been a right of parents and children after divorce. Its significance, however, as a factor in clinical intervention has been heightened because of the increased number of divorces and the growing acceptance of the principle of children's preference. Many custody arrangements are modified in voluntary arrangements between divorced parents and their children. In keeping with the value placed on the privacy of the family, these changes are rarely challenged by the courts unless the welfare of the child is in jeopardy. However, judicial opinion, whether governed by statute or precedent of case decisions, reflects a range of differing views on the extent to which children's preference should be made the basis of custodial change. One state may, for example, mandate children's preference as a matter of right for any child over a certain age, while another may require clear and convincing evidence that a change is in the best interests of the child before entering a new order or modification order overturning an established custodial environment. Thus, one court denied a request for modification and ruled that "less than usual weight to a child's preference shall be given if the court believes that the preference is based mainly on a desire for less discipline where such discipline is held to be in the child's best interests."[27] Another court granted a request for custodial change, "not because we think the children have not had a good home with their father and stepmother . . . but because of the wishes of the children themselves. . . ."[28] Because the remarried families with whom therapists work are vitally affected by these variations, practitioners must become aware of the circumstances and extent to which children's preference prevails in the state in which they practice, the advantages and disadvantages involved, and the implications for the particular family.

Practitioners often see remarried family clients after the fact. Custody modification has already either been granted or denied by the courts or modification has been made through some voluntary decision-making process between parents and children. Therapists are not likely to see those parent switches that have worked out well. Familiar, instead, are cases like the Maynor and Blake families, described in chapter two, where custodial changes generated a host of problems, not only for the individual child who made the change, but also for all members of the family, including those whom the child left and those to whom the child came. Thus, social and psychological issues of modification require an holistic approach, not only to the best interests of the child, but also to the best interests of the total family units involved. The tensions between individual rights and family rights must be faced squarely by legal and mental health professionals, as well as by the family members who are requesting that modification be made.

An analysis of remarried family applications for service indicates that adjustments related to custody modification, either into or out of the family, are frequent precipitants to requests for help. A predominant pattern of custody change is that of the adolescent boy who moves from the residence of his mother, who has sole custody and who may or may not have remarried since the divorce, into the home of the former noncustodial father, who has since remarried. Although such changes are usually made through legal proceedings, a substantial number are made through voluntary agreements.[29] These voluntary arrangements carry with them the risk of unpredictability, because such decisions are often more subject to change than those sanctioned by the courts. The complexity of the process of custody change is demonstrated in the following case example.

THE GREENE-JORDAN FAMILIES

Mrs. Greene, formerly Mrs. Jordan, applied for counseling at her local family service agency because her fourteen-year-old son, Dick, had requested a change in custody arrangements so that he could live with his father. She believed that the entire family needed help in dealing with their feelings of being rejected by Dick. On the other hand, she thought it was possible that Dick did not really mean to pursue a change in custody, but was upset because of her recent remarriage.

Dick, his sisters, Beverly, eleven, and Rhoda, nine, his mother, and his stepfather were seen. At this point, Dick was unwilling to discuss the reasons for his request to live with his father. He resented his mother's application for service and could not understand the "fuss being made about his simple request." In identifying the nature of the family structure and significant developmental events, the therapist learned that Dick's mother and stepfather were married seven months before the application for service. Mr. Greene's two children from a former marriage lived with his ex-wife in another state. Dick's mother and father were divorced when he was nine, and his sisters six and four. The mother was sole custodian of the children, and the father had weekly visitation rights. A minimal order for child support was made because the mother had a well-paying job. Dick's mother did not remarry for five years; his father remarried a widow with two children three years after the divorce.

After his parents were divorced, Dick, as the oldest child, assumed a great deal of responsibility for household chores and for the care of his sisters. He was deeply aware of how traumatic the divorce had been for his mother, and he tried in many ways to be the "man of the house." Fearful of adding to his mother's feelings of grief, Dick denied his own feelings of loss. Dick's mother and sisters said that he was like the Rock of Gibraltar. He was always cheerful and seemed not to have any problems. He was an active participant in family affairs, had an excellent school record, and had many friends. His present morose and withdrawn behavior was, therefore, in sharp contrast to what they had known.

Mrs. Greene dated the change in her son's behavior to a few months before her remarriage, when she informed the children of her plans. In retrospect, she realized that the telling had been abrupt, with insufficient preparation of the children. She had delayed seeking professional help because she had hoped that as Dick came to know her husband he would be less negative about her remarriage. She knew how important it was for adolescent boys to have a father figure with whom to identify and had hoped that her husband could fulfill that role. Beverly and Rhoda were also apprehensive about a change in their living situation, but they seemed more willing "to give her husband a chance to be a father." Although the mother, stepfather, and daughters agreed there had been many adjustments to make to having a father after five years of being a single-parent family, they believed that they were "making it," and that important attachments were being formed. Only Dick seemed to be having problems.

After several interviews, Dick was able to talk about the deep sense of loss he had experienced when his father first left home. He felt as though his father "had divorced me as well as my mother." He was so angry with his father that for almost a year he refused to see him. It was only within the last year that any regularity in visitation had been established, although his sisters had consistently observed the weekly visitation. In spite of his angry feelings toward his father, Dick revealed that he had often fantasied that he would someday be able to live with his father. As he got older, he saw that "fourteen" was a magic number of years, and that boys who had lived with their mothers for many years could change custody and live with their father simply by asking. Now that his mother was remarried and his sisters were establishing bonds with their stepfather, he believed he was no longer needed. Thus, he felt released from his responsibilities to his mother and sisters and free to pursue his hopes *of living with his father. Despite the assurance of his family that he was needed and loved, even if his responsibilities were changed, Dick continued to press for custody change. He insisted that his plans had been discussed with his father and his stepmother and that they had no objections.*

Practitioners who work with families such as the Greenes must explore the motivations that stimulate a request for custodial modification. They must seek answers to such questions as: What does the child hope to gain from the change and how realistic are these hopes? What unresolved psychological and developmental issues are embedded in the request? What is going on within the family that adds to an understanding of the nature and timing of the request for a parent switch? Often, this kind of exploration enables a child to become involved, in either individual or family therapy, in working through some of the issues that prompted the request. Other family members can also reevaluate their role and interaction with the child and consider ways in which to be more appropriately responsive to his or her needs.

This process often results in a greater commitment on the part of the child and the family to work on their problems, and a parent switch does not take place. But, at times, despite such a process, the request for custodial change stands—as it did for Dick Jordan. When the client and practitioner have clarified that the child's stated preference is not transient, they must then consider their next focus of activity. Some families may decide to terminate their contact with the clinician and work out the details of the custody change with an attorney or by mutual agreement with the child and the absent parent. Others may wish to have clinician explore the issues with the absent parent so that the transition can be as smooth as possible, in the best interests of all.

Unlike most clinical intervention with remarried families, which focuses on intrafamilial problems and processes, work on problems of custody modification moves the clinical process from an intrafamilial to an interfamilial focus. In some situations in which custody changes are being considered, it is desirable and necessary to work with both the custodial and the absent parent family. Often joint interviews with both families are productive and result in a mutually acceptable final arrangement. In other families, however, unresolved conflicts would interfere with this process, and, therefore, concurrent but separate interviews with both families is the treatment plan of choice. In the Greene-Jordan case, for example, the Greene family decided to remain in therapy to continue to work on the issues of family adjustment to Dick's feelings and plans. In addition, they wished the therapist to explore Mr. Jordan's view of Dick's plan and to arrive at some decisions about how the plan could be implemented. However, because Mrs. Greene did not wish to participate in joint interviews with her ex-husband, concurrent but separate interviews with the Greene and Jordan families were undertaken. Dick participated in interviews with both families, as both families would be vitally affected by the final plan.

A series of interviews with the Jordans was held in which many anxieties were expressed and questions raised. Mrs. Jordan wondered if Dick's needs would preempt the rights and needs of other family members. Would the close-knit family group they had established be threatened if Dick came to live with them? Would Mr. Jordan maintain his concerns and ties to her children or would his interest in Dick be paramount? How would she handle being a resident-stepmother? Dick had only recently begun to visit their home with any regularity, and she did not really know or understand him. She anticipated that it would take time to build bonds with Dick and that, at first, her bonds to her children would take priority over those with Dick.

Mrs. Jordan's fifteen-year-old daughter, Becky, asked if Dick would be expected to obey the family rules or if he would be "special" and "get away with doing nothing," as the stepbrother of one of her friends did. Ten-year-old Brian was excited about having a "big brother," but was fearful that Dick would change his mind and return to the "old" family if he did not like things in the "new" family. Mr. Jordan was concerned about the impact of Dick's departure on his two younger daughters, who would continue to live with their mother. He knew how important Dick had been to them during the years after the divorce. He did not want to participate in a plan that would hurt them further, yet he did want to be responsive to Dick's request. He hoped that some of this concern could be dealt with by frequent and regular visitation between Dick and the Greene family. As Dick participated in these family interviews, he verbalized that he would need to adjust his goals of getting to know his father better with the needs and goals of other family members. He laughed ruefully at his earlier perception that a custody change was a "simple" request. After several additional interviews in working on the normal expectable tensions and problems that could accompany the new arrangements, Dick left the Greenes and went to live with the Jordans.

The Greene and Jordan families continued in separate but concurrent treatment during the transition period. While the Greenes continued to deal with their feelings of loss and ways in which they could maintain and build positive bonds with Dick although he lived elsewhere, the Jordans worked on the problems of including Dick as a new member of their family. Each family sought to develop and maintain a new workable family balance. Finally, Dick worked on ways to balance and maintain ties with both families.

Essentially, the Greene-Jordan response to Dick's request for custody modification was to choose the divided custody option with a well-defined visitation arrangement. Child support had not been raised as an issue by either family. Given the continued strain between Dick's mother and father, as evidenced by Mrs. Greene's inability to be involved in joint interviews with her former husband, joint custody, with its heavy demand on parental sharing, did not appear to be an appropriate option. After all agreed to the new plan, the changes were approved by the court. The child's preference was honored in the context of best interests test.

It can be argued that children's preference in custodial changes or parent switches enable parents and children to avoid the commitment necessary in making family adjustments after divorce and remarriage. On the other hand, custody change permits a child to live with that parent who is more psychologically and socially necessary as the child's developmental and social needs change. Still again, it may be argued that custody change is an option that enriches the life of the child. The Greene-Jordan case suggests that none of these arguments stands alone and that all three have elements of truth. The case record shows that, when his mother remarried, Dick was unwilling to make the commitment to work on adaptation to the remarried Greene family. However, during the process of clinical intervention he did decide to work on problems of adaptation to the remarried Jordan family.

The record also indicates that when Dick was placed in maternal custody, at age nine, living with his mother as the primary residential guardian and keeping the family intact was the custodial plan of choice. By the time Dick was fourteen, however, his developmental needs had changed. He was ready to move into an adolescent boy's relationship with a father. The problems he experienced in having his stepfather assume this role appeared to preclude the possibility that his stepfather could function in the role of father. Therefore, the change in custodial relationships did provide Dick with the opportunity for reestablishing social and psychological bonds with his father on an ongoing daily basis that could potentially enhance his developmental growth toward maturity. It would further appear that if both families make the necessary adaptations to Dick's changed custodial arrangements, potential for enrichment for all may be realized.

VISITATION AND
CHILD SUPPORT MODIFICATION

Requests for modification of earlier decisions also occur in regard to child support and visitation arrangements without change in custody arrangements. At times, remarried fathers, financially burdened by support both for children who live elsewhere and for the remarried family unit, petition the courts to change existing child-support orders. Despite movements toward shared financial support of children by divorced parents, courts have consistently found that the change in circumstances introduced by remarriage does not absolve a father of responsibility to observe earlier child-support orders.[30]

Also, earlier decisions regarding visitation made at the time of divorce may be disruptive after remarriage. The custodial parent may then seek to modify visitation arrangements. Requests to terminate or modify visitation may be made because an absent parent has failed to meet child-support payments or to maintain a consistent and predictable visitation schedule. At times, a child may be uninterested in visitation and may ask for the change. Again, requests for change in visitation may follow efforts of an absent parent to undermine the new parental unit, as observed in the situation with Kim Dean described in chapter two. Requests for termination of visitation have also been made following documentation of charges of immoral, sexual, or abusive behavior toward a child. Although there is evidence of increasing flexibility in modifying visitation agreements, legal decisions have traditionally tended to deny requests to terminate visitation rights of absent parents on grounds that the parental rights of biological parents are a "sacred right."[31]

Critics of the emphasis on parental rights and responsibilities have argued that such decisions place biological parental rights above the best interests of the child. They have asserted that the custodial parent should be the ultimate decision maker about visitation with an absent parent, and that adoptive, foster, and, by analogy, stepparents, are psychological parents and should have prior rights over an absent biological parent.[32] Yet, it can be argued that the custodial parent is often acting on unresolved marital issues and could use the right to terminate visitation as a punitive measure that in no way is responsive to the child's developmental and growth needs. Moreover, studies indicate that children of divorce make better postdivorce adjustments if they have a continuing relationship with their absent parent.[33] Practitioners must often work with families in considering the ramifications of changes in custody and visitation arrangements. Often, they also work with families in clarifying the issues involved in stepparent adoptions of a stepchild.

ADOPTION ISSUES AFTER REMARRIAGE

Many remarried families have been able to resolve the adjustments to the new family situation and seek to formalize loving and responsible stepparent-stepchild relationships through a legal adoption. In this event, stepparent and stepchild are in the same legal relationship to each other as any adoptive parent and child, and all rights and duties vested in the biological relationship are acquired by the adoptive parent and the adopted child. According to the National Center for Social Statistics, 40 percent of all adoptions are between stepparent and stepchild.[34] However, views on the wisdom of adoption in remarried families are contradictory.

Proponents of adoption in remarried families believe that a child who has been adopted by a stepparent has a greater feeling of belonging and being more like his or her peers and other families. The child gains a feeling of permanence, and his or her rights are the same as those of biological children born to the remarried couple. The issue of "by what name shall I be known" is resolved for the child and his or her identity is more closely linked to the remarried family. In the event of the death of the biological parent or of a divorce of the remarried couple, the child has a greater likelihood of a continuing relationship with the stepparent who has adopted the child and stepsiblings who have become adoptive siblings. Thus, the trauma of loss and discontinuity may be reduced.

Those who have questioned the wisdom of stepparent-stepchild adoptions have argued that adoption, always a complex psychological phenomenon, is even more complicated in the remarried family. The legal process that establishes new ties with the adopting parent erases prior legal ties and also erases identity that is derived from biological and cultural ties to the past. The high incidence of adopted children who seek to reestablish contact with their biological parent reflects the basic need for connections to one's roots, and adoption is perceived as still another discontinuity in the child's life. Practitioners working with remarried families who are considering adoption will need to explore both the advantages and disadvantages as they are relevant to the particular family involved.

In remarried family situations where death has been the antecedent to remarriage, the adoption procedure is relatively simple. The biological parent, stepparent, and stepchild (if old enough) mutually agree on this plan and petition the court for a change in legal status to reflect adoption. At times, some of the children in a remarried household will choose the option of adoption, while others may prefer to remain unadopted, as in the case of the Bostwick family.

THE BOSTWICK FAMILY

Mr. and Mrs. Bostwick had been married for three years. Mrs. Bostwick had been widowed for two years before the remarriage. She brought two children with her to the remarriage, a ten-year-old son, David, and a six-year-old daughter, Lois. After some initial problems of adjustment to their stepfather, a warm and cohesive family unit was established. The issue of adoption arose because of differences in name between the children and their parents. This difference in name was especially complicated in the school situation. Lois was grateful when her stepfather presented the plan for adoption so that the entire family could have the same last name. David, however, was resistant. Familial tensions resulted because of the stepfather's feeling that he was unappreciated, Lois's anxiety that the plan would fall through, and the mother's concern that this reflected some unresolved hostilities between David and his stepfather.

In the process of clinical intervention, the positive feelings that David had toward his stepfather were clarified. His resistance was related to his fond memories of his father and, in no way, seemed to reflect repressed hostilities or lack of appreciation for all that his stepfather had done for him. He did, however, have strong feelings about maintaining the family name because he was the only son and he did not want his father's name to "die out." Lois, on the other hand, had only vague memories of her father and was eager to get beyond the questions of why her name was different from her mother's. During the course of therapy with the family, empathic bridges were built in which the needs and problems of each were explored. A happy resolution was reached when it was agreed that Lois would be legally adopted, but that, in accordance with his wishes, David would not.

In contrast to the relative ease with which adoptions between stepchild and stepparent take place when the dissolution of the nuclear family has occurred because of death, the process of step adoptions when there is a surviving divorced, noncustodial parent is much more difficult. The legal complexity derives from unresolved tensions between the doctrine of parental preference and the concept of the child's right to a psychological parent. Underlying is the issue of the right of the remarried family to conditions that will further family bonding and cohesion. Current adoption law and practice continue to favor the doctrine of biological parental preference over psychological, and the rights of the absent biological father over the rights of the remarried family unit.[35] Children with living parents can become available for stepparent adoption only through voluntary consent of both parents or through judicial termination of parental rights on the basis of unfitness or abandonment. There appears to be no consistent and coherent guidelines to determine adoptions that fall between these two extremes. In such cases, courts may request a mental health agency to make a study of the family situations so that they will have a fuller understanding of the relevent facts and dynamics involved before they render a decision. The following case was referred to a mental health clinic for such a study.

THE BURTON-REESE FAMILIES

The Burton family had lived as a remarried family for two years. Mr. Burton had two children who lived with their mother. Mrs. Burton and her only child, eleven-year-old Martin, lived with Mr. Burton. Martin, his mother, and his stepfather petitioned the court for legal adoption. Martin's father had never paid child support nor maintained any sustained visitation. In the absence of such involvement, the Burtons had developed a lifestyle and feeling about themselves "as if" there were no noncustodial father. They had assumed that the petition for adoption would not be challenged. But, the petition was contested, because Martin's father, Mr. Reese, stated that he was not willing to consent to the termination of his parental rights. He acknowledged that he had been remiss in meeting child-support payments and holding to a visitation plan, but explained to the court that he had been deeply depressed after the divorce and was not able to mobilize himself to work or to maintain regular visitation. Following a period of intensive psychotherapy, he was now working and felt able both to meet his support payments and adhere to a regular visitation plan. Because there were no grounds on which the court could declare the father unfit at the present time, and because Mr. Reese was unwilling to surrender his parental rights, the court asked that the child's preference be determined through a neutral investigation.

The clinician explored the nature of the stepparent-stepchild relation-ship and found that Martin had solidified a positive relationship with his stepfather and that the family had bonded together as a family unit. Mr. and Mrs. Burton declared that any involvement of the absent parent with Martin would be an intrusion in their family life.

When Mr. Reese was seen he gave evidence of a good job and ability to meet the child-support order. He was, in addition, highly motivated to establish a meaningful relationship with his son. Indeed, he explained that it had been this hope and goal that had enabled him to make the positive strides in working through his feelings of desolation at the time of divorce. He did not feel he should be further punished by being de-prived of his parental rights to be involved with his son.

As the linking person between his biological father and his mother and stepfather, Martin was the hub of the controversy. He felt deeply torn between his wish to maintain the harmonious family unit he was a part of and his strong empathy with the trauma his father had experienced after the divorce. He understood his father's lack of involvement. In the course of clarifying his feelings for the court study, Martin concluded that he would like to maintain the important emotional bond he had developed with his stepfather, as well as resume his relationship with his father.

When the report of Martin's preference was made, the court recommended that the Burton family be seen in ongoing therapy to help them accept the realities of a participating, noncustodial parent. In the event that Mr. Reese failed to fulfill his legal and social responsibilities to Martin, the petition for adoption could be reconsidered.

Such decisions regarding adoption of a stepchild by a stepparent are reminiscent of those that confront judges in difficult custody cases at the time of divorce. As yet, there do not appear to be any uniform standards to guide the courts in stepparent-stepchild adoptions when the divorced, absent, biological parent is legally fit and does not wish to surrender his biological rights. The Burton-Reese case, if heard in different states, might well bring different decisions. The more traditional decision would be the denial of the adoption petition in favor of the biological father, in accord-ance with the doctrine of parental preference. On the other hand, if the case were heard in a state that gives the courts the right to waive parental consent as a necessary condition to adoption when the parent is fit, the court might rule that it was in the best interests of the child to live in an adoptive relationship with his mother and stepfather.[36]

In contrast, an increasing number of case decisions demonstrate an expanded application of the doctrine of parental preference. Thus, unwed fathers are more frequently being accorded the same legal rights of consent to adoption as unwed mothers. They have been able to prevent adoptions when the unwed mother of their children has later married and agreed to the adoption of her children by a stepfather. In 1979, the case of Caban versus Mohammed gave an unwed father the same rights in regard to his children as a divorced, noncustodial biological father.[37]

The significance of this direction for the remarried family lies in the fact that many of the children who are involved in such contests are born of live-in or social marriages or unwed teenage marriages. If the relationships terminate, the children usually live with a single parent in a one-parent family unit. Just as the single parent who has been divorced or widowed reaffiliates in another two-parent, two-generational family unit, so do parent and children from prior live-in units or never-before-married, single-mother units. Although these may be legal first marriages, these family units have many of the same problems and dilemmas of the legally remarried family and, for purposes of analysis, have been considered socially remarried families in this book. Previously, mothers in socially remarried families could agree to adoption of their child by a third party, without the consent of the live-in or unwed father. With the extension of the doctrine of parental rights to prior live-in or unwed partners, the issue of legal adoptions in socially remarried families has implications for many children who formerly could be adopted with no question, but who are now denied this option. The issue of legal adoption is similar for socially and legally remarried families. Given the increasing numbers of socially remarried families, legal decisions that expand the doctrine of parental preference reinforce the doctrine of strangers. Social distance is supported and problems with role performance and bonding are fostered by the law.

The doctrine of parental preference, as well as being applicable in cases of divorced, noncustodial, and unwed fathers, also favors the divorced noncustodial parent who seeks to gain custody of a child when the custodial remarried parent has died. In such instances, the absent or noncustodial parent becomes the surviving parent. This parent acquires all the rights and responsibilities of sole care and custody of the children, just as would have been true if both parents had lived together in a nuclear family. The Blake family, discussed in chapter two, reflects such a situation.

When Amy Blake's mother died, her stepfather asked that she continue to live with him and her two half-sibs. Her father, however, refused, and Amy went to live with him and her stepmother. The problems introduced by the change in custody were the focus of clinical intervention.

Emphasis on parental preference in decisions about adoption or continued custody by stepparents if a spouse should die have made many stepparents reluctant to invest in strong emotional bonds to stepchildren. Fear that these bonds would be abrogated by the legal preference of biological parent rights has resulted in the tentative and uncertain assumption of parental roles by the stepparent. The potential for strong social and psychological bonds may, thus, be inhibited.

Two parallel tracks are apparent in legal doctrines and principles that have relevance to the rights and duties among remarried family members and between remarried family members and the noncustodial parent: one balances the rights and obligations of biological and legal parents toward their children after divorce and remarriage, the other protects the rights of children in these circumstances.[38] Both of these tracks reflect positive directions in the evolution of individual human values, but neither includes a focus on the family as a significant societal institution and milieu essential to the emotional health of its members. There is increasing recognition that a third track that seeks to establish criteria and principles to balance the values and functions of the family and the values and rights of individuals is needed.[39]

Practitioners, in their therapeutic role with remarried families, have the unique opportunity to identify current legal inequities, inconsistencies, and biases that contribute to recurrent remarried family problems and dilemmas. They can indicate legal principles and decisions that have reinforced structural divisions and barriers to the development of emotional bonds, and, in addition, have rigidified the cultural metaphor that "step is less." Through systematic accumulation of this information and participation on interdisciplinary judicial and mental health teams, practitioners may contribute to the formulation of criteria that will address these issues and further the work of developing the third track. The evolving nature of legal doctrines offers hope for new creative leaps that will result in principles that facilitate societal and remarried family goals for family cohesion, and recast cultural orientations toward the remarried family so that it is more realistically perceived and valued.

NOTES

1. Bernard Schwartz, *The Law in America* (New York: McGraw-Hill, 1974), p. 1.
2. Ronald C. Schiller, "Child Custody: Evolution of Current Criteria," *De Paul Law Review* 26 (Winter 1977): 243; and Allen Roth, "The Tender Years Presumption in Child Custody Disputes," *Journal of Family Law* 15 (1976–1977): 243–46.
3. John G. Brosky and John G. Alford, "Sharpening Solomon's Sword: Current Considerations in Child Custody Cases," *Dickenson Law Review* 81 (Summer 1977): 683–98.
4. See Henry F. Foster and Doris Jones Freed, "Life with Father: 1978," *Family Law Quarterly* 11 (Winter 1978): 321–28; and Robert H. Mnookin, "Child Custody Adjudication: Judicial Functions in the Face of Indeterminancy," *Law and Contemporary Problems* 39 (Summer 1975): 226–93.
5. See New York Court of Appeals, Finlay v. Finlay, *American Law Reports Annotated* (1925): 940 208, NYS. 585, rev. 240 NY, 429.
6. Sanford Katz, *When Parents Fail* (Boston: Beacon Press, 1971), p. 6.
7. "Parent and Child," 59, *American Jurisprudence*, 2d Sec. 26, p. 110.
8. Mnookin, "Child Custody Adjudication," pp. 226–93.
9. Uniform Marriage and Divorce Act, National Conference of Commissioners on Uniform State Laws, 1970.
10. "Parent and Child," 59, *American Jurisprudence*, 2d Sec. 24, p. 109.
11. Mnookin, "Child Custody Adjudication," p. 231.
12. Joseph Goldstein, Anna Freud, and Albert J. Solnit, *Beyond the Best Interests of the Child* (London: Free Press, 1973).
13. See Carol B. Stack, "Who Owns the Child: Divorce and Child Custody Decisions in Middle-Class Families," *Social Problems* 23, no. 4 (April 1976): 505–15; and Sheila Rush Okpaku, "Psychology: Impediment or Aid in Child Custody Cases?" *Rutgers Law Review* 29 (Summer 1976): 1117–53.
14. Robert Fainer and Dennis Matthew Wasser, "Child Custody and Visitation Disputes: An Overview," *The Los Angeles Lawyer* (July 1978): 80.
15. David M. Siegel and Suzanne Hurley, "Role of Child's Preference," 11 *Family Law Quarterly* (Spring 1977): 11.
16. See "Lawyering for the Child: Principles of Representation in Custody and Visitation Disputes Arising from Divorce," *Yale Law Journal* 87 (May 1978): 1126–90; James R. Devine, "A Child's Right to Independent Counsel in Custody Proceedings: Providing Effective 'Best Interests' Determination Through the Use of a Legal Advocate," *Seton Hall Law Review* 6 (Winter 1975): 303–35; Maurice K.C. Wilcox, "Child's Due Process Right to Counsel in Divorce Custody Proceedings," *Hastings Law Review* 27 (March 1976): 917–50; and Ruth-Arlene W. Howe, "Divorce: Critical Issues for Legal and Mental Health Professionals," *The Urban Social Change Review* 10, no. 1 (Winter 1977): 15–21.
17. Fainer and Wasser, "Child Custody and Visitation Disputes," p. 80.
18. Foster and Freed, "Life with Father," pp. 323–25.
19. Fainer and Wasser, "Child Custody and Visitation Disputes," p. 80.
20. Foster and Freed, "Life with Father," p. 331.
21. Mary Ann Glendon, "The American Family in the 200th Year of the Republic," *Family Law Quarterly* 10, no. 4 (Winter 1977): 335–55. See also Jarrett v. Jarrett, 78 Ill. 2d 337, 400 N.E. 2d 421 (1979), rehearing denied Feb. 1, 1980.

Appeal pending U.S. Supreme Court for a decision which remands custody of children to a father because a mother was in a live-in social remarriage situation deemed to be a harmful environment to her children.

22. Calif. Civil Code Sec. 5127 6; and N.Y. Domestic Relations Law Sec. 31, 32.

23. Brenda Maddox, The Half-Parent (New York: M. Evans and Co., 1975), p. 164.

24. "Attorney Reviews Private Schools' Rights and Obligations," Stepparent News (October 1980) :1.

25. "Parent and Child," 59, American Jurisprudence, 2d Sec. 37, p. 120.

26. Maddox, Half-Parent, p. 171.

27. Siegel and Hurley, "Child's Preference," p. 11.

28. Ibid., pp. 12–14.

29. Esther Wald, "Analysis of Custodial Modification in Remarried Families," unpublished study, 1979.

30. Homer Clarke, Law of Domestic Relations (St. Paul, Minn.: West Publishing, 1968), p. 502.

31. Benjamin Henszey, "Visitation by a Non-Custodial Parent: What is the 'Best Interest' Doctrine," Journal of Family Law 15 (1976–1977): 214–33; and Richard S. Benedek and Elissa P. Benedek, "Post Divorce Visitation: A Child's Right," American Academy of Child Psychiatry 16, no. 2 (Spring 1977): 256–71.

32. Goldstein, Freud, and Solnit, Best Interests of the Child, p. 38.

33. See Judith Wallerstein and Joan B. Kelly, "Children and Divorce," Social Work 24, no. 6 (November 1979): 471.

34. See National Center for Social Statistics, Adoptions in 1975, Report no. E-10 (Washington, D.C.: U.S. Government Printing Office, 1977), p. 7.

35. Andre P. Derdeyn and Walter J. Wadlington, III, "Adoption: The Rights of Parents versus the Best Interests of Their Children," American Academy of Child Psychiatry 16 no. 2, (Spring 1977): 238–55; and "Parent and Child," 59, American Jurisprudence, 2d Sec. 26, p. 110–15.

36. Mnookin, "Child Custody Adjudication," pp. 237–56.

37. See Caban v. Mohammed, 47 United States Law Week, 4462, 24 April, 1979.

38. Mnookin, "Child Custody Adjudication," p. 229.

39. See Mary Ann Glendon, "Power and Authority in the Family: New Legal Patterns as Reflections of Changing Ideologies," American Journal of Comparative Law 23 (Winter 1975): 27–33; and Glendon, "American Family in the 200th Year of the Republic," pp. 335–55.

9

BLENDING AND
BECOMING:
A PROBLEM-
PROCESS PROFILE

The detailed analysis of the specific dimensions of the schema
for study has laid bare a wide range of problems, processes,
issues, and dilemmas for the remarried family. A synthesis of this
information yields a generalized and composite view of the objective reality for this special case of family—and this chapter
focuses on that view. A profile of the locus and content of problems
and processes that are generated by this reality and frequently
encountered by practitioners is presented, and, in addition, specific and relevant bodies of knowledge that expand understanding
about these problems are suggested. The expectation is that such
an approach will enhance the practitioner's ability to make more
precise and informed diagnostic assessments, establish realistic
goals with the client, and facilitate the building of empathic
bridges and effective therapeutic intervention.

Along the specific dimensions suggested in the schema for
study, a comprehensive generalized view of the objective reality
of the remarried family requires that it be considered in terms of
a two-pronged perspective. The first and more long-range view

studies this family in terms of its broad historical, cultural, social, and legal context. The second and more immediate perspective compares and contrasts the remarried family with the nuclear family along cultural, legal, structural, and developmental dimensions of the here and now.

It is within this objective reality that the remarried family functions as an alive day-to-day family unit. The more particular reality of the family who comes for professional help can be derived from relevant aspects of the general objective reality. Each family will vary in the number, nature, and emphasis of the problems for which it seeks professional help. For some, legal problems may predominate; for others, problems will be related to the developmental, structural, or cultural dimension; for still others, the problems may overlap and be related to one or more dimensions of the schema for study.

Client and practitioner must work together within the particular reality of the specific remarried family. Together they must clarify and narrow the gap between the objective reality and the subjective views of the family situation held by each individual in the remarried family, and determine realistic goals that will promote a workable family balance.

The objective reality of the remarried family establishes the parameters within which the problems, issues, and dilemmas of this special case of family exist. How best to cope with these problems is, of course, the challenge for every remarried family.

A PROBLEM-PROCESS PROFILE

The range of problems that confront the remarried family is often diffuse and intertwined. It is not possible, therefore, to segregate problems as belonging to one dimension of the schema or as being discrete. Indeed, a given category of problem, such as role, may be diffused throughout all of the dimensions for study. Similarly, a problem that begins as a cultural problem may ultimately be experienced as an intrapersonal problem of low self-esteem or negative identity. Problems are interrelated, one giving rise to or resulting from another, each affecting and being affected by others. It is useful to provide the practitioner with some systematic classification that synthesizes and organizes problems from all of the dimensions of the schema for study.

The problem-process profile is offered as a beginning effort at such systematic classification. It focuses first on the *locus* of the problem or who is involved in the identified problem, and second on the *content* (or the *what*) of the problem. This classification by locus and content also suggests relevant bodies of knowledge that must be integrated with both the objective reality of the remarried family situation and the subjective perceptions of individual members. It has been developed for use by practitioners in formulating diagnostic assessments for work with remarried families.

The structural dimension, with its classification of formal and informal subsystems within the family, is useful for specifying the locus of the problem, and allows the practitioner to determine if the problem is primarily within the remarried family. If so, the problem may involve the total family unit or it may be limited to a specific subsystem, such as the marital, stepparent-stepchild, or any of the other multiple formal family subsystems. In addition, the locus of the problem may be between one or more members of the remarried family and extended or absent family members.

Most current research indicates that the primary locus of problems is within the remarried family and between stepparents and stepchildren or between stepsiblings.[1] The stepmother, more often than the stepfather, is named as the focal person in conflict with stepchildren.[2] Marital problems are often reverberations of problems between stepparent and stepchildren or between stepsiblings.[3] Through identification of the locus of the problem, therapists can determine whether the family with whom they are working affirms or denies prevalent findings.

The problem profile that follows was developed in the course of direct clinical practice with remarried families. Two predominant directions guided the development of the problem profile: (1) that the views of both parents and children should be reflected, and (2) that the problems identified by them early in the course of clinical intervention should be indicated. Therefore, the first verbatim taped family therapy interview held with the family, on or before the third contact with the therapist, was analyzed for content. In this way, the profile was limited to problems and processes identified by parents and children during the initial phase of therapy that they judged to be linked to or interfering with the reconstitution and reorganization of the family unit. Problems related to preexisting factors were not included in this profile, except as they were exacerbated by the current remarried family situation.[4]

THE REMARRIED FAMILY: A PROBLEM-
PROCESS PROFILE

I.   Environmental Problems
Problems may occur because of insufficient external resources
essential to family functioning or because of changes in how
these resources are acquired, distributed, or managed.

   A. Locus of Problem
      1. The entire family unit
      2. A subsystem or combination of subsystems within the
         remarried family
      3. An individual family member

   B. Content of Problem
      1. Space problems because of relocation, crowding, and
         issues of territoriality
         • Mrs. Brent and her two sons moved into the home of
           Mr. Brent and his two sons. Issues of territoriality
           were reflected in such statements as "This is my
           house and you do not belong here."
         • Marcia Carr felt that she "did not belong" in the house
           her husband had shared with his deceased wife. Her
           children resented leaving their old neighborhood,
           changing schools, and sharing space with stepsi-
           blings they hardly knew.
      2. Time problems
         • Mr. and Mrs. Carr complained that they did not have
           time to spend with each other because the children
           needed so much of their time.
         • Bob and Tom Brent resented the time their father
           spent with their stepbrother.
         •Jim Gray resented the time that his wife Ellen spent
           with her daughter, Nancy.
      3. Money problems because of maintenance of a prior and
         a current family unit
         • Janet Ronson felt resentful because her earnings were
           used to support her husband's children, who lived
           with their mother.
         • Jack and Marcia Carr both had to work and take extra
           jobs to make ends meet.

4. Other problems associated with external environmental issues in the remarried family

II. Individual Adjustment Problems
   Intrapersonal difficulties that are reactive to situational events or changes unique to the remarried family may occur. Such difficulties may be identified because of the intensity of symptoms of the internal state of the individual or in the performance of the individual with one or more of the significant social systems with which he or she interacts. Impaired intellectual, social, or emotional functioning may be observed in such symptoms as depression, anxiety, confused states, psychosomatic disorders, rage reactions, alienation, withdrawal, and daydreams.

   A. Locus of Problem
      1. Within a specific individual in the family system

   B. Content of Problem
      1. Reactive emotional responses and behaviors to loss of prior family structures, spouse, parent, or other significant caretaking persons, such as a grandparent, and changes in custodial arrangements
         • Billie was sad and confused because his parents no longer lived under one roof. His daydreams were concerned with ideas about getting his stepfather to leave home.
         • Tom and Bob Brent felt that life had been better for them when they "batched it" as a single-parent family.
         • Mr. Rossi's unresolved grief for his deceased wife was interfering with his relationships with his daughter and second wife.
      2. Self-concept and self-esteem problems because of the failure of an earlier marriage, disappointment in role performance of self as a stepparent, and negative comparisons of self with "the other spouse" or stepsiblings
         • Ginny Blake was disappointed in her attitudes and feelings as a stepparent to her stepdaughter.
         • Joan Peters said that she always ended up feeling like the "wicked stepmother."

3. School problems include deteriorating academic performance, excessive cutting of classes, suspension or expulsion, or other problems in the school setting that are shown to be related to some aspect of the remarried family situation
   - Nellie was distractible and unable to concentrate because she was confused by her new family situation.
   - Kim Dean was referred to the school social worker because of angry behavior associated with the new family situation.
4. Other problems associated with individual adjustment difficulties to the remarried family situation

III. Intrafamilial-Interpersonal Adjustment Problems
Problems are related to the transitional process of reorganization from prior single-parent family units into a remarried family. The reorganization process may be viewed as one of "blending" of prior family lifestyles and "becoming" a remarried family unit with its own identity and lifestyle.
The process of "blending" involves working on problems of achieving some workable degree of consensus on processes of decision making, socialization and care of children, distribution of power in the household, conflict resolution, and inclusion of new family members. Disturbances in these areas may be observed in role and bonding problems.

A. Locus of Problem
   1. The entire family unit
   2. A subsystem or combination of subsystems within the remarried family

B. Content of Problem
   1. Adaptation, acculturation, and integration of prior lifestyles into a "remarried family" lifestyle. Families often report problems in this area as "learning to live together as a new family." This situation requires attention to such problems as integrating values and priorities of earlier family units with those of the new family unit, defining new norms, rules, and regulations, and achieving consensus on views of child care, discipline, and communication patterns

- The Hanley children could not accommodate to the differences in the values and priorities of their step-mother from those that characterized the earlier family structures within which they had lived.
- Each of the Brent prior single-parent family units was having difficulties accommodating to the rules and regulations of the other.
- Mrs. Lewis felt that her husband was much too harsh in disciplining her children; he felt that she was much too lenient.
- Mrs. Maynor felt that the communication pattern in their home was such that her husband heard only his children's version of things.

2. Problems of establishing identity within and becoming a remarried family unit. An essential aspect of this process is achieving gratification from membership in this family unit. Problems of name and negative identity are barriers to the process of "becoming" a new family unit in its own right

- Mrs. Donahue was resentful that Leah would not call her "mother."
- The Smiths and the Jones solved the problem of "by which last name" by using a hyphenated combination of both family names; they became known as the Smith-Jones family.
- The Bostwicks solved the problem of a different last name for Lois by having the stepfather adopt her.
- Tom and Bob Brent resented living in a stepfamily.

3. Role problems involve difficulties around the reallocation of roles, learning new roles, and the resolution of differences resulting from lack of agreement between two or more persons within the family about appropriate role behavior, reciprocal role expectations, or role priorities. Ambiguity about specific steprole behavior is a frequent cause of remarried family difficulty

- Lynn Carr had a difficult time giving up to her step-mother her accustomed role as parent-surrogate and spouse companion of her father.

- Jim Gray had to learn how to be a stepparent to a child he hardly knew.
  - The Brents, Carrs, and Maynors had to learn to resolve the strains of the hybrid natural and stepparent roles they carried.
  - Mr. and Mrs. Maynor had problems in resolving their different perceptions about appropriate "step-role" behavior.
4. Bonding problems involve difficulties in forming attachments and establishing affiliations between two or more remarried family members. This category is differentiated from role problems in that it is related to the emotional or affective relationship between persons in the family rather than to definitions of specific behaviors. Problems would include bond preferences of children of prior marriages to other remarried family ties, bond shifts, bond cross-pressures (split loyalties), and residual bonds between formerly married partners
  - Mr. Maynor's priority attitude toward his bonds to his natural children created marital difficulties.
  - Ginny Blake was deeply troubled because she resented her stepdaughter's intrusion into her relationship with her newborn natural child.
  - Janet Ronson resented her husband's preference of his bonds to his children over his bonds to her.
  - Jennifer's feelings of rejection because of her father's interest in his new stepfamily were a crucial problem for her.
  - Mr. Maynor's growing positive relationship to his stepsons was stopped when his natural children came to live with him.
  - Mr. Hanley felt torn between his love for and understanding of his children's feelings about their stepmother and his loyalty to and love for his new wife.
  - Kim Dean felt unable to handle her split loyalties toward her absent father and the new remarried family in which she lived.
5. Other Intrafamilial-Interpersonal adjustment difficulties

IV. Interfamilial difficulties often occur around reconstitution, and involve acculturation, role, bonding, and legal issues.

A. Locus of Problem

1. Between one or more members of the remarried family and extended family members of either spouse in the remarried family unit

2. Between one or more members of the remarried family and absent parent family members

B. Content of Problem

1. Extended family members may have the same difficulties as members within the remarried family of inclusion of new persons of the remarried family, role definitions, and accommodation to different values, priorities, and other aspects of the new family lifestyle

   • The various sets of grandparents in the Allen family showed favoritism toward their natural grandchildren, thus creating problems of competition and jealousy among the children.

   • Joan Peters was resentful of the "special place" Mark had with his grandparents.

2. Absent parents may have difficulties with adjusting to coparenting apart as a new lifestyle, defining new roles for themselves, and allowing bonding to take place for their natural child within the new remarried family unit. In addition, there may be problems related to legal issues of child custody, child support, and visitation. These problems intrude on remarried family adjustment processes

   • Kim Dean's father used his visitation time with her to undermine her possible growing attachments to the remarried family.

   • Finding an appropriate balance between the legal
   . rights of the biological father and the psychological rights of the stepfather was a difficult problem for the Sexton family.

3. Other Interfamilial adjustment problems

A NETWORK OF RELATED THEORY

The objective reality and problems profile of the remarried family highlights the need for a network of related theory on which the practitioner can draw. This network must be specified and integrated with the generalized body of knowledge about the remarried family and with principles of clinical practice. Such an approach offers the practitioner some direction and focus in work with this special population.

Immediately apparent in work with the remarried family is the fact that problems revolve around issues of loss, family reorganization, and the working through of relationships with extended and absent family members. Given these recurrent problems, some interdisciplinary substantive bodies of knowledge that have broad application and are relevant to the remarried family will be specified. The concepts and theories of these bodies of knowledge may be used singly or in combination with the specific knowledge about the remarried family. Included in such a network would be theories about grief and moruning, mechanisms and processes by which adaptation and socialization to new life situations are facilitated, role theory, and the nature of the bonding process. It is necessary for all of this knowledge to be considered within the context of individual personality, family systems, and group process theory.

Theories of grief and mourning, as developed by John Bowlby, Elisabeth Kübler-Ross, Erich Lindemann, Bertha Simos, and others, are particularly useful. Their work supports the belief that unless and until individuals have traversed the stages of grief and mourning, their capacity for the formation of later meaningful relationships is seriously impaired.[5] Because loss is a recurrent phenomenon in working with members of the remarried family, some theoretical foundations that provide the therapist with a substantive knowledge base in this area are fundamental requirements.

Other important knowledge bases in the network of related theory are associated with theories about facilitation or processes of "blending" prior family units so that they "become" a unified remarried family unit. Sociologists and anthropologists, using such concepts as acculturation, accommodations, and socialization to new life situations, have put forth some useful understandings about these processes. Involved in these processes are the clarification and definition of present and future goals and the development of skills in resolving, living with, and integrating differences in values and priorities. In addition, the processes by which new norms and rules may be established and integrated with prior values and practices are suggested in these related theories. Because remarried families are often involved in work with these processes, the therapist will find that theories elucidating the processes of accommodation and socialization to new life situations will be useful adjunctive knowledge bases in clinical diagnosis and intervention.[6]

A particularly useful body of knowledge for work with the remarried family is role theory. Sociologists, anthropologists, social psychologists, and social workers have developed voluminous materials on such concepts as role ambiguity, role strain, role performance and role taking.[7] Because lack of definitions about appropriate step role behavior, role dissension, and role strain are frequent aspects of problems for which remarried families seek help, role theory is an important resource for the therapist in work with remarried families.

Another body of knowledge that has particularly important significance for the remarried family is that related to bonding theories. Many who work the field of group process have made important contributions to understanding group processes of affiliation, power, and control within a group, and the issues that need to be addressed so that bonds of positive affiliation may develop. The remarried family often begins as a collection of individuals with uncertain and tentative positive feelings toward each other (except the marital pair); this knowledge informs the practitioner that processes facilitating group attachment are of vital importance.[8]

In addition, knowledge about the bonding process between individuals within the group is also needed. Sociologists, ethologists, and practitioners are working toward a further understanding of the bonding processes between individuals.[9] Konrad Lorenz's study of bonding processes in animals and the broad range of current research in neonatal research offer beginning insights into the processes by which individuals bond with each other.[10] Ralph Turner's concept of "crescive bonding," the cumulative process of developed feelings of affiliation through shared experiences over time, is a particularly useful one in working with remarried families.[11] It offers the hope that if practitioners can intervene *before* destructive and nonproductive patterns of interaction are fixed, families may be helped to build crescive bonds. In this way, the social bond, which is the only symmetrical bond all family members share at the time of remarriage, can be strengthened.

This network of related theory merely highlights some of the theoretical foundations that are particularly responsive to recurrent problems of the remarried family, as shown in the problem-process profile. The next chapter will consider how the therapist, in work with individual families, selects and applies aspects of these theories to help the remarried family members meet the challenge of dealing more effectively with the problems for which they seek help.

NOTES

1. Lucille Duberman, "Step-Kin Relationships," *Journal of Marriage and the Family* 35 (May 1973): 283–92.
2. Ibid.
3. Lillian Messinger, "Remarriage Between Divorced People and Children from Previous Marriages: A Proposal for Preparation for Remarriage," *Journal of Marriage and Family Counselling* 2 (April 1976): 193–200.
4. Esther Wald, "A Problem-Process Profile." This profile is an adaptation of a problem typology developed for "The Reconstituted Family: A Special Case of Family" (diss. in process).
5. See Elizabeth Kübler-Ross, *On Death and Dying* (New York: Macmillan, 1969); John Bowlby, *Attachment and Loss* (New York: Basic Books, 1969); John Bowlby and C. Murray Parkes, "Separation and Loss within the Family," in *The Child and His Family*, ed. E. James Anthony and Cyrille Koupernick (New York: John Wiley, 1970), pp. 197–216; Barbara Snell Dohrenwend and Bruce P. Dohrenwend, *Stressful Life Events: Their Nature and Effects* (New York: John Wiley, 1974); Ira O. Glick and C. Murray Parkes, *The First Year of Bereavement* (New York: John Wiley, 1974); Geoffrey Gorer, *Death, Grief and Mourning* (London: Cresset Press, 1965); Erich Lindemann, "Symptomology and Management of Acute Grief," *American Journal of Psychiatry* 101 (1944): 140–148; C. Murray Parkes, *Bereavement* (London: Tavistock Publications, 1972); Bernard Schoenberg et al., *Loss and Grief* (New York: Columbia University Press, 1970); Bertha G. Simos, *A Time to Grieve: Loss as a Universal Human Experience* (New York: Family Service Association of America, 1979); and Heinz H. Wolff, "Loss: A Central Theme in Psychotherapy," *British Journal of Medical Psychology* 50 (1977) 11–19.
6. See J.W. Berry and R.C. Annis, "Acculturative Stress," *Journal of Cross Cultural Psychology* 5 (1974): 382–405; N.A. Chance, "Acculturation, Self-Identification and Personality Adjustment," *American Anthropologist* 67 (1965): 372–93; Barbara Snell Dohrenwend and Bruce P. Dohrenwend, "Toward a Theory of Acculturation," *Southwestern Journal of Anthropology* 18 (1962): 30–39; and Ralph Turner, *Family Interaction* (New York: John Wiley, 1970), especially sections on accommodation and socialization.

7. See Joan Aldous, *Family Careers: Developmental Changes in Families* (New York: John Wiley, 1978); Jerold Heiss, ed., *Family Roles and Interaction: An Anthology*, 2d ed., (Chicago: Rand McNally, 1976); Robert Merton, *Social Theory and Social Structure* (New York, Free Press, 1968); and Turner, *Family Interaction*, pp. 185–215, 283–313.

8. See Saul Bernstein, ed., *Explorations in Group Work: Essays in Theory and Practice* (Boston: Boston University School of Social Work, 1965); Dorwin Cartwright and Alvin Zander, *Group Dynamics: Research and Theory* (New York: Harper and Row, 1968); and Robert W. Roberts and Helen Northen, eds., *Theories of Social Work with Groups* (New York: Columbia University Press, 1976).

9. See Selma Fraiberg, *Birthright of the Infant* (New York: Bantam, 1977); Margaret Mahler, Fred Pine, and Anni Bergman, *The Psychological Birth of the Infant* (New York: Basic Books, 1975); and Wladyslaw Sluckin, *Imprinting and Early Learning*, 2d ed. (Chicago: Aldine, 1973).

10. Konrad Lorenz, *On Aggression* (New York: Harcourt, Brace and World, 1967).

11. Turner, *Family Interaction*, pp. 80–87, 161.

10

THE THERAPIST'S STORY

Remarried family members come for professional service when one or more problems have become sufficiently stressful to prod them to seek help. Some come soon after the process of family reconstitution has begun, in the hope that early intervention can prevent beginning problems from escalating. Others have weathered the early stages of "blending and becoming" only to have hard-won workable family balances disturbed by crisis events or by transitions into new individual and family developmental stages. Still others come in despair after years of unsuccessful efforts to resolve their difficulties. Their early hopes of fulfillment in the remarried family have faded and maladaptive responses to problems have become stereotyped and automatic.

Most who seek professional help are, however, at some interim point on the hope-despair continuum. They have had sufficient experience to know that their problems cannot be wished away, but they come with the hope and expectation that the therapist has an informed body of knowledge and the necessary skills of a professional counselor to help them to cope more effectively with their problems. This chapter comments on some values and assumptions that underlie practice with the remarried family and illustrates clinical interventions with three families discussed in chapter two. Finally, principles of intervention specific to the remarried family are summarized.

VALUES, ASSUMPTIONS, AND THE CLINICAL PROCESS

Several core values and assumptions about the remarried family, the helping process with such families, and the therapists who work with them, guide intervention with this family. The basic assumption is made that, despite earlier trauma and often overwhelming problems, individuals can grow and change in the context of the remarried family. Recent studies have found that later constructive life experiences in foster or adoptive families can compensate for or even reverse the effects on children of their early deprivation and trauma.[1] By analogy, it may be assumed that problems and processes related to earlier discontinuities and losses suffered by persons who become members of remarried families can be alleviated by later constructive emotional experiences in this family unit.

A basic assumption underlying the clinical orientation of work with all families, including the remarried family, is that the family has two primary internal functions: (1) the provision of emotional gratification for adults in the family, and (2) the socialization, care, and nurture of its children. It follows that when families, nuclear or remarried, experience difficulties in carrying out one or both of these functions, problems result. The problems and processes may be the same as those that occur in any family, those inherent in the remarried family situation, or a combination of both.

Another assumption is that the problems and processes remarried families experience can be dysfunctional but are not necessarily pathological. Often they are normal developmental and transitional processes of adaptation to the remarried family situation. It is assumed that clinical intervention with this family can address many of these problems in ways that alleviate stress and balance the two basic internal family functions. Thus, both adults and children have opportunities for normal growth, development, and gratification.

Assumptions related to the clinical process rest on the belief that the therapist is familiar with the place of today's remarried family in a historical, sociocultural, and legal context. Beyond this is the expectation that he or she has a general knowledge of the differences and similarities between remarried and nuclear families along dimensions of the schema for study as developed in the preceding chapters. Additionally, the therapist should be fa-

192

miliar with the significant variations among remarried families along these same dimensions. When the clinical process begins with this foundation, the therapist is more likely to be able to fulfill the client's hope and expectations for help.

A further assumption about clinical intervention with the remarried family is that the process should be guided by an orientation to the person-problem-situation context, because neither person nor situation can stand alone and tension between the two is the basis for many problems and processes in interaction. The therapist should be well-grounded in personality theory about individuals and have a working knowledge of family systems. Moreover, it is assumed that the therapist must be alert to his or her own cultural orientations about the remarried family in addition to those of the client so that unrealistic expectations are not sought.

The larger goals of blending and becoming can be fulfilled through therapeutic tasks that involve consideration of the possible in light of the unchangeable givens of the remarried family situation. Clarification of realistic goals will help remarried family members achieve a workable family balance. The achievement of this balance involves recognizing that although the ideal family situation may not be possible, a workable balance may be achieved through reduction of conflict, development of more effective ways of coping with special problems and processes, and recognition of the rights of all family members. During the clinical process, remarried family members will learn to perceive the remarried family as different from the idealized nuclear family, but nevertheless as a "real" family that has dignity, worth, and value in its own right.

Finally, it is assumed that a general systems or ecological orientation to clinical intervention with a flexible combination of crisis intervention, problem solving, and psychosocial approaches with individual, marital, parent-child, and total family units is most useful. Such an integrated approach focuses on the interactional and transactional processes between persons and situation, as well as on internal psychological tensions within each person. This approach must be synthesized with values and assumptions that underlie clinical practice, substantive knowledge about the remarried family, selective use of relevant interdisciplinary theory, and appropriate and sensitive use of principles of clinical intervention. It is anticipated that this stance will facilitate engagement, create an empathic and effective working alliance with family members, and encourage an ongoing therapeutic process that reduces tension, promotes problem solving, and fosters psychosocial gains.

CLINICAL PROCESS

In describing the clinical process with three families, the stories of the Brents, Maynors, and Blakes have been recast through the use of a four dimensional schema (structural, legal, cultural, and developmental) and the problem-process profile. The elaboration of the schema and the profile is limited to information from the first interview, as presented in chapter two. Additional information is included as it emerged during the process of clinical intervention. The details of the schema and the profile enable the practitioner to study and assess the specific objective reality of each family and draw from the more generalized body of information about the remarried family as necessary.

The process of clinical intervention is described from referral through termination. The rationale is given for who are seen and in what combinations and for the focus of intervention. In addition, the selection and application of relevant aspects of substantive knowledge about the remarried family that facilitates the definition of realistic goals and movement toward a workable family balance is demonstrated.

THE BRENT FAMILY

The Brents were referred to their local family service agency by a minister four months after their marriage. When Mrs. Brent telephoned to initiate service she explained that things were not going well in the new family situation. The Brents were seen in combined family and marital therapy for seven months.

SCHEMA FOR STUDY

Structurally, the Brents were a "his and hers" family unit. Mr. Brent, thirty-nine, and Mrs. Brent, thirty-five, had both been divorced. At the time of remarriage, Mr. Brent's two sons, Tom, sixteen, and Bob, fourteen, and Mrs. Brent's two sons, Rick, fourteen, and Fred, thirteen, became part of the remarried family. All family members were in "hybrid roles"; that is, they occupied both a natural and a step position characteristic of the "his and hers" family structure.

Legally, there was no ongoing active coparenting and no visitation activity with an absent spouse for either set of children. Each parent with whom the children resided had sole legal custody of the children. Although there was a legal requirement for child support from Mrs. Brent's first husband, these payments were irregular and inconsistent. Rick and Fred retained the legal name of their biological-legal noncustodial father.

Culturally, neither Mr. nor Mrs. Brent had been prepared for the objective realities and normal adjustment processes of the remarried family. They derived their expectations, goals, and values about the remarried family from the only reference group they knew—the nuclear family. Their orientation to the remarried family was that there was no difference between this family and the nuclear. They therefore assumed parent roles as if there were no need to redefine the parent role in the remarried family. In contrast, according to the cultural orientation of Bob and Tom, the remarried family was a "devalued" family situation. Rick and Fred's orientation was unclear.

Developmentally, the Brent family was in a very early stage of the remarried family life cycle. Developmental remarried family tasks involved reorganization from two prior single-parent family units into a remarried family unit. Subtasks involved blending prior life-styles, defining appropriate step role behavior, reciprocal including of new family members, and becoming a remarried family with its own unique identity. At the same time, the core family developmental tasks required the tandem mastery of appropriate parental release and separation-individuation of Tom, Bob, Rick, and Fred, who were at varying stages of adolescence and working on individual issues of identity. In addition, Mr. and Mrs. Brent were in an early stage of establishing themselves as a marital unit. This required mutual interpersonal accommodation and opportunity to rework unresolved earlier marital tasks. These familial and marital developmental tasks were interwoven with individual developmental tasks for both Mr. and Mrs. Brent, who were approaching middle adulthood. The tasks of this stage involve coming to terms with life's disappointments and making new commitments. Other developmental issues in this family were feelings of loss expressed by all of the children about structural and developmental discontinuities when the preferred single-parent family structure was changed to the remarried.

The age at which significant discontinuities and trauma occurred for each family member was noted. Mr. Brent was married

for seventeen years before he was divorced. He lived with his two
sons in a single-parent household for one year and remarried at
the age of thirty-five. Bob and Tom were fifteen and thirteen re-
spectively, at the time of the divorce. They had not had any contact
with their mother since that time. Mrs. Brent had been married
for thirteen years. She lived as a single parent with her two sons
for three years before she remarried. At the time of the divorce,
Rick was thirteen and Fred was twelve. They had not had any
contact with their father since that time.

PROBLEM-PROCESS PROFILE FOR ASSESSMENT
The *locus* of the problems and structural *alignments* when clinical intervention was initiated were between Tom and Bob versus
Mrs. Brent, and Tom and Bob versus Rick and Fred. Thus, the
major subsystem alignments were between stepsons versus stepmother and each natural sibling subsystem versus the other. In
addition, there was beginning stress between Mr. Brent and his
two sons, the natural father-child subsystem. Neither the marital
nor the natural mother-child subsystem were involved in problems presented at the time of application. Mr. and Mrs. Brent were
a united marital subsystem and Mrs. Brent and her two sons were
a united parent-child subsystem. Both Mr. and Mrs. Brent had
attempted to expand the boundaries of their natural parent-child
subsystems to include the spouse's children. Beginning positive
alignments were noted between Mr. Brent and his two stepsons;
attenuation of ties between Mr. Brent and his two sons was indicated.

The *content* of the problems the Brents articulated at the time
of application involved environmental, intrafamilial-interpersonal, and intrapersonal levels. On the environmental level, Tom
and Bob referred to problems about space and issues of territoriality, expressing feelings of being "invaded," while Rick and
Fred expressed resentment because of problems of relocation
when they moved into the Brent household from their former
community and had to change schools. On an intrafamilial-interpersonal level, problems centered on the developmental tasks of
family reorganization and the strains of blending two prior well-
functioning separate, single-parent households into a remarried
family household. Mr. and Mrs. Brent's lack of socialization to the
normal adjustment processes of integrating two families was a
major problem area. Difficulties of synthesizing different lifestyles
and values, formulating mutually acceptable rules and regulations

for management of the household, including new family members, and defining and achieving consensus on appropriate step role behaviors were paramount. Problems of exclusion of new family members and preference for the natural tie were apparent in Tom and Bob's resentment of Mrs. Brent, Rick, and Fred, as well as Rick and Fred's resentment of Tom and Bob. Mrs. Brent's efforts to recreate a lifestyle as if this were a nuclear family resulted in the superimposition of her values and routines so that an integration and accommodation of prior lifestyles of both families were not reflected. On an intrapersonal level, all of the children were dealing with problems of loss about the prior single-parent family structure. In addition, Bob and Tom experienced feelings of loss because of their father's involvement with their stepbrothers. Finally, all of the developmental issues of four adolescent boys in conflict with parental goals for family reconstitution were problem areas. These problems had been in existence since the beginning of the marriage. Their increased intensity and Mr. and Mrs. Brent's anxiety that it would disrupt their marriage precipitated the application for service.

CLINICAL INTERVENTION

Initial therapeutic intervention in work with the Brents involved decisions about the problem focus, who would be seen, and in what combinations. Exploration with the family about their perceptions of the most pressing problem for work resulted in consensus that the problems of family reorganization were most urgent. From the parents' perspective, feelings about the jeopardy of the new family unit made this a logical focus. Bob and Tom, eager to see some of the rules and routines revised, saw this focus as an opportunity for change, and Fred and Rick agreed in the hope that the effort would result in less tension for all.

This was a desirable initial focus from the therapeutic viewpoint because it defined the family as a unit and communicated the therapeutic position that the problem belonged to the entire family unit. However, because this was a new and vulnerable family unit, the marital-parental unit also needed explicit definition. Therefore, Mr. and Mrs. Brent were invited to consider additional bimonthly interviews focused on issues they wished to discuss as a separate unit. This demonstrated to the family the therapist's acceptance of Mr. and Mrs. Brent as the new marital unit in charge of the family. Also, the boys were offered the opportunity for individual or joint sessions with one or more other family members if they wanted them. The therapist reserved the right to ask for such sessions if it seemed in the interest of the therapeutic process. Such options provide important freedoms for remarried family members and for the therapist to deal with problems flexibly.

197

The Remarried Family

At times it may be necessary to shift the focus from the family to a natural parent-child unit, or to see a family member individually. The critical issue in setting up the plan for who is seen outside of the family interview and how often is to permit sufficient flexibility so that various structural combinations are possible, depending on the needs of the individuals and the issues involved in therapy. The therapeutic plan was for the total family unit to be seen in weekly family-unit therapy, and for Mr. and Mrs. Brent to be seen twice a month in addition. Other combinations were to be made if and when it was therapeutically indicated or desired by family members. Thus, clients and therapist determined through a mutual process of exploration the locus, content, and problem priority for immediate work.

In the first few interviews with the family, the therapeutic goal was to establish a working alliance with the family unit and, concurrently, to demonstrate empathy for the tensions and stress that each was experiencing in the new family structure. The therapist, therefore, conveyed some beginning information about the universal complexity of the remarried family situation, as evidenced through an analysis of the structural and developmental dimensions of this family.

As an entry into discussion of the tasks of family reorganization, the short time the family had lived together as a remarried family unit was made explicit in contrast to the duration of time spent in the nuclear and single parent family stages. This technique opened the way for discussion of the present very early phase of reconstitution and exploration of appropriate expectations of each other for family solidarity.

A primary purpose for the discussion of the structural and developmental issues in this particular family situation was to stimulate thinking about the differences between nuclear and remarried families in order to consider realistic goals. Another purpose was to emphasize that the tensions being experienced were normal and nonpathological at this stage of reconstitution. This approach contributed to the establishment of beginning empathic bridges among family members, as well as to a positive working alliance between the total family unit and the therapist. Moreover, such an approach contributed to hope for change and arrested the escalating spiral of despair that characterized the family at the time of application. Finally, the focus served as reference points for recurrent discussion of realistic roles and expectations of emotional attachments, which could be considered in light of the realities imposed on the Brent family by the structural and developmental "givens" of their specific situation.

As the process of clinical intervention moved into its middle phase, the focus was on several recurrent themes that were barriers to positive family reorganization. Primary was the cultural issue of lack of earlier socialization of the family to some of the built-in realities of the remarried family. This required that the therapist educate the family to some of the normal adjustment problems of blending two formerly successful single-parent family lifestyles. Another theme was centered on discussions of the stress because of discrepancies between the values and priorities of Mrs. Brent and those of Tom and Bob. Therapeutic intervention focused on the exploration of the meaning and effect of the superimposition of the lifestyle of one family member on the other, and alternative possibilities of mutual accommodation to each other's values and priorities. A slow but progressive process of mutual decision making about family rules and regulations evolved. Confusion about lines of authority was eliminated as the concept of the stepparent as the social parent was emphasized. This process was facilitated because each spouse was able to support the other in assuming the role of the social parent for his or her children and demonstrated that parenting was a shared responsibility. Ground rules that all could accept were established through family dialogue, and new avenues for effective communication were initiated.

Another recurrent theme was the stress of the disparate goals of the parents, who were deeply immersed in the early stages of family reconstitution and pressing for family togetherness, and those of the adolescents, who were pursuing the normal developmental tasks for separation and individuation. The laissez-faire lifestyle of Mr. Brent's single-parent household had been much more conducive to the adolescent effort for separation and individuation than was the new tightly run household. As the normal aspects of these tensions were elucidated, Mr. and Mrs. Brent felt less assaulted by Bob's and Tom's resistance to participation in family activities. Also, all of the boys were freed to pursue normal individual interests with less guilt and rebellion.

The step-by-step therapeutic process of unraveling the nature of the barriers to family reorganization and blending led to discussions of Tom's and Bob's as well as Rick's and Fred's recurrent references to feelings of loss for their prior single-parent family status. The therapist, using selective aspects from theories of grief and mourning, was able to help the boys move through a process of anger at the loss to one of beginning reconciliation as they were able to identify some of the gains that had been made in family interaction patterns. Another aspect of loss that was explored concerned feelings about absent parents. Early denial of loss yielded to feelings of rage at having been abandoned and disappointment that there were no current contacts with these parents. Mr. and Mrs. Brent were able to accept their children's feelings and share with them their own hurts that their first marriages had ended in divorce. Family pain, formerly repressed and avoided, was now articulated and shared. The shared grief became the matrix for developing new family bonds. It provided a shared past life experience for all family members and became the beginning of a shared history for the new family.

Finally, Tom's and Bob's emerging anger at their father for their perception that he had shifted his attachment from them to their stepbrothers was addressed. It became clear that part of Tom's and Bob's exclusionary behavior toward Rick and Fred was retaliative for what they felt they had lost from their father. Their efforts to compensate for this perceived loss also explained their twin-like behavior. They said that they felt all they had "was each other." Mr. Brent talked about his feelings of loss because the camaraderie he had experienced with his sons was no longer active. He explained that although he felt much internal pressure to include Rick and Fred in his emotional life, he did not intend it to displace or exclude his own sons. Rick and Fred clarified that they had not wanted to intrude on the relationship that Tom and Bob had with their father, yet they valued the developing relationship with their step-father.

The issue of therapeutic intervention became one of emphasizing the importance of maintaining prior ties so that bond shifts in the new family situation did not compound earlier losses. Mr. Brent was relieved that he could now resume some of his earlier activities with his sons without fear that this would be harmful to his stepsons. Discussions were sparked on how family members could preserve past meaningful relationships and, at the same time, be open to new relationships. In a lively dialogue, the common sports interests of Mr. Brent and all of the boys became the focus of "family days." In time, rituals for birthdays, holiday activities, and a shared family history were built into the family lifestyle. The Brent family began to develop its own traditions. The beginning of a shift from the "devalued" status of the remarried family was in evidence as Tom and Bob began to willingly participate to a greater extent in special family activities.

The conjoint marital sessions with Mr. and Mrs. Brent, interspersed with the family therapy sessions, expanded on themes being worked on in family therapy and reinforced the integrity of the marital subsystem as a unit in its own right. In addition, Mr. and Mrs. Brent used these sessions to work through some of the unresolved feelings of past marital failure. They talked about their frustrated hopes that the new remarried family unit would erase past feelings of stigma because of their divorces. In these sessions, Mrs. Brent dealt with her disappointment that it had not been possible to act as if this were the original nuclear family. Mrs. Brent's expectations that Tom and Bob would respond to her as "their own mother" were examined in the light of the differences of biological, legal, and developmental ties between stepchildren and stepparents from those between children and their biological parents.

The therapeutic task focused on helping Mrs. Brent deal with the differences in kinship ties and establish different self-other role and emotional expectations until relationships were stabilized and trust could begin. Mrs. Brent struggled with the reality that for the present she would have to accept that Tom and Bob were not ready to accept her willingness and eagerness to be their "real" mother. Moreover, they were at individual developmental stages, when normal developmental thrusts for differentiation were in opposition to Mrs. Brent's wish for family closeness. However, there was therapeutic emphasis on the importance of the social parent role. The hope was that over time shared life experiences would generate positive feelings toward each other; that the social parent tie would grow although the absence of a biological and a shared developmental tie since the birth of the child could not be changed. Thus, realistic goals for parenting involved consideration of the possible in the context of unchangeable "givens."

During the clinical process, Mr. and Mrs. Brent accepted that the new family was not a replacement of the nuclear family each had lost, but rather a new entity with its own identity and characteristics, and that they as a couple were a marital unit separate and apart from their children. There was a healing of old wounds and enhancement of self esteem as marital and family bonds were strengthened.

The termination interviews with the Brent family as a unit took place as they neared their first anniversary. In reviewing where they had been at the point of application and where they were at the time of termination they reflected that a process of mutual accommodation to the values, priorities, and lifestyle of each prior family unit had been initiated. The recurrent past theme of exclusion was no longer so dominant. Rather, family members were finding creative ways to maintain prior ties and, at the same time, include new family members. New cultural orientations to the family were in process, so that the remarried family was neither devalued nor idealized as being no different from the nuclear family. Processes of blending and becoming were well under way. Tom seemed to capture the family climate with his comment that "they were no longer a house of strangers, but instead were beginning to be a house of friends."

In the Maynor family situation, another constellation of family problems and processes existed. This case demonstrates the difficulties families often encounter when workable family balances are disrupted by parent switches and when the stresses and problems engendered are not addressed. Here, maladaptive patterns become stereotyped and automatic. A crisis that highlighted these problems became the point of entry into this family situation.

THE MAYNOR FAMILY

The Maynors were referred to a family service agency by the local crisis center. They sought professional help seven years after their remarriage when a crisis state was precipitated by the seating arrangements at a wedding (see chapter two). The predominant role of clinical intervention was crisis-oriented marital therapy over a four-month period. During this time, a number of parent-child therapy sessions were held. A brief period of individual therapy with one of the children in the family was implemented.

SCHEMA FOR STUDY

Structurally, the Maynors were a "his" and "hers" family unit at the time of the application. Mr. Maynor, forty-six, and Mrs. Maynor, forty-four, had each been divorced. At the time of their marriage, they were a "hers" family because only Mrs. Maynor's children lived in the remarried family household. Mr. Maynor's three children lived with their mother and stepfather. When Bert and Howard joined the Maynor household, in a parent switch, a "his" and "hers" remarried family structure resulted. Mr. Maynor's older son Bert, twenty-one, had been away at college, and had just married a fellow student. Still at home were Mr. Maynor's son Howard, eighteen, Mrs. Maynor's son Mike, seventeen, and daughter Beth, fourteen.

Legally, a divided custody arrangement existed at the time of application. Mr. Maynor had custody of his two older children; his former wife had custody of the youngest child, Jane. However, at the time of divorce, all of Mr. Maynor's children lived with their mother, who was, thus, sole custodian. Mr. Maynor observed regular visitation rights and fulfilled child support obligations. Two years after Mr. Maynor's remarriage, Bert and Howard exercised their right of children's preference and legal custody was changed from their mother to their father. Mr. Maynor's former wife had remarried soon after their divorce, but was divorced from her second husband by the time of the application. Mrs. Maynor had sole custody of her children, Mike and Beth, from the time of divorce to the time of application for service. The whereabouts of the father was unknown and neither child support obligations nor visitation rights was observed.

Culturally, both Mr. and Mrs. Maynor had grown up in nuclear family households. Mr. Maynor, in particular, felt greatly stigmatized because he was the only person in the family who had ever been divorced. Mrs. Maynor's children had taken their stepfather's last name and called him "Dad," although no legal name changes were made.

Developmentally, the Maynors had successfully mastered their initial remarried family developmental tasks of mutual accommodation and adaptation. However, when a change in living arrangements occurred because Howard and Bert came to live with the Maynors, it necessitated a reworking of these tasks—this was never successfully accomplished. Thus, developmental tasks still to be mastered remained at the same time that mastery of individual and family developmental tasks related to the launching stage were required.

Both Mr. and Mrs. Maynor were in the middle-adult phase of their individual developmental life cycles. This was a time of inventory for each in terms of past and future goals and values. All of the children who were still residing in the home were involved in individual developmental tasks of identity formation and separation. Individual and familial developmental tasks were complicated for all family members because of earlier unresolved issues of loss and reciprocal inclusion of steprelationships.

Mr. Maynor had been married thirteen years at the time of the divorce, when Bert was twelve, Howard was nine, and Jane was eight. Bert and Howard came to live with the Maynors two years after their remarriage. Mrs. Maynor had been married for eight years before her divorce, when Mike was six, and Beth was two. Mrs. Maynor lived with Mike and Beth in a single-parent family for five years before she remarried.

PROBLEM-PROCESS PROFILE FOR ASSESSMENT

The primary *locus* of the problems in this family at the time of application was between Mr. and Mrs. Maynor as a marital unit. Contributory to the marital problem locus were structural *alignments* of Mr. Maynor, Bert, and Howard versus Mrs. Maynor and Mike. In addition, Howard and Mike were in frequent conflict. Beginnings of positive alignments between Mr. Maynor and his stepchildren, Mike and Beth, were arrested when Bert and Howard, Mr. Maynor's sons came to live with him. At that time, Mrs. Maynor made efforts to establish ties with her stepchildren, but later withdrew when the strong alliance between Mr. Maynor and his children resulted in feelings of exclusion for Mrs. Maynor and her children.

The *content* of the Maynor problems was predominantly on intrafamilial and interpersonal levels involving the marital and parent-child subsystems. Mr. Maynor perceived the problem to be the immediate threat to the marriage because of his wife's intent to file for divorce. Mrs. Maynor perceived the problem to be a marital one stemming from Mr. Maynor's preferential treatment of and alignment with his children over his wife and her children, the efforts of Mr. Maynor's children to reunite their father (her husband) with his former wife, and the intensity of his tie to his children. On an intrapersonal level, both Mr. and Mrs. Maynor experienced feelings of low self-esteem; Mr. Maynor because of the threat of a first and now an impending second marital failure, and Mrs. Maynor because her husband's attitude of priority toward his natural tie to his children appeared to be a statement of her diminished importance to him. Another intrapersonal problem for Mr. Maynor was his guilt toward his children and his need to compensate for this with them. For Bert and Howard, intrapersonal problems were unresolved issues of loss reflected in their fantasies and behaviors to implement parental reunion. All of these problems resulted in the assumption by each parent of advocacy roles for the natural children.

CLINICAL INTERVENTION

The initial phase of work with the Maynors consisted of a crisis-oriented approach focused on a reduction of the high tension level that had been precipitated by the wedding seating arrangements. Mrs. Maynor's early resistance to professional help appeared to be neutralized by the therapist's recognition of the stress both spouses had experienced, and by the general complexity of the remarried family situation. This recognition expanded the focus from individual fault to examination of some of the built-in realities that contributed to dysfunctional interactional patterns. It acknowledged Mrs. Maynor's feelings of frustration and, concurrently, solidified Mr. Maynor's motivation for professional help. Nevertheless, Mrs. Maynor specified that she would agree to work with the agency for only a four-month period before she would make a final decision about divorce.

In keeping with the principles of crisis intervention, the therapist sought to establish the connection between the current crisis and earlier events and patterns of family relationships. Mr. and Mrs. Maynor agreed that the wedding seating arrangements encapsulated family dynamics that had been in process since Mr. Maynor's children had come to live with them five years ago. At that time, the earlier positive relationships characteristic of their "weekend" family were displaced by family tension and strain.

Both Mr. and Mrs. Maynor agreed that the most immediate and pressing problem for therapeutic intervention concerned patterns of parent-child interaction that were the source of tension and conflict in their marriage. Indeed, they believed that many of their marital tensions would subside if problems in the parent-child area were resolved.

The Maynor's belief that marital and parent-child problems are intricately interwoven and that parent-child problems create the marital problems is a view that is frequently held by remarried couples. From a clinical point of view, it is often desirable to begin work with the marital couple when parent-child issues have become intertwined with marital problems. The teasing apart of marital and parent-child problems permits clarification of the processes and sequences in which these problems arise. It is then possible to identify and rework dysfunctional parent-child issues and behaviors that are interfering with marital relationships.

It was agreed that the initial focus of work would involve exploration of the perceptions of all of the family members of the underlying meanings of the wedding seating arrangements. This approach was taken because it was the predominant concern of both Mr. and Mrs. Maynor and the immediate precipitant to the current marital stress and threat of divorce. As the therapeutic process unfolded, clinical evidence indicated that much of Howard's behavior was related to his inability to accept his parents' divorce. Mr. Maynor's response to Howard's behavior appeared to be related to his guilt about the divorce and the strains he experienced in balancing his love for his wife, his natural children, and his stepchildren.

Efforts at parental reunion have been frequently observed by psychiatrists, psychologists, and social workers in clinical practice with children of divorce. They have been interpreted as children's ways of coping with feelings of loss and helplessness when they feel that they have been in some way responsible for the parental divorce. Other interpretations are that children have denied their feelings of loss and helplessness by means of ideas that they have the power to restore the earlier family unit. The therapeutic expectation of educating the Maynors to the prevalence of such feelings among children whose parents were divorced was that it would build understanding of the psychological needs of children that underlie these fantasies. Such an approach frequently helps stepparents feel less rejected and better able to reexamine their responses in terms of the children's feelings. This was borne out by Mrs. Maynor's greater objectivity and lesser sense of personal injury. Meanwhile, Mr. Maynor was encouraged to consider the reasons for his inability to help his children give up this fantasy.

In reflecting on the reasons for his failure to deal more openly with this issue earlier in the remarriage, Mr. Maynor recognized the deep feelings of guilt he had because his children's lives had been disrupted by his decision to divorce—something over which his children had no control. During therapy, Mr. and Mrs. Maynor were able to share with each other the stress and pain of parental decisions that at times ran counter to their children's needs and wishes, and their own pain as parents in making such decisions. Therapeutic intervention focused on giving support to the idea that parents have a right and a need to make decisions that may not always coincide with their children's wishes. This support enabled each to begin a process of coming to terms with this reality. Mr. and Mrs. Maynor concluded that it was important to help Howard, in particular, deal with his inability to accept his parents' divorce.

To this end, Mr. and Mrs. Maynor asked that Howard be invited to participate in a few therapeutic sessions. This direction was appropriate because Howard's efforts to reunite his divorced parents and Mr. Maynor's pattern of reinforcement of Howard's actions were central to the marital conflict and the threat of divorce.

Several therapeutic sessions with Howard and the Maynors followed. The primary focus of these interviews was to provide a context in which Howard and Mr. and Mrs. Maynor could talk together about their individual feelings and the interactive patterns that these brought into being. The therapeutic goal was to facilitate the development of empathic bonds among them. During these sessions, Mr. and Mrs. Maynor shared with Howard the impact of the wedding seating arrangements on Mrs. Maynor as the stimulant to seeking professional help. This event was, however, linked to Howard's persistent efforts to reunite his mother and father. Howard talked about his unhappiness when he lived with his mother and stepfather and his consistent yearning that his parents would reunite. When his mother and stepfather were divorced he felt that such a reunion could take place. He recognized that he had actively pursued and created opportunities to bring his parents together in the hope that his step-mother, Mrs. Maynor, would leave.

During these sessions, Mr. Maynor expressed sensitive awareness that Howard had never truly accepted his parents' divorce. Moreover, Mr. Maynor acknowledged that his failure to help his children with this reality had contributed to their hopes of a parental reunion. He explained that although he hoped to continue a cooperative coparenting relationship with his former wife, he was firmly committed to his present marriage. This position, clearly enunciated by Mr. Maynor, gave Mrs. Maynor hope that the marriage could be salvaged and conveyed to Howard that his father and stepmother were an established marital unit. The dialogue opened the way for therapeutic exploration of the grief issues previously handled through the fantasy of parental reunion. Mrs. Maynor's supportive role with Howard during this process contributed to the reestablishment of an earlier positive relationship.

Furthermore, Howard was seen in individual therapy for several additional sessions. The focus of work with him was on his feelings of loss about the hope of parental reunion and the reality of his father's commitment to the present marriage.

Another aspect of therapeutic intervention with Mr. and Mrs. Maynor was centered on the maladaptive advocacy roles each parent assumed on behalf of his or her children. The focus on this pattern in the parent-child relationship and its implications for marital conflict led to exploration of the feelings Mr. and Mrs. Maynor experienced about their positions of being both natural and stepparents or in the hybrid parent role.

Explicit therapeutic validation of Mr. Maynor's earlier positive relationships with his stepchildren suggested that he did not have difficulties in parenting his stepchildren. Indeed, his willing assumption of their total financial support and consideration of their legal adoption suggested that he did not adhere to the legal doctrine of "stepparent as a stranger" and had assumed the role of the parent in loco parentis. Further evidence of the ongoing solidification of the social parent-child relationship was observed in Mike and Beth's spontaneous referral to their stepfather as "dad," and their assumption of his surname as their own. In addition, Mrs. Maynor reported that her children related well to Mr. Maynor. Neither her children nor her husband had difficulties in mastery of the critical early remarried family developmental task of "inclusion versus exclusion." The shift in this pattern after Bert and Howard came to live with the Maynors on a permanent basis became the issue for therapeutic exploration.

With the validation of Mr. Maynor's capacity to establish meaningful relationships with his stepchildren, Mr. Maynor was able to reflect on the stress he experienced in maintaining these ties when natural and stepchildren lived under one roof. He revealed that for the first time since his divorce he felt some return of self-esteem as a "true" parent when his children made the decision to live with him and he could once again care for them under his roof. Mr. Maynor referred to their decision as a "gift" they had given him. He felt that, therefore, he had to prove to them they had made the right choice. Mr. Maynor talked of the tremendous cross-pressures he experienced when he made decisions favoring "her" children over "his." Unable to tolerate this stress, he finally removed himself from these conflictual feelings by identifying with "his" children and avoiding decisions that involved balancing the rights of both "his" and "her" children.

On the other side of this interactive pattern was Mrs. Maynor's feelings of loss that the positive growing attachments between her children and her husband had been aborted. She said this was especially true in relation to Mike. Because Mike had never had a positive father image, she had been pleased to see this relationship with his stepfather grow. The abrupt termination of this relationship seemed to her to be a statement of her further failure to provide Mike with a "good" father. This had subjective meanings to Mrs. Maynor that she had not been a "good" mother. The addition of Mr. Maynor's children to the household had resulted in changes in family alignments and relationships that enhanced her husband's self-esteem, but were the source of loss of self-esteem for Mrs. Maynor. She felt that she had no choice but to ally herself with Mike and form a counter coalition when she perceived that Mike's welfare was jeopardized by her husband's preferential treatment of his sons or by conflict between Mike and Howard.

The therapeutic need to clarify the complexity of the hybrid parent role and to separate these realities from definitions of one's own self-esteem became the focus of the final phase of work with the Maynors. This involved a clarification of the hybrid-parent role and separation of the reality issues of this role from one's self esteem. Once accomplished, realistic family goals could be identified and a return to a workable family balance achieved. This time, however, the workable balance would include Mr. Maynor's and Mrs. Maynor's children living together under one roof.

As Mr. and Mrs. Maynor addressed the issue of the hybrid parent role, they clarified that they both felt differently toward their natural children than they felt toward their stepchildren. The mutual acceptance that such feelings were normal and did not define them as "bad" persons contributed to beginning definitions of realistic perceptions of hybrid role performance as well as reconsideration of self-esteem issues.

Therapeutic intervention consisted of delineating the two components of the hybrid role, the natural and the step, and clarifying that feelings related to each of these components were not necessarily the same. Mr. and Mrs. Maynor began to clarify that neither parent expected the other to give up attachments to his or her children. What was expected was some effort to avoid the predominance of preferential treatment of one's natural children and to observe the rights of all family members.

During the therapeutic process, the therapist clarified for the Maynors that at the present time there are no appropriate universal definitions or role models for the stepparent, in contrast to well-formulated and universally accepted expectations for the natural and adoptive parent. The step situation becomes even more complex when the same person is both a natural and a stepparent to children who live together under one roof. Tensions between the natural and step roles are normal and expectable, just as are differences in feelings for natural and stepchildren. To accept this reality is to redefine family goals as well as expectations of one's self and of other family members. In this way, prior mechanisms of retreat from the strains of the hybrid role and total identification with one's natural children, employed by Mr. Maynor, or the formation of counter coalitions, as practiced by Mrs. Maynor, could be modified and family polarization reduced.

The implications of polarized patterns, coupled with the highly intense quality of attachment between each parent and his or her child were examined in terms of the individual developmental tasks of Mike and Howard to separate and individuate. Although each parent had been able to observe dysfunctional aspects of the parent-child relationship in their spouse, they had been unable to be self-observant. Mr. and Mrs. Maynor initiated discussions of how each could be "objective eyes" and resources for the other in correcting dysfunctional patterns of behavior. With this recognition a complementary relationship of mutual support vis-à-vis each other's children began, in place of the former oppositional stance.

In the terminating interviews with the Maynors they recognized that there were many unexplored areas in terms of their own individual needs and feelings. However, there had been sufficient progress so that they wished to hold to their initial agreement on a four-month period of crisis-oriented marital therapy. They agreed instead to participate in a family life education course offered for remarried parents.

In the summing up process of where they had been at the time of application and where they were at the time of termination, the Maynors recognized that failure to seek help earlier in the reconstitution process had resulted in rigidification of polarized patterns and maladaptive advocacy roles. However, the crisis of the wedding seating arrangements had forced attention to previously unresolved issues. The Maynors now reported that the marriage was no longer in jeopardy. Improved relationships between Howard and Mrs. Maynor were also under way. Howard seemed to be coming to terms with his parents' divorce, and he no longer engaged in efforts to reunite his parents. Indeed Mr. Maynor perceived that Howard was relieved that he no longer felt responsible for bringing his parents together. He now could pursue his own interests and plan for his forthcoming departure for college.

Mr. Maynor, having dealt with some of his guilt about his divorce, began to modify his preferential treatment for Howard and to reestablish his earlier interest in and activities with Mike. As this occurred, Mrs. Maynor began to relinquish her intense bonds with and her advocacy role on behalf of Mike. Both Mr. and Mrs. Maynor expressed greater feelings of comfort and self-esteem in their parenting roles. The combatlike interaction of "his" versus "hers" that had characterized the family at the beginning of clinical intervention was less evident, and it appeared that the Maynors were well on the way to reestablishing a workable family balance.

Some months later, the therapist received a note from Mrs. Maynor advising that Howard was enjoying his first year in college. Mike was busy exploring the various college options he wanted to pursue, and Beth seemed to be doing well with friends, school, and family. Bert and his wife, now back in school, were in frequent contact with the family. Mrs. Maynor commented that the family life education program they had attended had been most helpful in clarifying how usual the problems they had experienced were for many remarried families. She concluded her note with the sentence, "Thank you from the bottom of our marriage."

The Blake family reflects yet another remarried family situation that portrays the stresses experienced when idealized images of appropriate steprole behavior do not conform with actual behavior. The multiple problems that emanated from self-confrontation with this reality was a central focus of clinical intervention with this family.

THE BLAKE FAMILY

Ginny Blake was referred to a local mental health center by her physician because of feelings of depression for which no organic basis had been found. At the time of the application, Ginny had been married for three years. She and other members of her family were seen over a period of almost two years.

SCHEMA FOR STUDY

Structurally, the Blake family at the time of application was a "his" and "ours" remarried family structure. The family comprised of George Blake, thirty-one, formerly divorced, Ginny, twenty-five, who had never been married before, Amy, eight, Mr. Blake's daughter of a prior marriage, and Jeff, nine months old, a child of the present marriage. Thus a newly formed two-parent, two-generational nuclear family (the first for Ginny and the second for George) coexisted with the remarried family structure.

Legally, there were no coparenting issues with an absent parent at the time of application because Amy's mother had died five months prior to the request for service. Prior to her mother's death, Amy lived with her mother, stepfather, two stepsiblings, and two half-siblings. Her mother had been sole custodian since the divorce. Her father honored financial obligations for child support but did not begin a weekly visitation program until Amy was almost two years old. At the time of her mother's death, Amy's stepfather had asked that Amy be allowed to continue to live with him and her siblings. However, George Blake exercised his right of parental preference as the biological parent and brought Amy to live with him and his new family.

Culturally, George Blake's orientation to the remarried family derived from the nuclear family. In contrast, Ginny's orientation was derived from her own life experience as a member of a remarried family. Because of her background, Ginny perceived herself to have been a "deprived" stepchild. As a consequence, she developed an early idealized image of how she would perform if she were ever in the role of stepparent.

Developmentally, the Blakes had been married three years at the time of the application for service and were technically beyond the initial stage of remarried family reconstitution. However, the structural changes that occurred when Amy came to live under their roof introduced remarried family developmental tasks consistent with the earliest stages of family reconstitution. These were inclusion versus exclusion, and role definition versus ambiguity. At the time that Amy came to live with the Blakes, George and Ginny were working on the core family developmental task (stage two) of expanding the marital boundaries to include their first-born child, Jeff, then four months old. The structural change introduced when Amy joined the family resulted in a need for the Blakes to combine developmental tasks of stages two and five of the remarried family life cycle. This need is inherent for families when a nuclear family exists with a remarried family.

On individual developmental levels, Mr. and Mrs. Blake were in the young adult stage working on developmental tasks related to intimacy and interpersonal accommodation as a marital unit. Amy, then eight, was dealing with normal developmental tasks of acquiring learning skills, relating to the broader world of peers and adults outside of the immediate family, and developing appropriate individuation and autonomy. At the same time, she had to deal with feelings of grief and mourning because of her mother's sudden death, loss of the family unit and significant relationships she had known since she was three years old, and loss of a familiar community and school. In addition, she had to make adaptations to a new family situation, community, and school.

Ginny Blake had suffered the sudden loss of her mother when she was nine years old. Two years later, her father remarried a woman who had been divorced but had no children. Ginny's half-brother was born when she was twelve years old.

PROBLEM-PROCESS PROFILE FOR ASSESSMENT

At the time of application, Ginny defined the *locus* of the problem to be within her. However, there were indications of problems between her and her husband as well as between her and Amy. In addition, she identified a problem locus between her and her father and stepmother. Thus, problems were identified at intra-personal, intrafamilial-marital parent-child levels, and inter-familial adult child-adult parent level. No significant *alignments* were indicated. However, distance and insulation were indicated by Ginny to exist between George and herself, and between George and Amy.

The *content* of problems at the time of application was Ginny's feelings of depression and low self-esteem. Other content areas were Ginny's negative feelings toward Amy, emergent feelings of guilt and remorse because of historical negative feelings toward her father and stepmother, and guilty resentment toward her husband for burdening her with the total care of his daughters. It was not possible to ascertain the locus, alignments, and content of problems from the perspective of any other family member because they were not seen at the time of the initial interview.

CLINICAL INTERVENTION

The initial focus of work with Ginny was on her feelings of depression and negative self-concept. These symptoms began a few weeks after Amy came to live with Ginny and her husband on a permanent basis. Ginny reflected that Amy's arrival had intruded on the privacy and feelings of closeness she had been experiencing with her "own" family unit. These negative feelings contrasted sharply with earlier positive feelings she had toward Amy. Ginny associated this change in feeling with disappointment in and dislike for herself. She felt that such feelings were irrational and that there was something wrong with her for having them. Ginny identified that this was a problem within her that required immediate attention. In view of the intrapersonal level of the problem identified as most pressing, its clinical implications for intensified depression, if not addressed, and Ginny's high motivation to look more closely at the meaning of her own feelings, individual weekly therapy was initiated. However, there was general discussion of the possibility of later inclusion of other family members if therapeutically indicated. The urgency of immediate intervention with Ginny on an individual basis was reinforced by the clinical consideration that dysfunctional patterns of interaction in this family had not yet become automatic and unquestioned. The hope was that clinical intervention at this time could prevent or modify dysfunctional and maladaptive familial interactive patterns before they became stereotyped.

In the therapeutic process that followed, Ginny was able to make appropriate connections between her depressed feelings and diminished self-esteem with the disparity between her idealized and actual stepmother behavior. The pain of this discrepancy was compounded as Ginny saw herself replicating many of the same kinds of behaviors and attitudes toward Amy that she had so bitterly resented as a stepchild from her stepmother. The dilemma this posed for Ginny was one of reconciliation of the gap between her idealized and actual step role behavior and resentment of her stepmother. The therapeutic task was to clarify the components of realistic steprole performance so that actual performance could be measured against current reality rather than against the ideal Ginny had constructed as a child. The therapeutic expectation was that such an approach would begin to set some limits on Ginny's self-castigation for perceived past and current failures.

The interrelationship of Ginny's perception of Amy as an intruder was explored in terms of the situational reality: a new baby and Amy's unexpected arrival. A therapeutic-educative examination of the core nuclear and remarried family developmental stages and tasks was initiated. Through this approach, Ginny learned that developmental tasks of inclusion of new family members are often stressful in any family and are not necessarily pathological. Moreover, Amy's arrival was precipitous and unplanned. Thus, Ginny had not had time to become emotionally prepared for Amy's becoming a part of the household as had been true with Jeff. With clarification of these realities, Ginny was better able to differentiate her resentment about situational aspects of Amy's arrival from her feelings about Amy as a person.

The more accurate placement of Ginny's resentment resulted in a gradual reemergence of her positive feelings toward Amy. Ginny became less critical of herself, self-esteem began to return, and the intensity of the depression subsided. During this process, Ginny recognized that Amy's grief about her mother's death had reawakened Ginny's sorrow about the loss of her own mother. Ginny speculated that perhaps she also resented Amy because of the reminder of an early painful part of her life. Ginny recounted that she had never been able to articulate her feelings of loss to her father because he was so sad and she was fearful of burdening him further with her feelings. Slowly, Ginny was able to express the feelings of abandonment and anger experienced because of her mother's death and her father's isolating grief. When her father remarried, Ginny fantasied that her stepmother would be a replacement for the "ideal" mother she had lost. When these fantasies were not realized, Ginny once again felt abandoned and angry. Through a supportive therapeutic process, the validity of Ginny's hopes and feelings were confirmed in the context of her childhood perspective.

The phenomenon of splitting the "good" and "bad" mother images was explored as it was relevant to Ginny's situation. The therapeutic goal was to help Ginny integrate and synthesize the "wholeness" of a person as not being all good (ideal) or all bad. These directions helped Ginny to be more accepting of her own limitations in not achieving the idealized performance she asked of herself. However, at the same time her remorse and guilt because she had not been more empathic to the pressures her father and stepmother experienced were heightened. Ginny's distress because of this, her wish to establish a more positive relationship with her father and stepmother, and family theory about the value of intergenerational therapy led to exploration of the possibility of sessions with Ginny and her father and stepmother. Ginny decided such a series of sessions would be useful if her parents would agree to participate. When they willingly came, it was agreed that three intergenerational interviews would be held. The therapeutic focus of these interviews was defined as helping Ginny and her parents relive some of the stress of those early years within the corrected framework of attention to the built-in realities of their situation. These would be examined as they had been barriers to the development of positive attachments.

In the adult-child to adult-parent exchange Ginny learned for the first time about her stepmother's early hopes for an integrated family unit. Her stepmother talked of her anguish that she could not "reach" Ginny and that in the end she had failed to measure up to Ginny's hopes and expectations. Ginny's father talked of his feelings of frustration in not knowing how to break the pattern of increasing distance between his wife and child, and the pressures he experienced as the "person in the middle." Ginny, now able to reevaluate the family dynamics in the light of her idealized expectations that her stepmother would be a "replica" of her deceased mother, could empathize with the frustration her step-mother and father experienced because they could not fulfill her hopes. All agreed that the crucial task before them was to grow beyond their early hurts and work toward positive attachments in the here and now. Following this series of intergenerational family interviews, individual therapy with Ginny was resumed.

During the next phase of individual therapy with Ginny, she continued to rework some of the grief issues she had never resolved in relation to her mother's death. In addition, she began to solidify a less idealized but more realistic perception of appropriate step role behavior. This percep-tion helped her to accept that neither her own nor her stepmother's behavior needed to be measured against an idealized childhood per-spective. As the issue of step role behavior was increasingly defined by Ginny in terms of current realities, she began to articulate more openly her resentment toward George for his uninvolvement with Amy and for "dumping" the entire parenting role with Amy on her. She was fearful that unless these problems were addressed, her resentment toward George would mount and increase the distancing already apparent in the marital relationship. When the possibility of a shift to marital therapy for a period of time was explored with Ginny, she believed that this would be the optimal plan if George would agree.

Following some preliminary work to facilitate the shift from individual to a conjoint focus, a period of marital therapy ensued.

During this period, intervention was focused on clarification of mutual expectations of each other in parenting Amy. Ginny, no longer burdened with an idealized image of what her step role performance "should" be, was able to set realistic goals for herself that acknowledged her physical and emotional capabilities.

George, meanwhile, explained that he felt a strong sense of duty toward Amy because she was his biological child and he had legal responsibil-ities toward her. For this reason, he had insisted that Amy come to live with him after her mother died. However, because Amy was only a few months old when he and Amy's mother were divorced, he had never felt close to her, in contrast to his feelings of closeness to his son Jeff. George also described his feelings of unresolved hostility toward Amy's mother. He therefore found it difficult to tolerate her sorrow about her mother's death. Finally, George wondered if he had been right to insist that Amy come to live with him.

The focus of clinical intervention involved recognition of the impor-tance of shared developmental bonds with a child from infancy in ad-dition to legal and biological ties in forging emotional attachments. Inasmuch as George had not lived with Amy since she was a few months old, there had been no opportunity for these bonds to develop as they normally do. It was apparent that while George and Ginny were in an asymmetrical parenting position with Amy in terms of biological and legal bonds, neither had early developmental bonds with her but could share in the process of establishing them. In addition, the problems engendered when a child mourns an absent parent while living with a parent who does not share these feelings was recognized from the perspective of both parent and child. Although more complex in the Blake situation because a formerly divorced spouse had died, therapists often work with remarried families where a child deeply mourns an absent divorced parent while living with a parent who does not share these feelings. In such cases, the therapist must deal with this discrepancy in feelings of loss through recognition of the different emotional experience each has had with the absent person. At the same time, the therapist must encourage an emotional climate and the development of a support system that encourages the working through of the grief. Such an approach is consistent with theories of loss and attachment that indicate that unless the individual has dealt with the different stages of grief and mourning and come to some reconciliation of the loss, new attachments are less likely to be formed.

The nonjudgmental, supportive, and educative focus of the interviews provided a safe context in which George and Ginny could explore their relationship to each other and to Amy. A process of redefinition of the mutual expectations each held of the other was initiated. The discrepancies in these perceptions were examined in terms of the individual needs of each, cultural parent-child patterns of families of origin, and optimal growth opportunities for all. The therapeutic goals were to work toward reduction of marital stress and distance, and, in addition, to help George and Ginny develop channels of communication that would be transferable to working through of differences in other areas. In order to clarify further expectations, but this time between parents and child, the therapeutic task became one of involving Amy because so much of the work in this case revolved around the reverberations of Amy's having come to this household.

As Amy told her story during the family interviews, she timidly revealed her feelings of "not belonging" and her constant fear that she "would do something wrong." She was lonely at school and also felt uncertain about her place there. In addition, Amy talked about her loneliness for her mother and her "other family." As George and Ginny learned about Amy's perceptions and feelings about her situation, they were increasingly able to integrate her needs and feelings with their own. Empathic bonds between parents and child began to emerge.

Therapeutic intervention during this phase focused on the development of support systems on which Amy could draw as well as on her growing bond with her father and stepmother. The possibility of regular contact with the "other" family was explored so that Amy would not lose contact with the family she had known and with which she had lived since she was three years old. She had made clear that the sorrow she experienced not only involved the loss of her mother but also included her stepfather and siblings. When consensus was achieved among all who would be involved in such a plan, arrangements were made for regular visits to the other family. The reciprocal advantage of this plan was that it gave Amy an opportunity to maintain important relationships and ties and to share with others the grief experienced over the loss of her mother. At the same time it gave George and Ginny some of the private time with each other and Jeff that they had lost when Amy came

Work with the school was also initiated to develop a supportive network so that Amy's situation could be more effectively understood by her teachers. The rationale for this approach was twofold: it would accelerate the adjustment to the school environment, and it would reduce tension and facilitate mastery of age-appropriate developmental tasks related to learning. This approach resulted in more active efforts of the teacher to involve Amy in participation with her classmates and reduction of Amy's feelings of dislocation and "not belonging."

Finally, a plan of individualized therapy with Amy was established so that she could work through the feelings of loss and adjustment to her new situation in a therapeutic context. Such a plan was seen to have preventive as well as here-and-now advantages in facilitating Amy's adjustment to her new family situation.

After a period of continued marital therapy with George and Ginny that solidified their mutual expectations of each other vis-à-vis parenting of Amy and increased their ability to "tell each other their feelings and needs instead of distancing," Ginny returned to individual therapy for a brief period in order to solidify her own individual gains.

At the termination of clinical intervention, almost two years after Ginny's initial interview with the agency, there was no evidence of the depression that had been the original reason for the referral. Overall, Ginny said she felt "good about herself." Although still able and willing to look at her own role in interactive processes she no longer needed to see problems as "totally her own." The idealized image of appropriate steprole behavior no longer haunted Ginny, and reality rather than the ideal became the measure of performance.

On a marital level, Ginny reported that she and her husband had been able to maintain the gains that had been initiated during the period of joint therapy. Communication was more open, expectations more explicit, and parenting roles shared in relation to both Amy and Jeff. The feelings of closeness between George and Ginny had been reestablished and the marital bond seemed secure once again.

As Ginny described the parent-child relationships, George and Amy were spending more time together and seemed to be enjoying each other. Ginny was more relaxed with Amy and did not castigate herself if she felt angry with Amy or even at times wished the family comprised only her husband, herself, and Jeff. However, these feelings were less and less frequent, and she and Amy seemed to be reestablishing the positive relationship they had known before Amy came to live with them.

Amy continued to visit her stepfather and her siblings regularly, but the intensity of her need to see then seemed to be lessening. In addition, Amy was no longer a "fringe child" unsure of her place with her peers. She actively enjoyed school and brought home report cards that gave evidence of mastery of learning skills appropriate for her age and grade.

Another gain for Ginny was the improved relationship between herself and her father and stepmother. She reported the growing comfort and warmth she experienced with her stepmother as they shared some now recognized and accepted realistic feelings. The bonus for Amy was grandparents who loved and cared for her as a "real" granddaughter. Thus, at the termination of clinical intervention with the Blakes all family members had been seen and the subjective meaning of the experience from the point of view of each family member was ascertained. The earlier insulation and distancing from each other had yielded to a beginning process of sharing feelings and thoughts, role expectations of each other and self were clarified, and the way for significant attachments and bonding had been opened.

The formulation of realistic goals that were sensitive to the individual needs and feelings of each had facilitated the development of a workable family balance. As evidence of this, Ginny proudly exhibited a mother's day card she had received from Amy with the inscription "to the best mother alive."

The therapist's story of clinical intervention with the Brents, the Maynors, and the Blakes portrays the curious blend of the unique yet recurrent problems for which remarried families seek help. Each of these families was characterized by variations of "hybrid" role structures; remarried family developmental stages and tasks, cultural orientations, and legal realities.

The resolution of strains inherent in the hybrid role was a common problem, yet it was manifested in different ways with each family. Also present in all of the families were problems because of unrealistic or ambiguous role expectations of self and others. This problem, combined with unresolved issues of loss and mourning, resulted in barriers to the formation of remarried attachments and bonds. Ultimately, the Brents, the Maynors, and the Blakes were able to clarify realistic goals for remarried family living. This clarification resulted in greater congruence between expectations and reality so that each family terminated therapy with a reduction in tension and conflict, improved interpersonal relationships, and intrapersonal gains. Finally, each family achieved a workable family balance.

Not all stories of clinical intervention with remarried families work out as well as those of the Brent, Maynor, and Blake families. The therapist's understanding, however, of the built-in realities of the remarried family situation appropriately shared with family members provides a context in which they can determine their best solution to their problems. For example, when the Ronsons, described in chapter two, applied for help after their participation in a family life education course, they clarified that neither could meet the expectations of the other in balancing "old" and "new" ties. They concluded that divorce was their best solution. Similarly, the Deans (chapter two) concluded that compatible coparenting with Kim's absent father was not possible. They decided to move to another state in an effort to solidify the remarried family unit.

Although Ellen Gray's solution was not as drastic as that of either the Ronsons' or the Deans', she concluded that a workable family balance for her would mean coming to terms with the reality that her husband and Nancy might never love each other "just because they loved her." Clearly, clinical intervention that draws from substantive knowledge about the remarried family can help this family improve its situation, accept its limitations, or make informed decisions to charge its environment.

BASIC PRINCIPLES OF INTERVENTION

From an analysis of the clinical process with remarried families who, at termination, had achieved a workable family balance as defined earlier, some basic principles to guide intervention have evolved. These principles derive from a therapeutic commitment to help families balance and fulfill two basic functions: the care, nurture, and socialization of children, and the provision of emotional gratification of adults. In addition, these principles of intervention are implemented through the use of generic practice skills that have been the foundation of clinical intervention with multiple populations in a wide range of settings. Specific to work with the remarried family situation, however, are the following principles:

1. Stress nonpathological, developmental, and transitional aspects of remarried family situational adaptations and adjustments that are related to the two major processes of "blending" and "becoming."

   a. Explore the subjective meanings of the problems for which remarried family members seek help.

   b. Illuminate the objective reality of the remarried family situation as it is relevant to the problems for which they seek help through a cognitive-educative therapeutic process.

   c. Individualize the unique objective reality of each family.

   d. Relate the uniqueness of each family to the more generalized substantive knowledge about the remarried family.

   e. Focus on narrowing the gap between the subjective meanings of the problems to the clients and the objective reality of the remarried family situation.

2. Clarify realistic goals to promote "blending."

   a. Help family members articulate ideas about and achieve consensus on reciprocal role expectations consistent with the objective reality of the remarried family.

   b. Help family members formulate realistic expectations of each other in terms of new attachments.

   c. Help family members establish rules and regulations, communication and socialization patterns, and decision-making and conflict resolution strategies that are sensitive to the values and prior lifestyles of family members.

3. Recognize the structural and legal complexities of the remarried family system.

   a. Affirm the marital unit as a subsystem in its own right by encouraging parents to safeguard time and energy to nurture the marital relationship.

   b. Support the social parent role of the stepparent as appropriate and legitimate.

   c. Emphasize that the marital unit is the parental unit.

   d. Recognize the strength of prior biological, legal, and developmental ties of children toward the absent parent.

   e. Validate the maintenance of prior ties between parents, children, and siblings at the same time that attachments between steppersons are encouraged.

   f. Discourage the maintenance of dysfunctional alignments such as assumption of child advocacy roles by the natural parent for his or her child(ren).

4. Recognize the importance of the unique remarried family developmental life cycle stages and the impact of changes in custodial arrangements on remarried family interaction.

   a. Recognize the near-universality of issues of loss within remarried families for prior family structures and significant absent or deceased persons.

b. Develop information about the ages and sex of each family member at the time of each remarried family developmental stage.

c. Anticipate with remarried family members the range of meaning that changes in custodial arrangements have for the child making the change and for the families.

d. Correlate significant life events unique to the remarried family with family and individual developmental tasks.

e. Identify barriers to the mastery of remarried family and individual developmental tasks.

f. Involve remarried family members in grief and mourning work to deal with issues of loss and to facilitate the development of remarried family attachments and bonds.

5. Facilitate the remarried family process of "becoming." Identify archaic and current dysfunctional cultural orientations that are barriers to positive family identity, individual self-concept, affiliation and attachment with the new family unit, and the development of a workable family balance.

a. Demyth expectations that the remarried family is "no different" from the nuclear family.

b. Demyth fantasies of instant love.

c. Demyth fantasies of parental reunion.

d. Demyth stereotypes of the "wicked" stepparent.

e. Demyth orientations that "step is less."

f. Demyth expectations that remarried family adjustments are easy.

Unfortunately, no blueprint exists for unfailing success with remarried families. The above principles, however, have general applicability to most remarried family situations. They have been observed to facilitate realistic perceptions, to help formulate realistic goals, to promote effective problem solving, and to enhance opportunities for psychosocial growth of all family members. Thus, practitioners have a role in helping remarried families with processes of blending and becoming as these families achieve workable family balances and identities of worth and dignity.

NOTES

1. See Alfred Kadushin, *Adopting Older Children* (New York: Columbia University Press, 1970; and Barbara Tizard, *Adoption: A Second Chance* (London: Open Books, 1977).

11

BEYOND THERAPEUTIC
INTERVENTION

The preceding chapters have focused on the development of a
knowledge base about and therapeutic intervention with the
remarried family. However, more is needed. Although direct clinical intervention is the treatment of choice for many remarried
families, it is, in addition, necessary to move beyond therapeutic
intervention toward broader goals. These include widespread dissemination of knowledge about the remarried family, outreach
programs for those who do not know about or seek direct professional services, and preventive approaches that facilitate the remarried family's achievement of a workable family balance and
cohesion. This concluding chapter discusses some of the methods
and programs by which work toward these goals can begin.

COLLABORATIVE NETWORKS

Collaborative networks between practitioners and other professionals or institutions who may be working with the same individual, family, or group is a long-standing clinical approach that
builds mutual support systems of complementary services for
clients. It has the potential to enhance relevant information sharing (when the client's permission has been obtained), to clarify
goals and services each professional can offer, and to expand em-

pathic understanding of the client's situation by each professional. The combination of these factors contributes to more effective intervention by each discipline because of the synergistic effect that is frequently produced by harmonious collaborative intervention.

An important method through which dissemination of knowledge about the remarried family has been accomplished is the development of case-by-case collaborative networks with professionals in mutual work with remarried families. This approach is useful because it includes key persons who are also working with the remarried family. In this joint effort, practitioners who are informed about the remarried family have the opportunity to educate professionals of related disciplines to the unique aspects of this family situation. This knowledge can then become part of an accumulating body of knowledge that is transferable to other remarried family situations, from which these professionals can draw in later work.

Collaborative networks between mental health and school professionals, appropriate at all levels of education, are particularly important because children's problems are often first noted in school settings. Despite the increased numbers of children who live in remarried families, few schools have mechanisms by which to identify these children or knowledge to help them understand the objective reality of remarried families. Yet, children who are preoccupied with tensions and dilemmas of the remarried family situation are often not able to learn effectively or to deal constructively with peer relationships and with authority. Early detection of these children can result in the development of appropriate support systems in the school and referrals that will facilitate improvement in a child's learning and social adjustment patterns.

In case-by-case collaboration, practitioner and school can work together on behalf of a specific child and clarify those issues that are interfering with the child's academic and social adjustment. In addition, differential diagnostic assessments about which behaviors are aspects of normal childhood development, which reflect long-standing internal dysfunctional dynamics, and which are transitional problems of adaptation to the remarried family situation can be made. Although many teachers, sensitive and concerned about their students, contact social agencies, school social workers, or counselors when a child in the classroom appears to be troubled, an informed body of knowledge about the remarried family would enable them to be even more quickly alerted to the stress encountered by many children in remarried families.

Because increasing numbers of preschool children become members of single-parent and remarried families, the practitioner and the nursery school teacher are often involved in collaborative efforts that focus on the interrelationship of behavior in the nursery school with loss and bonding issues. Through these networks, the nursery school teacher gains a fuller understanding of the family situation and often becomes the "significant other" for these children, within the limits of his or her function as a teacher.

On a more generalized level, it is necessary to develop networks for school administrators for knowledge dissemination about the inherent realities, issues, and dilemmas that are unique to the remarried family. Forecasts that one out of every four children will be a stepchild for some period of time before 1995 underscore the need for a knowledge base about the remarried family that will help schools to develop policies relevant to this special case of family.[1] School personnel, faced with the primary task of educating children in the face of financial stress, time constraints, and heavy work loads, have often not been able to address the special issues of the remarried family that would help them better educate the child who is their educational charge. This situation, combined with interest in not being discriminatory, has contributed to school policies that treat all families as if they were intact nuclear families. On the other hand, hidden assumptions that "step is less" has, at times, been the unspoken communication. In these circumstances, children and parents have been hesitant to declare their identity as members of remarried families.

Central to the development of appropriate school policy is a philosophic orientation that recognizes the unique identity of the remarried family and the need for the school to have certain information in order to deal effectively with the children who live in this family situation. Sensitive to issues of family privacy, confidentiality, and the frequent conflictual relationships between divorced parents, schools have hesitated to seek this information. Yet, confusion about surnames, circumstances when stepparents can make emergency decisions, and the school's relationship with the noncustodial parent are only a few of the many reasons why schools need this information.

Some school administrators have instituted procedures for the use of hyphenated names and cross-referencing when there is no legal entitlement to a child's use of the stepfather's name. Others have been wary about such procedures out of concern about biological parent's rights, while still others have no consistent policy and follow the family's preference.

The uncertain role and limited legal status of stepparents have created difficulties for schools when they have needed to be in contact with the child's family. Although such contact has been welcomed by many stepparents, others have resisted such involvement because they have felt uncomfortable about their stepparent status and role. The lack of information about the family's preference in these situations has resulted in the school's having to make these decisions. This has often resulted in contacts that have bypassed an interested and concerned stepparent or stimulated feelings of anxiety and discomfort if a stepparent has been uncertain of his place in these contacts.

There has been similar, if not even greater, confusion in regard to contact with the noncustodial parent. The growing numbers of fathers' rights movements that seek to establish procedures to make them a more integral part of their children's lives, and remarried families who wish to exclude the noncustodial parents from involvement with the children result in the schools' becoming increasingly the ground on which families debate these issues.

As school personnel expand their understandings of the remarried family, they can begin to clarify what information they need to have and can legitimately request in order to fulfill their obligations. They can then develop objective and routine mechanisms by which to obtain this information. This approach has the value of reducing the anxiety of the student, the family, and the school personnel so the charge of educating the child is not burdened by these additional stresses that do not exist for the nuclear family.

Dissemination of knowledge about the objective realities of the remarried families is also necessary for other institutions that serve remarried families, such as protective and child welfare services. The high incidence of stepchildren who run away or become known to the police for other reasons is currently documented in youth service agencies and court records. Often a police officer sensitized to the complexity of the remarried family is able to make early and appropriate referrals to social agencies. The high numbers of stepchildren in foster homes suggests the need for knowledge dissemination about the complexity of the remarried family situation to child welfare agencies as well as the development of programs that help the child reenter the remarried family system at a later date with greater hope of achievement of a workable family balance that incorporates the stepchild.

PROFESSIONAL EDUCATION

Professional education has been another vehicle for expanded dissemination of substantive knowledge about the therapeutic intervention with the remarried family. Many professional associations and universities have sponsored courses for practitioners in a broad range of social services in this special area of the family in continuing education programs. Social agencies have organized regional conferences and brought specialists into their community to lead staff development workshops and seminars aimed at teaching theory and practice skills for work with the remarried family. In recognition of the need for such specialized knowledge, some universities are currently including courses on the remarried family (by whatever name—blended, merged, reconstituted, or step) as part of their clinical practice curriculum. All of these activities signal that professionals are becoming increasingly aware of the vulnerability and high-risk potential of this population.

FAMILY LIFE EDUCATION

Another direction that has been taken by many social service agencies is family life education programs for socially and legally remarried families. These programs provide an opportunity for participants to explore their problems with others in a similar situation, much as is done in self-help groups. They are led by staff members or, at times, by persons specifically trained in a special interest area. Family life education programs have the advantage of structured clinical leadership that is informed about this population. Participants in family life education groups have usually been recruited through recommendations from agency workers or outreach efforts to the general public.

The concept of family education, originally introduced in 1880 by the Child Study Association, has expanded from an early specific focus on child development to programs concerned with the total gamut of human relationships.[2] Some groups may concentrate on problems of well-defined, vulnerable populations, such as the physically or mentally handicapped, or the single parent; others may focus on a broad societal problem, such as drug abuse, teenage pregnancy, or family violence.

As defined by the Family Service Association of America, family life education has the purpose of enhancing and facilitating family and individual functioning. This purpose is carried out through group learning that combines intellectual and emotional experiences for its members.[3] The general goals of such programs have been to help participants understand and anticipate the patterns and stresses of family and community living in order to prevent or reduce the results of situational crises and to improve interpersonal relationships. Given the barometer-like response of family life education to social change, social problems, and vulnerable populations, its present interest in the remarried family is consistent with its purpose and goals.

The value of the family life education approach to work with the remarried family population lies in the recognition that, for many, the door of entry into the examination of concerns is through participation in a supportive group process that stresses normative aspects of a life situation. Through this process of group sharing under competent leadership, more effective ways of coping with problems are often identified.

As in work in the individual or family unit in direct clinical intervention, many remarried parents ask why the adjustment processes are so difficult when there are children of a prior marriage. The transmission of knowledge about the remarried family situation and an understanding of frequently related problems often lead to finding more effective ways to cope with normal nonpathological processes. Often members of family life education groups follow up their activity in this program with application for individualized or family help. Conversely, practitioners working with remarried family parents sometimes make referrals of these couples to family life education programs as an adjunct to clinical intervention.

Some family education groups have been carried out with stepchildren. Such programs have been formed through youth service organizations, church groups, and schools working independently or in collaboration with social agencies. Significantly, the formation of such groups has, at times, originated as grass-roots efforts of adolescent stepchildren asking for help in learning to live in the step situation. In addition, teachers, counselors, and school social workers have identified students who were having difficulties in academic performance and social relationships and were also having problems in adjusting to the remarried family situation. Additionally, many elementary schools are making such peer groups, led by trained clinical persons, available to children who are observed to be having social and academic difficulties and are in remarried families. The groups help children articulate their feelings and identify their concerns. At times, these groups are extended to include parents, in order to encourage dialogue between parents and children. When difficulties require additional therapeutic intervention, referral to appropriate resources can be made. As in work with remarried parent family life education groups, the normative aspects of the adjustment processes are emphasized. Ways of living more comfortably in the remarried family have been the focus of discussion.

On a preventive level, family life education programs have been developed for the single parent planning remarriage and for never-before-married persons expecting to become stepparents. The purpose of these programs has been to initiate a process of anticipatory socialization. The frequency of remarried parents' comments that they had no preparation for some of the normal processes of adjustment and adaptation to their family situation has emphasized the importance of this effort. Although the confrontation with the realities of some typical adjustments has occasionally resulted in a single parent deciding not to remarry, most who have been queried about their participation in such programs have found that the information helped them to make decisions that avoided stereotyped myths.

Many agencies have, in addition, provided services of their professional staff to self-help groups such as Parents Without Partners and stepparent self-help groups, to explore the issues of remarriage as aspects of prevention and early intervention. The broadened spectrum of intervention on behalf of the remarried family from that of therapist to builder of collaborative support systems with relevant other professions and to group leader in family life education thus begins to reach ever-widening segments of the remarried family population. However, still more is needed—this time in the form of education to the larger community.

EDUCATION OF
THE LARGER COMMUNITY

The interest of the general community in the remarried family is made evident through television programs, human interest stories, special editions of newspapers and magazines, and the proliferation of self-help books written by stepparents. However, many of these presentations reflect polar extremes of idealized family reconstitution or victimized steppersons. Once again, it is important to bring the objective reality of this family situation before the general public so that archaic misconceptions that "step is less" and new popular myths of "no difference" can be reexamined in the light of reality.

At the heart of such misconceptions is the need to break down stereotypes that have been part of the lore for centuries and, in addition, prevent the solidification of new myths based on denial mechanisms that seek to ignore the differences between the nuclear and remarried family situations. The critical and fundamental issue that underlies these myths, archaic and newly fashioned, is that of family identity—a concept basic to the remarried family process of becoming a family in its own right.

Erik H. Erikson has helped us to understand that the significant thrust of all individuals to establish one's identity is a lifelong developmental task.[4] Family theorists have identified the status-conferring aspect of the family as a cultural issue crucial to family identity. It is anticipated that identity issues will continue to be dominant cultural and psychological themes of postindustrial society.[5] Thus, issues of identity are expected to continue to be of key importance to individual and family development.

The inescapable professional task requires that a groundwork be laid for appropriate redefinitions and cultural reorientations toward the remarried family. Professionals have contributed to this endeavor through television and lecture appearances, written articles, interviews, and participation on panels of public interest forums and community service programs. The expectation is that as the general public becomes better informed, it will be in a better position to evaluate existing ideas and formulate new outlooks on the remarried family that are congruent with reality.

INTERDISCIPLINARY RESEARCH AND FAMILY POLICY

Still needed in the broadened spectrum of service on behalf of the remarried family are the coordinated efforts of mental health professionals and the social science community. More extensive clinical research to test practice wisdom and existing theories is needed. Such research could elaborate and refine knowledge and discover additional understandings about this special case of family. Practitioners, historically reluctant to disrupt the natural flow of the therapeutic process, have often been unwilling to pursue the research aspect of clinical practice. Increasing attention to research designs that are congruent with and build on the clinical process as it naturally occurs suggest directions that will combine research and clinical goals that advance practice.

On a clinical level, studies are needed to identify factors that help families achieve a workable family balance and therapeutic interventions are needed that could facilitate the strengthening of these factors. Research is also needed to explore the adjustments of remarried family members in the various custodial arrangements and their association with the achievement of a workable family balance. Finally, studies are necessary to identify those factors that have contributed to successful "blending and becoming" in remarried families who have not sought professional help.

On a global level, large-scale sociological studies are needed to identify the role of specific aspects of social change on cultural and legal orientations toward the remarried family. In addition, cross-national and cross-cultural studies are needed to explore possible differences among remarried families who seek help according to ethnic and racial backgrounds, rural and urban environments, socioeconomic status, and specific aspects of family culture and background.

Creative interdisciplinary teams could launch such studies and add to a further understanding of all families in general and the remarried family in particular. This knowledge could then be used by legislators and social policymakers to evaluate social problems and develop family policy at state and federal levels.

Policies are currently needed that foster cultural reorientations about the remarried family and individualize and institutionalize it as being *different* from the nuclear family, but still a real family of worth and value. Such issues as selecting a uniform name for the remarried family and differentiating it from the nuclear family in census counts would represent beginning attempts to validate this variation in the constellation of families.

Also needed are legal doctrines that do not regard stepparents as strangers and, instead, value them as involved and interested social parents who can and do make constructive contributions to the developmental and psychological growth of their stepchildren. This recognition must ultimately be reflected in family law that balances children's rights, natural parents' rights, and step-parents' rights. Perhaps the future creative leap is in legal and social doctrines that recognize the "best interests of all."

A FINAL NOTE

The family today is in a kaleidoscopic explosion of alternative lifestyles and multiple family forms. The end of the nineteenth century saw the erosion of the extended family and the emergence of the nuclear family as the dominant family form. Today, toward the end of the twentieth century, the erosion of the nuclear family and the increased numbers and visibility of the remarried family have been documented. Yet, the nuclear family, despite encroachment on its space by many different family structures, will continue to be the building block of society unless and until medical technology finds more feasible and expedient ways to provide for the continuation of mankind. The family, whatever its form, has continued to be a key societal institution that contributes to the mental helth of its members, and, consequently, to the well-being of society. In addition, it is known that all individuals and families share common human needs. Basic among these has been man's enduring need for meaningful human relationships in the context of the family. The remarried family, reflective of man's search for meaningful relationships, will continue as a companion structure to the nuclear family, sharing more or less of its space with other family structures depending on changing values and ideologies.

It is not possible to know which of the many evolving family forms will be the dominant family form of the future or what other vulnerable structures may yet emerge. What is known is that there is a continuum of change in family structure and function over time. The clinical mission of identifying those who are in jeopardy and high-risk populations is an ongoing one. The search for answers to questions that enhance knowledge and understanding of newly identified vulnerable populations must continue; so also must the process of testing the applicability of this knowledge in clinical intervention. In time, the broader spectrum of dissemination of such knowledge, constantly refined and expanded by further research, must proceed. Ultimately, such knowledge must filter into the decision-making and legislative processes to strengthen the family through effective and integrative family social policy.

Thus, a continuous process has been identified, one that is a necessary aspect of the best possible service the professional can offer to the client. Through this process, practitioners will be consistently involved in helping clients meet the challenge that their unique situations may impose and in helping those they serve realize the promise of meaningful relationships.

NOTES

1. Personal communication with Paul G. Glick, senior demographer for the United States Bureau of the Census, August 1980.
2. Roberta H. Wooten, "Family Life Education," *Encyclopedia of Social Work* (Washington, D.C.: National Association of Social Workers, 1977), p. 423.
3. Ibid.
4. See Erik H. Erikson, *Childhood and Society* 2nd ed. (New York: W.W. Norton, 1963); and Erik H. Erikson, *Identity: Youth and Crisis* (New York: W.W. Norton, 1968).
5. See Burkhart Holzner and John H. Marx, *Knowledge Application* (Boston: Allyn and Bacon, 1979), pp. 313–17; and Daniel Bell, *The Coming of Post-Industrial Society* (New York: Basic Books, 1973).

BIBLIOGRAPHY

Ackerman, Nathan. *Psychodynamics of Family Life*. New York: Basic Books, 1970.

Adams, Bert N. *The Family: A Sociological Interpretation*. Chicago: Rand McNally, 1980.

Aldous, Joan. *Family Careers: Developmental Change in Families*. New York: John Wiley, 1978.

Anderson, Ralph E., and Carter, Ira. *Human Behavior in the Social Environment: A Social Systems Approach*, 2d. ed. Chicago: Aldine, 1978.

Anthony, E., James, and Koupernick, Cyrille, eds. *The Child in His Family*. New York: John Wiley, 1970.

Antonucci, Toni. "Attachment: A Life Span Concept." *Human Development*, vol. 19 (1976).

Barash, Meyer, and Scourby, Alice, eds. *Marriage and the Family: A Comparative Analysis of Contemporary Problems*. New York: Random House, 1970.

Batt, John. "Child Custody Disputes: A Developmental-Psychological Approach in Proof and Decision Making." *Wilamette Law Journal*, vol. 12 (1976).

Bell, Daniel. *The Coming of the Post-Industrial Society*. New York: Basic Books, 1973.

Bell, John E. *Family Therapy*. New York: Jason Aronson, 1974.

Bell, Norman W., and Vogel, Ezra F., eds. *The Family*, rev. ed. New York: Free Press, 1968.

Benedek, Richard S., and Benedek, Elissa P. "Post-Divorce Visitation: A Child's Right." *American Academy of Child Psychiatry*, vol. 16, no. 2. (Spring 1977).

Berman, Claire. *Making It as a Step-parent*. New York: Doubleday, 1980.

Bernard, Jesse. *Remarriage: A Study of Marriage*. New York: Dryden Press, 1956.

Bernstein, Saul, ed. *Explorations in Group Work: Essays in Theory and Practice*. Boston: Boston University School of Social Work, 1965.

Berrien, Kenneth F. *General and Social Systems*. New Brunswick, N.J.: Rutgers University Press, 1968.

Berry, J.W., and Annis, R.C. "Acculturative Stress." *Journal of Cross-Cultural Psychology*, vol. 5 (1974).

Bertalanffy, Ludwig von. *General Systems Theory*. New York: George Braziller, 1968.

The Remarried Family

Bettelheim, Bruno. *The Uses of Enchantment: The Meaning and Importance of Fairy Tales.* New York: Alfred A. Knopf, 1976.

Block, Joel D. *To Marry Again.* New York: Grosset and Dunlap, 1979.

Blood, Robert O., Jr. "A Situational Approach to the Study of Permissiveness in Child-Rearing." *American Sociological Review,* vol. 18 (February 1953).

Blumer, Herbert. *Symbolic Interactionism: Perspective and Method.* Englewood Cliffs, N.J.: Prentice-Hall, 1969.

Bohannan, Paul. *Divorce and After.* Garden City, N.Y.: Doubleday/Anchor Books, 1971.

Bossard, James H.S. *The Large Family System.* Philadelphia: University of Pennsylvania Press, 1956.

———, and Boll, Eleanor S. *Family Situations.* Philadelphia: University of Pennsylvania Press, 1943.

Boszormenyi-Nagy Ivan, and Framo, James. *Intensive Family Therapy.* New York: Harper and Row, 1969.

———, and Sparks, Geraldine. *Invisible Loyalties.* New York: Harper and Row, 1973.

Boulding, Kenneth. "General Systems Theory: The Skeletons of Science." In *Modern Systems Research for the Behavioral Scientist,* edited by Walter Buckley. Chicago: Aldine, 1968.

Bowen, Murray. *Family Therapy in Clinical Practice,* New York: Jason Aronson, 1978.

Bowerman, Charles E., and Irish, Donald P. "Some Relationships of Stepchildren to Their Parents." *Marriage and Family Living,* vol. 24 (May 1962).

Bowlby, John. *Attachment and Loss.* New York: Basic Books, 1969.

Brosky, John G., and Alford, John G. "Sharpening Solomon's Sword: Current Considerations in Child Custody Cases." *Dickenson Law Review,* vol. 81 (Summer 1977).

Burchinall, Lee G. "Characteristics of Adolescents from Unbroken, Broken and Reconstituted Families." *Journal of Marriage and Family Living,* vol. 26 (February 1964).

Burgess, Ernest. "Unity of Interacting Personalities." *The Family,* vol. 7 (March 1926).

Caban v. Mohammed. *United States Law Week: 4462,* vol. 47 (April 1979).

California Civil Code, Sec. 5127.6. St. Paul, Minn.: West Publishing, 1981.

Carrierri, Joseph R. and Murawski, Walter. "Proposing Standards for Child Custody: The Proceedings, The Role of the Agency, and the Best Interests of the Child." *Fordham Urban Law Journal,* vol. 6 (Winter 1978).

Carr, Lowell J. *Situational Analysis: An Observational Approach to Introductory Sociology.* New York: Harper and Brothers, 1948.

Cartwright, Darwin, and Zander, Alvin. *Group Dynamics.* New York: Harper and Row, 1968.

Cavalho-Neto, Paulo de. *Folklore and Psychoanalysis.* Translated by Jacques M. P. Wilson. Coral Gables, Fla.: University of Miami Press, 1972.

Chance, N.A. "Acculturation, Self Identification and Personality Adjustment." *American Anthropologist,* vol. 67 (1965).

Charny, Israel W. "Integrated Individual and Family Psychotherapy." *Family Process,* vol. 5 (September 1966).

Chin, Robert. "The Utility of Systems Models and Developmental Models for Practitioners." In *The Planning of Change,* edited by Warren Bennis, Kenneth

Bibliography

Benns, and Robert Chin. New York: Holt, Rinehart and Winston, 1961.

Churchman, C. West. *The Systems Approach.* New York: Delta, 1968.

Clarke, Homer H., Jr. *Law of Domestic Relations.* St. Paul, Minn.: West Publishing, 1968.

Clayton, Richard R. *The Family, Marriage and Social Change.* Lexington, Mass.: D.C. Heath, 1975.

Cooley, Charles H. *Human Nature and the Social Order,* rev. ed. New York: Scribner's, 1922.

Coser, Rose Laub, ed. *The Family: Its Structure and Functions,* 2d. ed. New York: St. Martin's Press, 1974.

Coyle, Grace Longwell. "Concepts Relevant to Helping the Family as a Group." *Social Casework,* vol. 43 (July 1962).

Dahl, Barbara A.; McCubbin, Hamilton I.; and Lester, Gary R. "War-Induced Father Absence: Comparing the Adjustment of Children in Reunited, Non-reunited and Reconstituted Families." *International Journal of Sociology of the Family,* vol. 6 (1976).

Derdeyn, Andre P. "Child Custody Contests in Historical Perspective." *The American Journal of Psychiatry,* vol. 133 (December 1976).

————, and Wadlington, Walter J., III. "Adoption: The Rights of Parents versus the Best Interests of Their Children." *American Academy of Child Psychiatry,* vol. 16, no. 2 (Spring 1977).

Deutsch, Helene. *The Psychology of Women: Motherhood, A Psychoanalytic Interpretation.* New York: Bantam, 1973.

Devine, James R. "A Child's Right to Independent Counsel in Custody Proceedings." *Seton Hall Law Review,* vol. 6 (1975).

Dohrenwend, Barbara Snell, and Dohrenwend, Bruce P. *Stressful Life Events: Their Nature and Effects.* New York: John Wiley, 1974.

————. "Toward a Theory of Acculturation." *South Western Journal of Anthropology,* vol. 18 (1962).

Dorsen, Richard, ed. *Folkways and Folklife.* Chicago: University of Chicago Press, 1972.

Duberman, Lucille. "On Becoming a Family," doctoral diss. Case Western Reserve University, 1973.

————. "Step-Kin Relationships." *Journal of Marriage and the Family,* vol. 35 (May 1973).

Duvall, Evelyn. *Family Development,* 2d. ed. New York J.B. Lippincott, 1962.

Edwards, John, ed. *The Family and Change.* New York: Alfred A. Knopf, 1960.

Erikson, Erik. H. *Childhood and Society,* rev. ed. New York: W.W. Norton, 1963.

————. *Identity and the Life Cycle. Selected Papers.* New York: International Universities Press, 1959.

Euripides. "Hippolytus." In *The Complete Greek Tragedies,* vol. 3, edited by David Green and Richard Lattimore. Chicago: The University of Chicago Press, 1960.

Fainer, Robert, and Wasser, Dennis Matthew. "Child Custody and Visitation Disputes: An Overview." *The Los Angeles Lawyer,* July 1978.

Farber, Bernard. *Family and Kinship in Modern Society.* Glenview. Ill.: Scott, Foresman, 1972.

Fast, Irene, and Cain, Albert C. "The Step-parent Role: Potential for Disturbance in Family Functioning." *American Journal of Orthopsychiatry,* vol. 36 (April 1966).

Foster, Henry F., and Freed, Doris Jones. "Life with Father: 1978." *Family Law*

Quarterly, vol. 11 (Winter 1978).

Fortes, Meyer. "Step-Parenthood and Juvenile Delinquency." *Sociological Review*, vol. 25 (1933).

Fox, Robin. *Kinship and Marriage: An Anthropological Perspective*. Harmondsworth, Middx.: Penguin Books, 1971.

Fraiberg, Selma. *Every Child's Birthright: In Defense of Mothering*. New York: Bantam, 1978.

Freeman, David Simon. "Social Work with Families: A Systems Approach to a Unified Theoretical Model," doctoral diss. University of Southern California, 1973.

Freeman, Nora L. "Remodeling Adoption Statutes After Stanley v. Illinois." *Journal of Family Law*, vol. 15 (1976–1977).

Fromm, Erich. *The Forgotten Language: An Introduction to the Meanings of Dreams Fairy Tales and Myths*. New York: Grove Press, 1957.

Gardner, Richard A. *The Boys and Girls Book about Divorce*. New York: Service House, 1970.

Gaskell, Elizabeth. *Wives and Daughters*. 1864, reprint. New York: Penguin Books, 1979.

Geertz, Clifford. "Blurred Genres." *The American Scholar*, vol. 49 (Spring 1980).

Germain, Carel B. "Social Casework: An Historical Encounter," In *Theories of Social Casework*, edited by Robert Roberts and Robert Nee, Chicago: University of Chicago Press, 1970.

———. "Social Study: Past, Present and Future." *Social Casework*, vol. 49 (July 1968).

Gill, Margaret M. "Adoption of Older Children: The Problems Faced." *Social Casework*, vol. 59 (May 1978).

Girardot, N.J. "Initiation and Meaning in the Tale of Snow White and the Seven Dwarfs." *Journal of American Folklore*, vol. 90 (July-September 1977).

Glendon, Mary Ann. "The American Family in the 200th Year of the Republic." *Family Law Quarterly*, vol. 10 (Winter 1977).

———. "Power and Authority in the Family: New Legal Patterns as Reflections of Changing Ideologies." *American Journal of Comparative Law*, vol. 23 (Winter 1975).

Glenn, Norval D., and Weaver, Charles N. "The Marital Happiness of Remarried Divorced Persons." *Journal of Marriage and the Family*, vol. 39 (May 1977).

Glick, Ira O.; Weiss, Robert S.; and Parkes, C. Murray. *The First Year of Bereavement* New York: John Wiley, 1974.

Glick, Paul C. "Children of Divorced Parents in Demographic Perspective." *Journal of Social Issues*, vol. 35 no. 4 (1979).

———. "First Marriages and Remarriages." *American Sociological Review*, vol. (December 1949).

———. "Living Arrangements of Children and Young Adults." Revision of a paper presented at the Annual Meeting of the Population Association of America, United States Census Bureau. Washington, D.C., 1975.

———. "Some Recent Changes in American Families." In *Current Population Reports* Washington, D.C.: United States Government Printing Office. 1976.

———, and Norton, Arthur J. "Marrying. Divorcing and Living Together in the United States Today." *Population Bulletin*, vol. 32, no. 5 (October 1977).

———, and Spanier, Graham. "Married and Unmarried Cohabitation in the United States." *Journal of Marriage and the Family*, vol. 42 (February 1980).

Bibliography

Goldstein, Joseph; Freud, Anna; and Solnit, Albert J. *Beyond the Best Interests of the Child.* London: Free Press, 1973.

————, and Katz, Jay, eds. *The Family and the Law.* New York: Free Press, 1965.

Gorer, Geoffrey. *Death, Grief and Mourning.* London: Cressett Press, 1965.

Goode, William J. *After Divorce.* Glencoe, Ill.: Free Press, 1956.

Gordon, Michael, ed. *The American Family in Historical Perspective.* New York: St. Martin's Press, 1978.

Grinker, Roy R., Sr., ed. *Toward a Unified Theory of Human Behavior,* 2d. ed. New York: Basic Books, 1967.

Guerin, Philip. *Family Therapy: Theory and Practice.* New York: Halsted Press, 1976.

Habenstein, Robert W., and Queen, Stuart A. *The Family in Various Cultures,* 4th ed. Philadelphia: J.B. Lippincott, 1974.

Hamilton, Gordon. *Theory and Practice of Social Case Work.* New York: Columbia University Press, 1940.

Handel, Gerald, ed. *The Psycho-social Interior of the Family: A Sourcebook for Study of Whole Families,* 2d. ed. Chicago: Aldine, 1972.

Hansen, Donald A., and Hill, Rueben. "Families Under Stress." In *Handbook of Marriage and the Family,* edited by Harold T. Christenson. Chicago: Rand McNally, 1964.

Hartman, Ann. "Diagramatic Assessment of Family Relationships." *Social Casework,* vol. 59 (October 1978).

Hearn, Gordon, ed. *The General Systems Approach Contributions Toward an Holistic Conception of Social Work.* New York: Council on Social Work Education, 1970.

Heilpern, Else. "Psychological Problems of Step-Children." *The Psychoanalytic Review,* vol. 30 (April 1943).

Heiss, Jerold, ed. *Family Roles and Interaction: An Anthology,* 2d ed. Chicago: Rand McNally, 1976.

Henszey, Benjamin. "Visitation by a Non-Custodial Parent: What is the 'Best Interest Doctrine." *Journal of Family Law,* vol. 15 (1976–1977).

Hollis, Florence. *Casework: A Psychosocial Therapy,* 2d ed. New York: Random House, 1972.

Holzner, Burkhart, and Marx, John H. *Knowledge Application.* Boston: Allyn and Bacon, 1979.

Homans, George C. *Social Behavior: Its Elementary Forms.* New York: Harcourt, Brace and Jovanovich, 1961.

Horracks, John E. *The Psychology of Adolescence.* Boston: Houghton Mifflin, 1969.

Howe, Ruth-Arlene W. "Divorce: Critical Issues for Legal and Mental Health Professionals. *Urban Socal Change Review,* vol. 10 (Winter 1977).

Hunter, Evan. *Me and Mr. Stenner.* Philadelphia: J.B. Lippincott, 1976.

Ibsen, Henrik. *Little Eyolf. In The Complete Major Prose Plays of Henrik Ibsen.* Translated by Rolf Fjelde. New York: Farrar, Strauss and Giroux, 1978.

Janchill, Sister Mary Paul. "Systems Concepts in Casework Theory and Practice." *Social Casework,* vol. 50 (February, 1969).

Jenkins, Shirley. *Planning for Children of Divorce.* New York: Child Welfare League, 1976.

Jeter, Helen R. *Child Problems and Services in Child Welfare Programs.* Children's Bureau pub. 403. Washington, D.C.: United States Government Printing Office, 1963.

The Remarried Family

Jung, Carl. *The Archetypes and the Collective Unconscious*. Princeton, N.J.: Princeton University Press, 1981.

———. *Man and His Symbols*. New York: Doubleday, 1964.

Justice, Blair, and Justice, Rita. *The Broken Taboo*. New York: Human Sciences Press, 1979.

Kadushin, Alfred. *Adopting Older Children*. New York: Columbia University Press, 1970.

———. *The Social Work Interview*. New York: Columbia University Press, 1972.

Kahlique, Nazre. "A Study of Insecurity Feeling and Anxiety in Stepchildren and Non-Step Children." *Journal of Psychological Research*, vol. 5 (1961).

Kalter, Suzy. *Instant Parent*. New York: A. and W. Publishers, 1979.

Kamerman, Sheila B., and Kahn, Alfred J., eds. *Family Policy: Government and Families in Fourteen Countries*. New York: Columbia University Press, 1978.

Kanter, David, and Lehr, William. *Inside the Family*. San Francisco: Jossey-Bass, 1978.

Katz, Sanford. *When Parents Fail*. Boston: Beacon Press, 1971.

Kenniston, Kenneth. "Social Change and Youth in America." *Daedalus*, vol. 91 (Winter 1962).

———, and the Carnegie Council on Children. *All our Children: The American Family Under Pressure*. New York: Harcourt, Brace Jovanovich, 1977.

Kephart, William M. *The Family, Society, and the Individual*, 3d ed. Boston: Houghton Mifflin, 1972.

Knox, David. *Exploring Marriage and the Family*. Glenview, Ill.: Scott Foresman, 1979.

Kristen, M. Williams. *Remarriages, United States*. Rockville, Md.: National Center for Health Statistics, 1973.

La Roche, Shirley. "The Role of the Stepfather in the Family," doctoral diss. University of New Mexico, 1974.

Landis, Judson T. "The Trauma of Children When Parents Divorce." *Marriage and Family Living*, vol. 22 (February 1960).

Landis, Paul H. "Sequential Marriage." *Journal of Home Economics*, vol. 42 (October 1950).

"Lawyering for the Child: Principles of Representation in Custody and Visitation Disputes Arising from Divorce." *Yale Law Review*, vol. 87 (May 1978). (Note.)

Leslie, Gerald R. *The Family in Social Context*, 3d ed. London: Oxford University Press, 1976.

Levi-Strauss, Claude. *The Elementary Structures of Kinship*. Boston: Beacon Press, 1969.

Levinger, George, and Moles, Oliver C. *Divorce and Separation: Context, Causes and Consequences*. New York: Basic Books, 1977.

Levinson, Daniel J. *The Seasons of a Man's Life*. New York: Alfred A. Knopf, 1978.

Lewis, Jerry M. et al. *No Single Thread: Psychological Health in Family Systems*. New York: Brunner/Mazel, 1976.

Lidz, Theodore. *The Person: His Development Throughout the Life Cycle*. New York: Basic Books, 1968.

Lindemann, Eric. "Symptomatology and Management of Acute Grief." *American Journal of Psychiatry*, vol. 101 (1944).

Locke, Harvey J., and Klausner, William J. "Marital Adjustment of Divorced Persons in Subsequent Marriage." *Sociology and Social Research*, vol. 33 (November 1948).

Bibliography

Maddox, Brenda. *The Half-Parent*. New York: McEvans and Co., 1975.

Mahler, Margaret S. *The Psychological Birth of the Human Infant*. New York: Basic Books, 1975.

Maier, Henry W. *Three Theories of Child Development*, rev. ed. New York: Harper and Row, 1969.

Maisch, Herbert. *Incest*. Translated by C. Bearne. New York: Stein and Day, 1972.

Marschall, Patricia H., and Gatz, Margaret J. "The Custody Decision Process: Toward New Roles for Parents and the State." *North Carolina Central Law Journal*, vol. 7 (Fall 1975).

Masterson, James F. *Psychotherapy of the Borderline Adult*. New York: Brunner/Mazel, 1976.

Mayleas, Davidyne. *Rewedded Bliss*. New York: Basic Books. 1977.

McCarthy, James. "A Comparison of the Probability of Dissolution of First and Second Marriages." *Demography*, vol. 5 (August 1978).

McGough, Lucy S., and Shindell, Lawrence M. "Coming of Age: The Best Interests of the Child Standard in Third-Party Custody Disputes." *Emory Law Journal*, vol. 5 (1978).

McHugh, Peter. *Defining the Situation*. Indianapolis Bobbs-Merrill, 1968.

Mead, George C. *Mind, Self and Society*. Chicago: University of Chicago Press, 1966.

Mead, Margaret. *Culture and Commitment*. Garden City, N.Y.: Doubleday, 1978.

Meiselman, Karin C. *Incest*. San Francisco: Jossey Bass, 1978.

Merriam, Adele Stuart. "The Stepfather in the Family." *Social Service Review*, vol. 14 (December 1940).

Messinger, Lillian. "Remarriages Between Divorced People and Children from Previous Marriages: A Proposal for Preparation for Remarriage." *Journal of Marriage and Family Counseling*, vol. 2 (April 1976).

Minuchin, Salvador et al. *Families and Family Therapy*. Cambridge, Mass.: Harvard University Press, 1974.

Mnookin, Robert H. "Child Custody Adjudication: Judicial Functions in the Face of Indeterminancy." *Law and Contemporary Problems*, vol. 39 (Summer 1975).

Monahan, Thomas P. "The Changing Nature and Instability of Remarriages." *Eugenics Quarterly*. vol. 5 (June 1950).

———. "How Stable are Remarriages?" *American Journal of Sociology*, vol. 58 (November 1952).

vol. 5 (June 1950).

Moore, Bernece Milburn, and Holtzman, Wayne H. *Tomorrow's Parents: A Study of Youth and Their Families*. Austin, Tx.: University of Texas Press, 1968.

Moore, Maurice J., and O'Connell, Martin "Perspectives on American Fertility." In *Current Population Reports*, special studies series P-23, no. 70 Washington, D.C.: United States Government Printing Office, July 1978.

Moroney, Robert M. *The Family and the State: Considerations of Social Policy*. London: Longman, 1976.

National Center for Social Statistics. "Adoptions in 1975." Report no. E-10. Washington, D.C.: United States Government Printing Office, 1977.

Neugarten, Bernice L., ed. *Middle Age and Aging*. Chicago: University of Chicago Press, 1975.

New York Court of Appeals, "Finlay v. Finlay." *American Law Reports Annotated*, *208 N.Y.S. 585, rev. 240 N.Y. 429, 1925.*

New York Domestic Relations Law., Secs. 31 and 32. New York: McKinney, 1980.

The Remarried Family

Newcomb, Paul R. "Cohabitation in America: An Assessment of Consequences." *Journal of Marriage and the Family*, vol. 41 (August 1979).

Noble, June, and Nobles, William. *How to Live with Other People's Children*. New York: Hawthorne Books, 1977.

Nock, Stephen. "The Family Life Cycle." *Journal of Marriage and the Family*, vol. 41 (February 1979).

Nye, Ivan F. "Child Adjustment in Broken and in Unhappy Unbroken Homes." *Journal of Marriage and Family Living*, vol. 19 (November 1957).

————, and Berardo, Felix M. *Emerging Conceptual Frameworks in Family Analysis* New York: Macmillan, 1966.

O'Neill, Eugene."Desire Under the Elms." In *Three Plays* New York: Random House, 1959.

Okpaku, Sheila. "Psychology: Impediment or Aid in Child Custody Cases?" *Rutgers Law Review*, vol. 29 (1972).

Paredes, Americo, and Bauman, Richard, eds. *Toward a New Perspective in Folklore*. Austin, Tx.: University of Texas Press, 1972.

"Parent and Child." *American Jurisprudence*, vol. 59 (1978 Supplement).

Parkes, C. Murray. *Bereavement*. London: Tavistock Publications, 1972.

————. "Psycho-Social Transitions: A Field of Study." *Social Sciences and Medicine.*, vol. 3 (1971).

Parsons, Talcott, and Bales, Robert F. *Family, Socialization and Interaction Process*. New York: Free Press, 1955.

Perlman, Helen H. *Social Casework: A Problem-Solving Process*. Chicago: University of Chicago Press, 1957.

Pfleger, Janet. "The Wicked Stepmother in a Child Guidance Clinic." *Smith College Studies in Social Work*, vol. 17 (1946–1947).

Podolsky, Edward. "The Emotional Problems of the Stepchild." *Mental Hygiene*, vol. 39 (1955).

Radcliffe-Brown, Alfred R. *Structure and Function in Primitive Society*. New York: Free Press, 1965.

Reingold, Carmel. *Remarriage*. New York: Harper and Row, 1976.

Rice, Robert M., ed. *American Family Policy: Content and Context*. New York: Family Service Association of America, 1977.

————. *Family Listening Post*. New York: Family Service Association of America., 1977.

Roberts, Robert W., and Nee, Robert H., eds. *Theories of Social Casework*. Chicago: University of Chicago Press, 1970.

————, and Northen, Helen, eds. *Theories of Social Work with Groups*. New York: Columbia University Press, 1976.

Robinson, Margaret. "Stepfamilies: A Reconstituted Family System." Unpublished paper, 1979.

Roosevelt, Ruth, and Lofas, Jeanette. *Living in Step*. New York: Stein and Day, 1976.

Rosen, Robert. "Complexity as a System Property." *International Journal of General Systems*, vol. 3 (1977).

Rosenbaum, Jean, and Rosenbaum, Veryl. *Stepparenting*. New York: E.P. Dutton, 1978.

Roth, Allen. "The Tender Years Presumption in Child Custody Disputes." *Journal of Family Law*, vol. 15 (1976–1977).

Bibliography

Sampson, Edward E. *Social Psychology and Contemporary Society*, rev. ed. John Wiley, 1976.

Sander, Fred M. *Individual and Family Therapy: Toward an Integration*. New York: Jason Aronson, 1979.

Schlesinger, Benjamin. "Husband-Wife Relationships in Reconstituted Families." *Social Science Quarterly*, vol. 52 (Summer 1977).

——. "Remarriage—An Inventory of Findings." *The Coordinator, col.* 17(October 1968).

Schneider, David M. *American Kinship: A Cultural Account*. Englewood Cliffs, N.J.: Prentice-Hall, 1968.

——, and Smith, Raymond T. *Class Differences and Sex Roles in American Kinship and Family Structure*. Englewood Cliffs, N.J.: Prentice-Hall, 1973.

Schorr, Alvin L. "Views on Family Policy." *Journal of Marriage and the Family*, vol. 41 (August 1979).

Schulman, Gerda. "Myths That Intrude on the Adaptation of the Stepfamily." *Social Casework*, vol. 53 (March 1972).

Schwartz, Bernard. *The Law in America*. New York: McGraw-Hill, 1974.

Schiller, Ronald C. "Child Custody: Evolution of Current Criteria." *DePaul Law Review*, vol. 26 (Winter 1977).

Schoenberg, Bernard et al. *Loss and Grief*. New York: Columbia University Press, 1970.

Schultz, Duane. *Theories of Personality*. Monterey, Calif.: Brooks/Cole, 1979.

Schutz, David A. *The Changing Family: Its Functions and Future*. Englewood Cliffs, N.J.: Prentice-Hall, 1972.

Schutz, William C. *The Interpersonal Underworld*. Reprint of *Firo: A Three Dimensional Theory of Interpersonal Behavior*. Palo Alto, Calif.: Science and Behavior Books, 1966.

Sherif, Muzofer, and Sherif, Carolyn W. *Interdisciplinary Relationships in the Social Sciences*. Chicago: Aldine, 1969.

Siegel, David M., and Hurley, Suzanne. "Role of Child's Preference." *Family Law Quarterly*, vol. 11 (Spring 1977).

Simon, Anne W. *Stepchild in the Family*. New York: Odyssey Press, 1964.

Simos, Bertha G. *A Time to Grieve: Loss as a Universal Human Experience*. New York: Family Service Association of America, 1979.

Siporin, Max. "Situational Assessment and Intervention." *Social Casework*, vol. 53 (February 1972).

Sluckin, Wladyslaw. *Imprinting and Early Learning*, 2d ed. Chicago: Aldine, 1973.

Smith, William Carlson. *The Stepchild*. Chicago: University of Chicago Press, 1953.

Somers, Mary Louise. "Group Process Within the Family Unit." *The Family is the Patient: The Group Approach to Treatment of Family Health Problems*, monograph 7. New York: National Association of Social Workers, 1965.

Spanier, Graham, and Sauer, William. "An Empirical Evaluation of the Family Life Cycle." *Journal of Marriage and the Family*, vol. 41 (February 1979).

Stack, Carol B. "Who Owns the Child? Divorce and Child Custody Decisions in Middle-Class Families." *Social Problems*, vol. 23 (April 1976).

Stanford, Barbara, and Stanford, Gene. *Myths and Modern Man*. New York: Simon and Schuster, 1972.

Stepparent News, vol. 1 (September and October 1980).

Stinson, Janet Sinberg. *Now I have a Stepparent and It's Kind of Confusing*. New York: Avon, 1979.

241

The Remarried Family

Sullivan, Harry Stack. The Fusion of Psychiatry and Social Science. New York: W. W. Norton, 1964.

———. The Interpersonal Theory of Psychiatry. New York: W.W. Norton, 1953.

Sussman, Marvin B. "Family." In Encyclopedia of Social Work. Washington, D.C.: National Association of Social Workers, 1977.

Thomas, William I., and Thomas, Dorothy S. The Child in America. New York: Alfred A. Knopf., 1928.

———, and Zaniecki, Florian. The Polish Peasant in Europe and America. New York: Alfred A. Knopf, 1927.

Thompson, Stith. The Folktale. Berkeley, Calif.: University of California Press, 1977.

Thomson, Helen. The Successful Stepparent. New York: Harper and Row, 1966.

Tizard, Barbara. Adoption: A Second Chance. London: Open Books, 1977.

Turner, Ralph. H. Family Interaction. New York: John Wiley, 1970.

Tyler, Ralph W. "Social Policy and Self-Help Groups." The Journal of Applied Behavioral Research, vol. 12 (July-September, 1976).

Uniform Marriage and Divorce Act. National Conference of Commissioners on Uniform State Laws, 1970.

United States Bureau of the Census. "American Families and Living Arrangements." Population Division. Prepared for the White House Conference on Families. Washington, D.C.: United States Government Printing Office, 1980.

———. "Divorce, Child Custody and Child Support." Current Population Reports. Series P-23, no. 84. Washington, D.C.: United States Government Printing Office, 1979.

———. "Marital Status and Living Arrangements: March 1979." Current Population Reports, Series P-20, no. 349. Washington, D.C., United States Government Printing Office, 1980.

———. "Marital Status, Number of Times Married and Duration of Present Marital Status: April 1948." Current Population Reports, Series P-20 no. 23. Washington, D.C.: United States Government Printing Office, 1949.

———. "Number, Timing and Duration of Marriages and Divorces in the United States: June 1975." Current Population Reports, Series P-20 no. 297. Washington, D.C.: United States Government Printing Office, 1976.

———. "Population Profile of the United States: 1979." Current Population Reports, Series P-20, no. 350. Washington, D.C. United States Government Printing Office, 1980.

Van Den Berghe, Pierre L. Man in Society: A Biosocial View. New York: Elsevier, 1978.

Verdi, Guiseppi. "Don Carlos." In Kobbé's Complete Opera Book, rev. ed., edited by the Earl of Harewood. New York: Putnam, 1972.

Whitaker, James K. Social Treatment: An Approach to Interpersonal Helping. Chicago: Aldine, 1974.

Victor, Joan Berg, and Sander, Joelle. The Family. Indianapolis: Bobbs-Merrill, 1978.

Wald, Esther L. "The Blended Family." Children in Contemporary Society, vol. 12 (1979).

———. "Family: Multi-Parent." In Encyclopedia of Social Work. Washington D.C.: National Association of Social Workers, 1977.

———. "The Non-Nuclear Family." The Many Dimensions of Family Practice: Proceedings of the North American Symposium on Family Practice, 1978.

Bibliography

New York: Family Service Association of America, 1980.

Wallerstein, Judith, and Kelly, Joan B. "Children and Divorce." *Social Work*, vol. 24 (November 1979).

Westoff, Leslie Aldridge. *The Second Time Around: Remarriage in America.* New York: Viking Press, 1977.

White, Annie M. "Factors Making for Difficulty in the Step-Parent Relationship with Children." *Smith College Studies in Social Work*, vol. 14 (1943).

Wilcox, Maurice K.C. "Child's Due Process Right to Counsel in Divorce Custody Proceedings." *Hastings Law Review*, vol. 27 (March 1976.)

Williams, Kristen M., and Kuhn, Russell. *Remarriages, United States.* Rockville, Md.: National Center for Health Statistics, 1973.

Wilson, Kenneth L. et al. "Stepfathers and Stepchildren: An Exploratory Analysis from Two National Surveys." *Journal of Marriage and the Family*, vol. 37 (August 1975).

Winch, Robert F. *Identification and Its Familial Determinants.* Indianapolis: Bobbs-Merrill, 1962.

———, and Spanier, Graham, eds. *Selected Studies in Marriage and the Family.* New York: Holt, Rinehart and Winston, 1974.

Winnicott, D.W. *The Family and Individual Development.* London: Tavistock Publications, 1965.

Wolff, Heinz H. "Loss: A Central Theme in Psychotherapy." *British Journal of Medical Psychology*, vol. 50 (1977).

Wooten, Roberta H. "Family Life Education." In *Encyclopedia of Social Work.* Washington, D.C.: National Association of Social Workers, 1977.

Yorburg, Betty. *The Changing Family.* New York: Columbia University Press, 1973.

Zainaldin, Jamil S. "The Emergence of a Modern American Family Law: Child Custody, Adoption and the Courts, 1796–1851." *Northwestern University Law Review*, vol. 73 (1979).

Zuk, Gerald. "Values and Family Therapy." *Psychotherapy: Theory, Research and Practice*, vol. 15 (1978).

INDEX

Index

Index

Conflict and dissension, 27-28
Coping and adaptation, iii, 122
  problem-solving abilities, 13
Court records, 224
Cox family, 129-130
Cultural orientation, 40-41, 67-86
  client and therapist, 83-86
  family members, 67-85
    mixes of images and myths, 67-75
  step relationship, 45-62
  step theme in folklore, 52-62
Custody of children, 5, 50, 93, 123
  best interest of the child doctrine,
    150-153
  children's preference, 153-154
  divided, 155-156
  financial responsibility, 149-150
  joint, 156-157
  legal decisions, 148-173
  maternal preference, 148-150
  modification after remarriage, 160-
    167
  parental preference, 151-152
  psychological parent role in, 153-
    154
  sole, 155-156
  visitation rights, 150, 155, 167-168
  noncustodial parent, 150

Dean family, 167, 182, 184-185, 218
  initial interview, 23-24
Decision making, 27
Defiance and rebellion, 23
Degh, Linda, 61
Depression, 24
Deutsch, Helene, 58-59
Developmental approach, 37, 40-41
Developmental issues and tasks, 113-
    142
  balance of old and new bonds v.
    schism, 126-127, 136
  connection v. detachment, 138-140
  coping v. disorganization, 122
  decision v. ambivalence (divorce),
    120
  emotional bonding, 115-116
  enmeshment, 119, 129-131
  inclusion v. exclusion, 119, 126,
    131, 138
  life cycle stages, 113-142

marital interest v. self-interest, 118,
    125-126
  mourning v. denial, 121, 123, 138
  RF identity v. prior family identity,
    124-129
  renewal v. boredom, 140-142
  role definition v. role ambiguity,
    126
  separation-individuation v.
    enmeshment, 119, 129-131, 138-
    142
  single-parent families, 124-129
  stabilization v. dissolution, 119,
    125-127
  therapeutic intervention, 127-128
Diagnostic assessment, 5, 67
  problem-process profile, 10
Divorce
  changing ideologies and, 68
  children's hope for parental
    reunion, 18-19, 123-125, 131
  church control over, 49
  colonial period, 49-50
  effect on children, 7-8
  first marriages, 7
  life cycle stages, 120
  no-fault divorce laws, 152
  primary cause of marital
    dissolution, 51, 120
  rate after remarriage, 8
  remarriage after, 48-49
  shifting outlooks, 51-52
  social stigma, 50
  stepchildren of, 7-8
  therapeutic intervention, 121
Donahue family, 79-81, 183
Dorsen, Richard, 56

Ecological processes, iii
Ego ideal, idealized self-image, 73
Emergency medical decisions, 159
Emotional difficulties, 29
  bonding process and, 115-116
  step situations, 8
Empathy, developing, 80
Environmental stresses, 25-26, 29,
    180-186
Erikson, Erik H., 228
Expectations
  of instant love, 72-73

Index

stranger phenomenon, 158-160
Uniform Marriage and Divorce Act,
 152
visitation rights, 123, 150, 155, 167-
 168
Levinger, George, 120
Lewis family, 81-82, 183
Life cycle stages and tasks, 113-142
 developmental perspective, 114-116
 nuclear families
  contraction-launching, 117, 141
  establishment, 116-118, 141
  expansion, 117-119, 141
  stabilization, 117
 remarried families, 117
  contraction, 121-124, 141
  dissolution (death or divorce),
   119-121, 141
  establishment, 141
  expansion, 124-129, 141
  launching-contraction, 138-140
  stabilization, 140-142
 therapeutic interventions, 113
Lifestyles, 68
 alternative, 230
 blending, see Blending different
  lifestyles
 integration of prior, 182
Literature on remarried family, 68
 review of, 32, 34-35
Live-in or socially remarried families,
 2
 adoption issues, 172
 lack of statistical data, 7
Lofas, Jeanette, 68
Loneliness, 4
Lorenz, Konrad, 187
Loss, grief and mourning, 186
Love issue
 multiple parents, 22
 myth of instant love by affiliation,
  72-73
Loyalties, split, 5, 76, 105, 136-138
Lynd family, 106-107

Mangold, Margaret, vi
Mapping family positions and roles,
 97-102
 technique, 97-98
Marriage

concept, 47-48
crisis-oriented therapy, 204-209
cultural orientations, 52
difficulties, 34
dissolution and remarriage, 48
marital interest v. self-interest, 118,
 125-126
marital satisfaction, 34
marital subsystems, 90-91
parental consent, 50
threats to, 29
 See also Remarriage
Maynor family, 96, 121, 183, 184, 217
 initial interview, 19-21, 29
 intervention, 204-209
 problem-process profile for
  assessment, 203-204
 schema for study, 202-203
 support payments, 19
Mead, Margaret, 71, 78
Merton, Robert, 32
Mnookin, Robert, 152-153
Money problems, 28, 180
Morgan family, 71-74
Mother-child relations, 60
 See also Parent-child relations
"Mother Holle," 54
Mother-in-law, 60
 in fairy tales, 54
Mothers
 archetype, 60-61
 attachment to natural, 26
 natural, 26, 59, 60
 See also Stepmothers
Motivation among remarried families,
 vi, 8-9, 84
Mourning and denial, see Grief and
 mourning
Multiple parent problems, 22-23
Myths and fantasies, 29, 67-86
 of children, 17-19
 denial and unrealistic expectations,
  69
 myth of instant love by affiliation,
  72-73
 myth of "no difference," 228
 old images and new myths, 67-86
 parental reunion fantasies, 18-21,
  123-125, 131
 problems created by, 9, 14

Index